REGULATING THE BODY

Regulating the Body

*Autonomy, Control, and the
Broken Promise of Equality
in American Law*

Edited by
Austin Sarat *and* Susanna Lee

NEW YORK UNIVERSITY PRESS
New York

NEW YORK UNIVERSITY PRESS
New York
www.nyupress.org

© 2025 by New York University
All rights reserved

Library of Congress Cataloging-in-Publication Data
Names: Sarat, Austin, editor. | Lee, Susanna, editor.
Title: Regulating the body : autonomy, control, and the broken promise of equality in American law / Austin Sarat, Susanna Lee.
Description: New York : New York University Press, 2025. |
Includes bibliographical references and index.
Identifiers: LCCN 2024039907 (print) | LCCN 2024039908 (ebook) |
ISBN 9781479830626 (hardback) | ISBN 9781479830633 (paperback) |
ISBN 9781479830640 (ebook) | ISBN 9781479830671 (ebook other)
Subjects: LCSH: Human body—Law and legislation—United States. | Human body—Moral and ethical aspects—United States. | Equality before the law—United States.
Classification: LCC KF390.5.H85 R44 2025 (print) | LCC KF390.5.H85 (ebook) |
DDC 342.7308/5—dc23/eng/20240828
LC record available at https://lccn.loc.gov/2024039907
LC ebook record available at https://lccn.loc.gov/2024039908

This book is printed on acid-free paper, and its binding materials are chosen for strength and durability. We strive to use environmentally responsible suppliers and materials to the greatest extent possible in publishing our books.

The manufacturer's authorized representative in the EU for product safety is Mare Nostrum Group B.V., Mauritskade 21D, 1091 GC Amsterdam, The Netherlands.
Email: gpsr@mare-nostrum.co.uk.

Manufactured in the United States of America

10 9 8 7 6 5 4 3 2 1

Also available as an ebook

For Stephanie, my sweet love (A. S.)

For Charlotte, Ryan, and Thomas, with all my love (S. L.)

CONTENTS

Introduction: Regulating the Body   1
Susanna Lee and Austin Sarat

1. The "Gift of Life": Regulating the Sale of Gametes in the United States   21
Kimberly Mutcherson

2. My Genetics, My Choice? Parents, Children, and Pediatric Genetic Testing   61
Allison M. Whelan

3. Mask-Shaming: On Private Enforcement and Disability Politics   100
Doron Dorfman

4. Vaccines and Abortion: Congruence, Divergence, and the Elusive Meaning of Medical Freedom   125
Wendy E. Parmet

5. Trans Disabled Inclusion: Disability Rights Include Trans Disabled People   166
Claudia Center and Victoria Rodríguez-Roldán

6. Controlling Condemned Bodies: Regulation and Dehumanization of Death Row Inmates   187
John H. Blume and Allison Franz

About the Contributors   227

Index   229

Introduction

Regulating the Body

SUSANNA LEE AND AUSTIN SARAT

From fertilization to gestation, from birth to puberty, sexual maturation to procreation, illness to treatment, the chance to live to the right to die, individuals make decisions about what to do, or not to do, with their own bodies every day. They do this in the name of self-expression, love, ritual, art, emotion, recreation, or survival. At the same time, American law now takes an intense interest in the body, its needs and its uses. Alongside a Constitution that promises individual liberty and accompanied by incendiary discourse that both vaunts and undermines principles of personal freedom, legal regulations surrounding the body are becoming increasingly complex and contested.

Regulation of the body in the United States has been and continues to be famously uneven. For instance, 49 of 50 states require seatbelts to be worn in cars, but fewer than half of states require all motorcycle riders to wear helmets.[1] Recreational and medical marijuana are legal in some states and not in others.[2] Death row prisoners may have the right to volunteer for execution, but most states impose criminal penalties on those who assist another to commit suicide.[3]

Since the COVID-19 pandemic, and in some cases because of it, the production of laws regulating the body has accelerated. And with them, legal acrobatics and inconsistencies have also multiplied. In the domain of gender expression, a teenage girl may seek a breast reduction but a transgender boy in some states cannot. As this volume goes to publication, several states are seeking to ban gender-affirming care for adults as well as children.[4] Some of these same states have sought to ban drag shows, though so far such bans have failed in the face of First Amendment challenges.[5]

Virulent arguments against state-mandated masking and vaccination in response to the pandemic have deployed the principle of bodily autonomy. But such appeals are often made by legislators and public officials who oppose bodily autonomy in other realms.[6] In June 2022, the United States Supreme Court reversed the constitutional right to abortion and enabled states to compel a person to carry a pregnancy to term, whether or not that pregnancy is wanted or viable.[7]

In this volume, we examine practices and discourses used in arguments about regulating the body. We want to understand why law takes such an active interest in our bodies and what we do with them. Throughout, the contributors focus on what legal regulation of bodies claims to do and on what, amid worsening discursive incoherence, it actually does.

What Does Regulation Do?

Few people would deny that regulation of various aspects of our lives is a crucial component of any functioning society. The state regulates economic markets, infrastructure and the environment, interpersonal conduct, and even in some cases speech. In theory, regulation produces: financial or physical security and improved health and well-being. When the site of regulation is the body itself, questions around what regulation produces become significantly more fraught.

Throughout America's history, the state has regulated bodies. In some cases, one person's bodily autonomy has been restricted to preserve other bodies. Vaccine mandates are one instance of this kind of regulation, as are all regulations around physical violence. In other cases, bodily autonomy is restricted to preserve or protect the body being restricted: motorcycle helmet laws are of this sort.

Still other regulations insinuate that certain individual conduct is wrong, even when no harm is done: laws against homosexual sex were of this type, as are laws around gender-affirming care for adults. As the last examples make clear, the regulation of bodies does not fall evenly across society. The bodies of some groups have been much more strictly regulated than others. The most extreme of these were regulations around slavery, where entire human existences were placed in permanent servitude to a "society" that was defined to exclude them. The Black body has long been more harshly regulated than its white counterpart, as has the female body in comparison with the male. One mark of social subjugation is the way bodies are regulated.

Even within the frame of these abiding inequalities, though, regulation of the body has moved in historical waves, and regulatory regimes have long tended to take certain ideological forms. Broadly stated, the 1973 decision in *Roe v Wade* belonged to, and signaled, an era of deregulation in the name of privacy and freedom. Crucially, as subsequent criticisms have noted, the *Roe* decision did not address questions of sex discrimination head-on but rather relied on and centered the principle of personal autonomy, not only for the woman seeking abortion care but also for the physician treating her. That choice of foundation defined the regulatory regime that produced it, but it would bear problematic fruit in the decades to follow.

As critics like John Hart Ely famously noted, the Supreme Court's response was "not adequate."[8] Ruth Bader Ginsburg, another critic, stated: "The *Roe* decision might have been less of a storm center had it both homed in more precisely on the women's equality dimension of the issue and, correspondingly, attempted nothing more bold at that time than the mode of decision making the Court employed in the 1970s gender classification cases."[9] In the years following *Roe*, antiabortion voices promptly seized on statements like Ely's as evidence of *Roe*'s basic wrongheadedness, but in so doing they rode the pendulum to an opposite extreme. That is, they "homed in on" and went after autonomy, which *Roe* in its chosen reasoning (privacy and autonomy, as opposed to equal protection) had set up for a great fall.

Because autonomy rather than gender discrimination had been front and center in *Roe*'s reasoning, the post-*Roe* regulatory regime can be characterized as one in which autonomy was cast as an actual or potential harm. (It can also be characterized as one in which gender discrimination, or discrimination full stop, seemed forever relegated to dissents). During the 1980s, various laws increased the state's ability to regulate the body. They included such measures as seatbelt legislation, which started with New York in 1984,[10] and the 1986 *Bowers v. Hardwick* decision, which affirmed the criminalization of sex between adult men.[11] The war on drugs mandated harsher criminal penalties for possession and use of certain drugs, and age restrictions on alcohol purchase increased.[12] In sum, while the tide of economic regulation was turning in a libertarian direction under President Ronald Reagan, it was also simultaneously turning in favor regulating the body.

Now, fifty-plus years after *Roe*, the current ideological landscape is as blunt in its denigration of autonomy as the *Roe* landscape was enthusiastic in its embrace of it. To be clear, we aim in this discussion not to elevate autonomy per se or simply to celebrate Justice Harry Blackmun's opinion in *Roe v. Wade*. Rather, we wish to point out the extent to which our current regulatory moment is retributive in nature and, at least with respect to abortion, radically disconnected from the needs and lived experiences of the people being regulated.

The transition from *Roe* and its respect for privacy and autonomy to the current selective distrust and demonization of those values was made possible by various kinds of narrative manipulation and misrepresentations from various corners: legal decisions, political discourse, media stories, medicine, and popular culture. It was also made possible by a confluence of historical circumstances. The Supreme Court's decision in *Dobbs v. Whole Women's Health Center* overturning *Roe*, announced in June 2022, came at a time of considerable controversy about regulation of the body.

During the COVID pandemic, progressives wanted bodies regulated, in the form of vaccine and mask mandates, while conservatives for the most part did not. At the same time, conservatives wanted bodies of trans adolescents and even adults to be regulated, while progressives did not. Progressives wanted women to have the right to make reproductive decisions for themselves, free from state interference, while conservatives did not.

The COVID pandemic was not the first public health circumstance where regulation of the body represented a crucial and immediate public good and autonomy (in the form of vaccine and mask resistance) represented a danger to society. But it was the first in decades. Furthermore, it fed—however clumsily and imprecisely and from an improbable political place—into a narrative about regulation that antiabortion politicians had been pushing for a long time. As one of the contributors to this volume notes, the slogan "My body, my choice" was being taken up simultaneously by antivaccine and anti-masking activists and by women fighting to retain reproductive autonomy. It has served whoever has had the strongest judicial platform.

The *Dobbs* decision, combined with the COVID pandemic, signaled that the regulation of bodies was entering a rhetorically extreme phase, wherein bodies are regulated for the *potential* harm that their autonomy could cause or, more precisely, for the potential harm that their autonomy could—given some discursive acrobatics, anachronistic arguments, alarmist tactics, and pure invention—be *said* to cause.

Again, to measure the substance and value of regulation, it is necessary to consider its actual consequences. In December 2023, a pregnant American mother of two, Kate Cox, whose fetus had a fatal condition and who would have suffered infertility and even death if she were forced to continue the pregnancy—was denied an abortion in Texas. As Ms. Cox was twenty weeks pregnant, there was no chance that her fetus could survive outside the womb. After a lower court granted an exception to the Texas ban on abortion, which allows the procedure in medical emergencies, the state Attorney General intervened, threatening the woman's doctors and hospitals with first-degree felony prosecution.

The state Supreme Court sided with the state Attorney General, stating: "No one disputes that Ms. Cox's pregnancy has been extremely complicated. Any parents would be devastated to learn of their unborn child's trisomy 18 diagnosis. Some difficulties in pregnancy, however, even serious ones, do not pose the heightened risks to the mother the exception encompasses."[13] Because Ms. Cox had been in and out of the emergency room several times in deteriorating health, she was forced to leave the state to obtain reproductive health care.[14]

As numerous commentators have stated, Ms. Cox's case undercuts the "pro-life" argument for criminalization of abortion. A popular political slogan claims that "the cruelty is the point," and for the purposes of this volume we would postulate that, increasingly, regulation is the point. In September 2022, a New York woman seeking treatment for severe headaches was denied treatment because she was of "childbearing age" and the medication could cause birth defects. The patient's insistence that she did not want children and would abort if she became pregnant did not change the doctor's opinion, and she remained untreated.[15] In yet another example, in December 2023 an Ohio woman who miscarried a nonviable fetus, and who went to the hospital seeking care, was reported to the police and arrested for abuse of a corpse.[16]

The examples just cited have to do with reproductive freedom, but regulation has also accelerated in other areas, including in the domain of gender-affirming care.[17] Numerous states have prevented parents from seeking gender-affirming care for their trans children, even as they seek to empower parents to remove books with gay protagonists from schools and public libraries.[18] Repeated attempts have even been made (and so far thwarted on free-speech grounds) to prevent men from dressing as women for the purposes of entertainment.[19] These are instances of regulation for regulation's sake—and what is more, regulation with a carceral bent. Such multifaceted, uneven, and punitive regulations are ultimately made possible by narrative manipulations and misrepresentations. These make it hard to trace the real interests served when law regulates bodies and signal a serious crisis of legitimacy for the law.

What Do We Mean to Accomplish by Writing About Regulation Now?

Much as regulatory regimes have traced a fifty-year arc that seems at the moment to be bending toward constriction, scholarly writing about regulation has chased and examined that arc. Among the earliest of such scholarship is David Meyer's *The Human Body and the Law*. Meyer's book, published in 1970, was a "medico-legal study" treating such topics as genetic engineering, fetal rights, transplantation, and euthanasia. It discussed questions of regulation in the domain of reproduction without mentioning sex discrimination at all. In 1997, Alan Hyde's *Bodies of Law* theorized the body as a legal-discursive invention, invoking gender theory and feminism (Kristeva and Butler) and citing Foucauldian notions of regulation to describe "just which bodies law currently constructs and when and how it comes to construct different bodies for different purposes" (5). Hyde stated: "Perhaps what we need is not a new right, but a bringing into consciousness of the multiple constructions already immanent in law" (6).

This century has seen numerous efforts to illuminate and dismantle discrimination in such constructions, but it has also seen accelerating endeavors to enable such discrimination in the name of limiting bodily autonomy. The retrograde nature of recent legislation, and the movement toward a focus on regulation that is preemptive and punitive rather than protective in nature, has generated a new body of scholarly and popular work on regulation of the body. Much of that work focuses on reproduction—Sara Clarke Kaplan's *The Black Reproductive* (2021), Michele Goodwin's *Policing the Womb* (2020), Anita Bernstein's *The Common Law Inside the Female Body* (2019)—or medical ethics—John Fabian Witt's *American Contagions* (2021), Jill Fisher's *Adverse Events* (2020), Jesse Wall's *Being and Owning* (2015). Many of these works raise the important analytical framework of intersectionality to point out that identity politics—however maligned as a ground for ideology—are alive and well in regulatory regimes. Increasing scholarly attention to racial and gender discrimination points out that regulation is often deployed as selective punishment.

In *The Black Reproductive*, Sara Clarke Kaplan describes "the transformation from slavery's punitive systems of captivity, enslavement, and dispossession to the burdened individuality of nominal freedom, with its attendant regulation, containment, and subordination" (182). She argues that the specter of captivity and dispossession is ever present for individuals of color in a white-supremacist society. The fact that captivity and dispossession were visceral experiences for some Americans and merely lines in history books for others has been brought into focus through sustained scholarly attention to discrimination. Similarly, the fact that medical, physical, and legal vulnerability are visceral experiences for women in a patriarchal society has been illuminated by increasing concentration on the lived experience of inequality. When we speak of systemic inequality, we are talking about inequality that operates within and through regulatory systems or, in other words, about regulatory enforcement of inequality.

Hyde wrote in 1997: "Most people who have not been defined as marginal—the 'general population' we will encounter particularly when we construct diseased bodies—are subject to social regulation and coercion largely through two great disciplines of power, the discipline of sexuality and gender, about which Foucault wrote so much, and the discipline of the market and economic activity, about which he did not." Since the time Hyde wrote those words, changes in the regulatory regime have—sometimes subtly, sometimes not—treated large numbers of people as dangerous, either actually or potentially, to either actual or potential others, and thus reasonably subject to control.

As we see from the examples of the Texas mother seeking a lifesaving abortion or the Ohio woman arrested for miscarrying, such regulatory systems create a growing, and increasingly marginalized, class of reprobates. Our book thus adds not only to scholarly literature about regulation of the body in the medical or public health domains but also to discussion about regulation as a carceral practice. When regulation increases, actions that avoid regulation become punishable offenses, and regulated persons—now cast as offenders—become subject to ever-increasing regulation as punishment. This book thus aligns philosophically with such studies as Michelle Alexander's 2010 *The New Jim Crow* and Elizabeth Hinton's *From the War on Poverty to the War on Crime: The Making of Mass Incarceration in America*, both of which examined inequalities in and around the carceral system.

Dobbs, or the Importance of Focusing on Material Consequences of Regulation

The chapters in this volume examine the reasons for and practical consequences of regulation. They investigate what is enabled or produced when a regulatory regime transitions from a paradigm that respects autonomy to a paradigm that views autonomy as actually or potentially harmful. Taken together, they analyze and respond to the myriad regulatory practices and discourses operating today.

Before reviewing the individual contributions to this volume, we would like to return to our earlier point about *Roe*'s "incomplete foundation." A commonly told story about abortion access in the United States is that *Roe* was a clumsily argued decision—giving insufficient justification and overstepping the proper boundaries of constitutional interpretation—and that *Dobbs* represents the culmination of decades of legal and ideological hostility to *Roe*. Critics say *Dobbs* overturned *Roe* in a move that was as faulty (albeit in different ways) as its predecessor. This is an accurate depiction of events, but it glosses over the ways in which the antiabortion movement, including *Dobbs*, consciously, methodically, and repeatedly depended on faulty reasoning. *Dobbs* authorized regulation of the body in the name of democracy, which the Court itself has helped to cripple in many other cases (notably voting rights, gerrymandering, and presidential immunity).

Numerous critics have noted that privacy and autonomy were not the most durable ground on which to build *Roe*.[20] The antiabortion movement has jumped on those acknowledgments. At one point, the *Dobbs* opinion cites an internal memorandum from the legal team representing *Roe* in the early 1970s. That memorandum, according to Justice Samuel Alito, advocated reliance on a prochoice article by Cyril Means even though it only wore "the guise of impartial scholarship while advancing the proper ideological goals."[21] Alito cites this memorandum (in fact a memo from a law student) as evidence of bad faith among *Roe*'s legal team (as in fact have countless right-to-life publications and websites since *Roe*), then states in the *Dobbs* opinion that "[c]ontinued reliance on such scholarship is unsupportable" (27).

If "such scholarship" means "writing that wore the guise of impartial scholarship while advancing the proper ideological goals," then Alito's calling it "unsupportable" is incredibly cynical. The entire *Dobbs* opinion is itself an example of a Supreme Court "advancing the proper ideological goals," which in this case meant banning abortion and reducing women to a childbearing function. It arrives there through an astoundingly misleading series of citations and misrepresentations that undermine its pretense to root regulation of women's bodies in a secure framework of legal reasoning.

To give one example of *Dobbs*'s "ideological goals," Alito mentions that two articles by a "pro-abortion advocate" (Cyril Means) "have been discredited," and he cites several sources as evidence of that assertion.[22] It is worth pointing out that the voices "discrediting" Means are themselves relentless ideologues, more cravenly devoted to their desired end than Means ever was. One of these voices, Robert Destro, is a frequent contributor to *Human Life Review* and authored a "Catholics for the Common Good" brief against marriage equality and in favor of California's Proposition 8 (the amendment that would have banned same-sex marriage).[23] As Donald Trump's assistant secretary of state for democracy, human rights, and labor from September 2019 to January 2021, he met with election deniers on January 6 but then declined to talk "about the details of those meetings."[24]

Still another cited scholar, Robert Byrn, called himself New York's "[n]umber one foe of abortion" and, in 1971, when answering a hypothetical question about "whether a 10-year-old girl who is raped by a mental defective should be forced to bear the child," responded: "That's the toughest case. The implication is usually that the mental defective is black. My answer is that the wrong to the girl has already been done[] and that we ought not to compound that wrong by killing a life."[25] A third named source in Alito's opinion is Joseph Dellapenna's 2006 *Dispelling the Myths of Abortion History*. When a female law professor, Carla Spivack, published an article in the *William and Mary Law Review* critiquing Dellapenna's book, Dellapenna's response was to eviscerate the review article not in a law journal but in the religious journal *First Things* and to defend himself by pointing to another pro-life reviewer who had published a positive review of his book in *First Things*.[26] This was not a dialogue among legal scholars but an open ideological departure from the realm of legitimate legal discourse.

Nonetheless, while standing on this most biased of foundations, Alito sets himself out as the arbiter of legitimacy, sound reasoning, and precedent. He declares: "Stare decisis plays an important role and protects the interests of those who have taken action in reliance on a past decision. It 'reduces incentives for challenging settled precedents, saving parties and courts the expense of endless relitigation.'" He repeats this quote further on, pointing out: "It has been said that it is sometimes more important that an issue 'be settled than that it be settled right,'" then adding, "we place a high value on having the matter 'settled right.'"[27] Alito's opinion thus insinuates that calling previous abortion law "settled" was hasty and careless, a sort of bandying about by those interested only in expediency. (The dissent removes the quotes, noting for instance that the Court has linked abortion rights "for decades to other settled freedoms involving bodily integrity, familial relationships, and procreation.") The quotations in *Dobbs* serve to set the idea of what is settled out of reach of all other interpreters and lawmakers, reducing it to a nullity and making Alito the sole arbiter of its validity and of what is legitimate in the realm of bodily regulation.

The fact that the *Dobbs* decision attacks the *Roe* opinion for putting ideological consistency above constitutional reasoning—and then proceeds without a pause to do the same thing, moving even farther and more shamelessly afield—underscores the role that narrative manipulations and misrepresentations have played in the transition from a regulatory regime that elevated autonomy and privacy and glossed over equality to one that undermined both autonomy and equality. There is something almost novelistic in the opinion's decision to reach back across five centuries to land on the men he calls "eminent common-law authorities" and to cite their ideas as foundational and determinative. There is something insidious in the decision to criticize judicial activism while practicing it.

Alito's opinion is also striking in its move to cast the individuals it harms—women—as marginal characters in its drama of historical revisionism *and* to claim methodological superiority in the process. It is almost a banal observation, in this historical moment, to say that regulation is an ideological phenomenon, but this is all the more reason for its bases and biases to be exposed to critique since the opinion in *Dobbs* was handed down. The reasons for regulation—and for individual regulations, one at a time—must continually be interrogated and its actual consequences reevaluated for humanity and consistency.

Savage Inequalities

We know that the relationship of the human body to the law has been radically uneven throughout American history. The law names rights as self-evident and then limits, removes, or protects them for some people and not others. It can also be seconded in this endeavor through nonstate actors—agents and forces that can complement (and even determine) the reach of state laws. We know that those inconsistencies are sublimated by, or perhaps are even truly invisible to, the very individuals who create regulations. The critic Michael Holquist observed of Dostoevsky's famous novel *Demons*, a chronicle of political manipulation and pathological egotism: "The relation of the novel's protagonists to each other is essentially that of an author to the characters he invents."[28]

So it is with some regulators' relation to the individuals they are regulating; so it is with Alito's relation to women, many of whose lives in the time since *Roe*'s reversal have been devastated by his ruling. This is why it is important to concentrate on what regulation *does*, including the consequences it has for individuals and society as a whole. It is not our intent to advance a broad liberal argument for autonomy as a fundamental good but rather to train our eyes on what is wrought, on what is made possible, as a result of the current regulatory regime.

Today, what the individual can or cannot do with her own body, and what the government can and cannot do to regulate that body, varies according not only to race and gender but also to class and geography. In the United States, with its federal system, getting access to the care needed to sustain or control one's body depends almost entirely on where one lives. Because abortion proscriptions are state-specific (as of the time this volume was going to publication), for instance, women who can travel to states where reproductive health care is legal cannot be forced to give birth. Those who cannot may experience a very different regime of bodily regulation.[29]

However, such movement in itself has already become the focus of regulatory ambitions, creating more and wider nets of regulated subjects.[30] (What is more, the Supreme Court's consideration of the abortion pill indicates a willingness not to "leave the issue to the states.") Resistors of repressive regulations may be portrayed by those seeking to use law to control the body as a threat to the social order. Increased regulation, in other words, responds to the endeavors of disfavored individuals and groups to achieve autonomy.

The chapters in this volume explore that fact and the relation of laws' regulation of the body to various aspects of social inequality. They are organized according to a chronology of the cradle to the grave. The regulations examined range from the sale of gametes to parental rights over children's genetic information, to debates about masking, to the discourse of bodily autonomy regarding vaccines and abortion, to the rise of anti-transgender legislation, to the intimate regulation of the bodies of inmates on death row. Some chapters deploy a traditional legal understanding of regulation—effectively using it as a synonym for formal law. Others exhibit a more legally pluralistic understanding of regulation—as something that could include, but that might also exceed, formal laws. Our book brings together leading scholars in law and the humanities to examine the practices and discourses used to regulate the body through various modalities, concentrating on those scenarios where ethical and legal inconsistencies abound. It then situates those examinations within a cultural-political environment that increasingly values regulation and punishment over long-standing constitutional protections and even jurisprudential soundness.

Each chapter in this book examines the material consequences of regulation while at the same time analyzing the reasoning that produces those consequences. This means that each contribution addresses the disparate lived experiences of various individuals subjected to regulation of their bodies.

* * *

In chapter 1 ("The 'Gift of Life': Regulating the Sale of Gametes in the United States"), Kimberly Mutcherson examines the regulations surrounding the sale of gametes. Such transactions have constituted a long-standing and, in some countries, a long-contentious trade, especially when done anonymously. While some countries have banned the practice or allow only noncommercial gamete exchanges, the United States has long leaned in to the commercial aspect of the practice, and law and policy have been fairly hands-off in how this practice has been regulated. For a variety of reasons, though, that stance has been challenged in the first quarter of this century.

Controversies involving reproductive endocrinologists who commit fertility fraud; donor-conceived people demanding access to information about their genetic origins and an end to anonymous sales of gametes, mostly sperm; the advent of serial sperm donors who work outside the fertility industry; and the soft cap on compensation for women who sell ova have all created pressures for new industry regulations. The two big questions arising out of this issue—whether to allow individuals to sell their gametes and, if so, how to regulate those sales—remain complicated and controversial.

Mutcherson explores the loose regulatory landscape for gamete sales in the United States; efforts to create more law and policy, including individual states banning the anonymous sale of gametes; and regulators attempting to crack down on serial donors. Her discussion acknowledges the basic principle that the sale of gametes, unlike the sale of other body parts or fluids, leads to the creation of new human beings, which demands a level of exacting review that is not warranted for sales that do not lead to this end result. Even so, regulatory regimes must balance that reality with respect for the rights of individuals to sell their gametes for their own benefit and for the benefit of those who want to use those gametes to create babies. Ultimately, Mutcherson argues that, while law can and should play a role in the conditions under which gametes get sold (for instance by requiring more exacting medical histories from gamete sellers for the benefit of future human beings), the industry itself should be protected and sustained.

In chapter 2 ("My Genetics, My Choice? Parents, Children, and Pediatric Genetic Testing"), Allison M. Whelan explores the regulation of children's bodies and futures, with a specific focus on their genetics, predispositions for future disease, and the choices made in light of genetic testing. American law and jurisprudence have long recognized a significant role for parents in making decisions about myriad aspects of their child's life: education, religion, health care, and much more. Buttressing this tradition is a long-standing recognition by the United States Supreme Court that parents have a constitutional right to direct the care, custody, and control of their children. And even while these rights are not absolute and exceptions exist, the line between permissible and impermissible parental control over decisions for their children remains murky.

Existing law and jurisprudence do not clearly answer whether minors have—or should have—control over their genetic futures. Importantly, children represent a vulnerable population because, legally speaking, they are considered incapable of providing consent and thus often remain voiceless in decision-making. In turn, this renders their bodies and minds subject to regulation and control by others.

One such domain where these questions come to the fore is "pediatric predisposition genetic testing" (PPGT). This phrase is used in chapter 2 to describe genetic testing done on a minor, consented to by their parent(s), for the purpose of (1) determining whether the minor has any genetic mutations that will result in an adult-onset disease that lacks a known cure or method of prevention, such as Huntington's disease or amyotrophic lateral sclerosis (Lou Gehrig's disease); or (2) assessing the risk that the minor will develop an adult-onset disease including those with known curative treatment options, such as various types of cancer. While American law and tradition have long recognized the rights of parents to consent to myriad types of health care services for their children, PPGT may provide unwanted information about a nonconsenting child—information that must be lived with for the rest of that child's life. Children have too often become pawns in larger sociopolitical battles fought primarily between parents and the state, with their rights and interests cast aside. With this consideration in mind, the chapter explores whether and how to protect children's bodily autonomy, integrity, and privacy in this new era of genetic technologies.

Chapter 3 ("Mask-Shaming: On Private Enforcement and Disability Politics") by Doron Dorfman examines public and private enforcement of mask regulations during the COVID-19 pandemic. Masks were the most visible and obvious symbol of the COVID-19 pandemic, an effective and cheap preventive measure for stopping the spread of the coronavirus. Despite becoming part of people's daily routines for quite some time, masking once again has become rare in public spaces. Since the April 2022 Florida federal district court decision in *Health Freedom Defense Fund, Inc. v. Biden* that struck down the Centers for Disease Control and Prevention's transit mask order and entered a nationwide injunction against it, common carriers and transportation hubs stopped requiring masks, as did other places of public accommodation.

By February 2023, no states were requiring people to wear masks in public places or even in hospital settings. Almost overnight, masking became an individualized-voluntary practice of regulating one's own body to protect against variants of the coronavirus. Since then, there has been a growing number of incidents of harassment, shaming, and ridicule for wearing a mask in public, spurred by an ongoing political campaign against preventative COVID measures. It is as if masking in public has become stigmatized and penalized.

Chapter 3 explores the effects of the shift in masking from a mandatory practice to one that is individualized and voluntary. Those who continue to mask are mostly immunocompromised and disabled individuals, older people, caregivers, and friends of the disability community. Thus masking sends strong signals about the wearer's identity. Through a process Dorfman calls "penalizing prevention," those who wear masks are stigmatized and penalized in a variety of ways. Such practices create structural stigma for masking as well as a chilling effect on those doing so, thereby frustrating the goal of improving public health and disability inclusion.

Wendy E. Parmet's chapter 4 ("Vaccines and Abortion: Congruence, Divergence, and the Elusive Meaning of Medical Freedom") analyzes the shared history and a common rhetoric of vaccine mandates and abortion bans. In the nineteenth and early twentieth centuries, the medical establishment embraced vaccine mandates and abortion bans as consistent with science and public health. During this same period, opponents of each type of regulation argued for bodily autonomy and "medical freedom." In both cases, courts rejected most autonomy claims, viewing both abortion bans and vaccine mandates as reasonable exercises of the states' police power.

Since *Roe v. Wade*, however, the politics and legal regulation of abortion and vaccination have diverged. For example, even after the Supreme Court in *Roe* established a constitutional right to an abortion, courts routinely upheld vaccine mandates. In effect, the right to bodily autonomy that *Roe* recognized did not include the right to reject vaccination.

Courts today have favored autonomy-based challenges directed at vaccine mandates. In the same year that the Supreme Court in *Dobbs v. Whole Women's Health Center* held that the United States Constitution does not protect a right to an abortion, the Court used the language of autonomy to hold that OSHA lacked authority to compel large employers to mandate vaccination or COVID testing and masking. Further, several justices in *Dobbs*'s conservative majority have questioned the constitutionality of state vaccine mandates and the authority of the precedent that supports them. To these justices, at least, individual autonomy extends to vaccination but not to the termination of pregnancy.

Parmet's chapter examines the shared history and rhetoric of the abortion rights and vaccine freedom (antivax) movements and seeks to explain their contradictory contemporary politics, geography, and legal regulation. It also argues that, despite their mutual employment of the phrase "my body, my choice," opponents of vaccine mandates and abortion bans accept significant limitations on bodily autonomy. They just have very different views as to whom the body is obligated and how the scope of that obligation should be determined. The chapter concludes by discussing what these differing views may mean for public health and law moving forward.

Chapter 5 ("Trans Disabled Inclusion: Disability Rights Include Trans Disabled People") by Claudia Center and Victoria Rodriguez-Roldán, examines the intersecting regulations imposed on transgender and disabled individuals. It focuses on the experience of transgender individuals who are also disabled, exploring the myriad regulatory questions posed by that experience. Even when laws do not explicitly target trans people with disabilities, state officials deploy discriminatory reasoning in litigation defending anti-trans laws.

The government's experts argue that the existence of other disabilities prior to transition means that people should not be able to access gender-affirming care, implying that trans people with disabilities are somehow not truly trans. The government has in many cases presented itself as the arbiter of who can and cannot receive care; at times, this role can also be filled—and sometimes exploited—by a parent or state-appointed conservator who does not support the idea of gender-affirming care. Living without such care, however, can disrupt education and employment, exacerbate trauma and poverty, worsen existing disabilities, and cause new disabilities.

In chapter 5, the authors interrogate the rhetoric used by lawmakers attempting to bar disabled individuals from accessing gender care, paying particular attention to their selective citations of scientific literature or their reliance on questionable or biased sources of allegedly scientific data. At issue in the overlapping regulations imposed on trans disabled individuals is an aggressive narrative, casting trans disabled individuals as both incapable of consent and undeserving of care. Also at work is what can be called "indirect" regulation, which amounts to control of bodies and minds through omission or even criminalization of care. The chapter also contains some reparative propositions for providing accommodation, support in decision-making, and respectful care to disabled and trans individuals.

Chapter 6 ("Controlling the Condemned: Regulation and Dehumanization of Death Row Inmates") by John H. Blume and Allison Franz analyzes regulations of the bodies of death row inmates. Blume and Franz note that in the world outside death row states exert control over citizens' bodies in the form of abortion regulations, bans on physician-assisted suicide, and qualified immunity for police officers who use force in the name of preserving the sanctity of life. On death row they mandate similar bodily regulation, particularly of Black bodies, for exactly the opposite reason. While such policies can seem directly contradictory, state mechanisms of body regulation serve a common purpose: to silence marginalized groups, primarily people of color, through constant and consistent messaging that their bodies are never free from state regulation. Nowhere is this purpose more blatantly displayed than on death row.

As chapter 6 demonstrates, the bodies of death row inmates are regulated at every step. Condemned prisoners are told where to go, when to go there, when to sleep, when to wake up, what, when, and how much to eat or drink, whether they can go outside, when and how often they can shower, and even whether and how often they receive access to natural light. They can be forcibly medicated during the legal proceedings needed to procure a death sentence, and such forced medication can continue throughout their lives. The list continues. In some states, this lifelong body regulation culminates in an illusory choice of the manner in which the state will kill the inmate, a decision that the state frames as a grant of the "privilege" of bodily autonomy, however temporary and however limited.

Death row prisoners are one part of a continuum of the legal regulation of bodies. People seeking abortions, terminally ill people seeking to end their life on their own terms, people severely injured or killed by police who then face no consequences, and people on death row are all forced to cede control of their bodies to the state in service to a broader system of societal control that seeks to disempower marginalized or disfavored groups. Every carefully constructed day on death row is a reminder that states' "pro-life" policies belie the underlying reality that those states view life not as sacrosanct but an object to be regulated in the service of the societal status quo.

In the end, the work compiled in this book shows the complex web of regulations governing the body. It illustrates the push and pull of different values and how it plays out in law, politics, and the daily lives of the people whose bodies are the subject of regulation. We hope that this work reminds us of all the work that needs to be done to protect bodily autonomy, political equality, and human dignity.

NOTES

1 Insurance Institute for Highway Safety, "Motorcycle Helmet Use Laws," modified July 2024, www.iihs.org.
2 Council of State Governments, "State Approaches to Marijuana Policy," , February 13, 2023, www.csg.org.
3 G. R. Strafer, "Volunteering for Execution—Competency, Voluntariness," *Journal of Criminal Law and Criminology* 74, no. 3 (Fall 1983): 860–912; Cornell Law School, "Physician-Assisted Suicide," Cornell Law School, updated March 2024, www.law.cornell.edu.
4 Maham Jahid, "New State Bills Restrict Transgender Health Care—For Adults," *Washington Post*, March 1, 2023, www.washingtonpost.com.
5 Alejandro Serrano and William Melhado, "Texas' Ban on Certain Drag Shows Is Unconstitutional, Federal Judge Says," *Texas Tribune*, updated September 27, 2023, www.texastribune.org.

6 Alice Miranda Ollstein and Megan Messerly, "Republicans Clash with Prosecutors Over Enforcement of Abortion Bans," *Politico*, February 12, 2023, www.politico.com.
7 Dobbs v. Jackson Women's Health Organization et al., 597 U.S. ___ (2022).
8 Ely noted that *Roe* "is bad because it is bad constitutional law, or rather because it is not constitutional law and gives almost no sense of an obligation to try to be," and also pointed to women's historical subordination. John Hart Ely, "The Wages of Crying Wolf: A Comment on *Roe v. Wade*," *Yale Law Journal* 82, no. 5 (April 1973): 920–49, 947.
9 Ruth Bader Ginsburg, "Speaking in a Judicial Voice," *New York University Law Review* 67, no. 6 (December 1992): 1185–209, 1200. Catharine MacKinnon commented on the failure to address sex discrimination, describing *Roe* as an "insult got up as a gift" because "under conditions of gender inequality [abortion] does not liberate women; it frees male sexual aggression." Catharine Mackinnon, "Privacy and Equality: Notes on their Tension," *Tocqueville Review* 21, no. 2 (2000): 77–85.
10 Center for Disease Control and Prevention, "MV PICCS Intervention: Primary Enforcement of Seat Belt Laws," updated May 16, 2024, www.cdc.gov.
11 Bowers v. Hardwick, 478 U.S. 186 (1986).
12 Alcohol Policy Information System, a project of the National Institute on Alcohol Abuse and Alcoholism, "The 1984 National Minimum Drinking Age Act," https://alcoholpolicy.niaaa.nih.gov.
13 Supreme Court of Texas, No. 20-0994 (2023), www.txcourts.gov.
14 Eleanor Klibanoff, "Texas Supreme Court Blocks Order Allowing Abortion; Woman Who Sought It Leaves State," *Texas Tribune*, December 11, 2023, www.texastribune.org.
15 Kelly Rissman, "Woman Sues Hospital for Denying Her Treatment for Debilitating Headaches Because She's 'Of Childbearing Age,'" *Independent*, October 9, 2023, www.independent.co.uk.
16 Maham Javid and Kim Bellware, "She Miscarried in Her Bathroom. Now She's Charged with Abuse of a Corpse," *Washington Post*, December 15, 2023, www.washingtonpost.com.
17 Human Rights Campaign Foundation, "Map: Attacks on Gender Affirming Care by State," updated May 2024, www.hrc.org.
18 Hannah Gross, "Rallying Against Attempts to Challenge LGBTQ+ Books at NJ Libraries," *New Jersey Spotlight News*, July 19, 2023, www.njspotlightnews.org.
19 Adam Gabbatt, "'Subtle And Sinister': Republicans' Anti-Drag Crusade Seen as Assault on LGBTQ+ Rights," *The Guardian*, September 19, 2023, www.theguardian.com.
20 Ruth Bader Ginsburg, "Some Thoughts on Autonomy and Equality in Relation to *Roe v. Wade*," *North Carolina Law Review* 63 (1985): 375.
21 *Dobbs*.
22 Cyril C. Means, "The Law of New York Concerning Abortion and the Status of the Foetus, 1664–968: A Case of Cessation of Constitutionality," *New York Law Forum* 14 (1968): 411; Cyril C. Means, "The Phoenix of Abortional Freedom: Is a Penumbral or Ninth-Amendment Right About to Arise from the Nineteenth-

Century Legislative Ashes of a Fourteenth-Century Common-Law Liberty?" *New York Law Forum* 17 (1971): 335–410, 335.

23 Catholics for the Common Good, "CCG Marriage Brief: Overturning Prop 8 Violates Voters Rights; Repudiates Attacks on Religion," January 29, 2013, posted by the Gay and Lesbian Alliance Against Defamation (GLAAD) in 2018, https://s3.us-west-2.amazonaws.com.

24 Rosalind S. Helderman, "Senior Trump Official at State Met with Election Denial Activists Jan. 6," *Washington Post*, May 17, 2022, www.washingtonpost.com.

25 Judy Klemesrud, "He's the Legal Guardian for the Fetuses About to Be Aborted," *New York Times*, December 17, 1971, www.nytimes.com.

26 Joseph Dellapenna, "Recycling the Myths of Abortion History," *First Things*, August 5, 2008, www.firstthings.com. When the positive reviewer Michael Uhlmann passed away in 2019, his obituary underscored his pro-life bent, recalls him making sexual comments to the wives of graduate students, and remembers him sending a toy pistol to the newborn son of a colleague so he would "appreciate his second amendment rights from the start." Greg Piper, "Professor Who Saved Electoral College and Shaped Pro-Life Movement Celebrated by Students And Colleagues," *The College Fix*, November 18, 2019, www.thecollegefix.com.

27 *Dobbs*.

28 Michael Holquist, *Dostoevsky and the Novel* (Princeton: Princeton University Press, 1977), 135. Nancy Anderson describes this sort of invention as everywhere present in *Demons* in the narrator's description of Varvara Petrovna's relationship to Stepan Trofimovich ("She invented . . . him, and was the first to believe in her invention" (15)) and in the narrator's comments about Peter ("I tell you, sir, it's very easy for Pyotr Stepanovich to live in the world, because he imagines a man and then lives with him the way he imagined him. (259, 362)." Nancy Anderson, "The Perverted Ideal in Dostoevsky's *The Devils*" (Peter Lang: 1997).

29 Frances Stead Sellers, "Her Baby Has a Deadly Diagnosis. Her Florida Doctors Refused an Abortion," *Washington Post*, updated May 19, 2023, www.washingtonpost.com; Elizabeth Cohen and John Bonifield, "Texas Woman Almost Dies Because She Couldn't Get an Abortion," *CNN*, updated June 20, 2023, www.cnn.com.

30 Aria Bendix, "Idaho Becomes One of the Most Extreme Anti-Abortion States with Law Restricting Travel for Abortions," *NBC News*, April 6, 2023, www.nbcnews.com.

1

The "Gift of Life"

Regulating the Sale of Gametes in the United States

KIMBERLY MUTCHERSON

The creation of the technology to freeze sperm for use in artificial insemination (AI) and the later invention of in vitro fertilization (IVF) led to a booming, worldwide business in recruiting men and women to sell sperm and ova to would-be parents. In our modern world there are thousands of commercial transactions each year involving the sale of gametes or sex cells. This unique form of commerce raises practical, ethical, and normative issues around whether and, if so, how the government should regulate this trade, including whether and how to regulate the bodies and choices of those who sell their gametes.

Even though the use of purchased gametes to create pregnancies in the face of infertility is a long-standing global practice, it remains mired in controversy. In many countries, the sale of gametes raises questions about appropriate compensation, if any, for individuals who are selling their gametes; the responsibilities of gamete-selling banks and health care providers to protect the physical and emotional well-being of those sellers; ethical quandaries, created when parts of the body are commodified; and the human rights implications of creating children who may never know their genetic origins. The many dilemmas have led some countries to ban the sale of gametes and allow only noncommercial gamete exchanges, but most states in the United States have leaned into the commercial aspect of the practice, and policymakers have largely let the gamete market self-regulate.

Over time, some advocates, consumers, lawmakers, and gamete sellers have challenged this laissez-faire attitude by raising concerns about fraud perpetrated by the purchasing banks or the sellers, harm to children, harm to sellers and buyers, and ethical concerns about how selling the tools of conception might degrade families and societies through the commodification of reproduction. Reproductive endocrinologists committing fertility fraud; donor-conceived[1] people demanding access to information about their genetic origins and an end to anonymous gamete sales; coverage of serial sperm donors who donate their sperm to dozens of women without any middleman; and the soft cap on compensation for women who sell ova have all generated pressure to create new and more binding industry regulations.

This chapter explores the loose government generated regulatory landscape for gamete sales in the United States; efforts to create more law and policy to formally regulate the industry, including individual states banning the anonymous sale of gametes; and attempts to crack down on serial donors who work outside of existing gamete-selling banks. The entire discussion rests on the principle that, because the sale of gametes leads to the creation of new human beings, the reasons and ways to regulate deserve exacting review, and proposed forms of new regulations, must balance potentially conflicting goals. Factors to be considered in that balance include:

- that a person's creation story can have physical and psychological impacts throughout their lives;
- the state's obligation to protect those who cannot protect themselves;
- respect for an individual's right to sell their gametes for their own benefit;
- the right of individuals to purchase those gametes once on the market to effectuate their constitutionally protected right to procreate; and
- societal concerns about the corrosive risks of commodifying bodies and body parts, the process of procreation, and the reality of parenting.

The law can and should play a role in ensuring minimum standards of conduct in the gamete market, but there are existing bodies of law that regulate parts of the practice in the absence of a single regulatory regime focused on the gamete-selling industry. If there is to be more regulation—and it is not clear that this is necessary—it is vital to ensure that the industry is sustained not primarily for those who make money in it but to benefit those who, through chance or circumstance, must or choose to use its tools to create children.

Infertility

The gamete industry began as a way to satisfy the procreative desires of the medically infertile, specifically opposite sex, married couples.[2] Infertility is a substantial issue in the United States, with the Centers for Disease Control and Prevention estimating that about one in five women of reproductive age in the United States is infertile.[3] In keeping with a tendency to discuss infertility as a women's issue, the same agency offers no estimate for the number of infertile men in the United States, although "33% of infertility involves the partner with a uterus and ovaries, 33% of infertility involves the partner with a penis and testicles; [and] 33% of infertility involves both partners or is unexplained."[4]

The phrase "medical infertility" means the inability to conceive after one year of trying to do so, typically through unprotected sex with an opposite-sex partner. For women over the age of 35, a medical diagnosis of infertility can be made after six months of trying to conceive because fertility decreases for women after this age.[5] For men, fertility begins to decrease closer to 50.[6] Medical infertility can be caused by a range of factors, some attributed to a male partner such as low sperm count, and others attributed to a female partner such as polycystic ovary syndrome.

The costs of infertility treatment can be exorbitant depending on what level of care is needed. Consequently, many people living with infertility in the United States are unable to successfully access treatment.[7] Private health insurance does not routinely cover this treatment. About 20 states and the District of Columbia mandate varying levels of insurance coverage for treatment of infertility, with different exceptions to the mandates including carveouts for religious employers and small businesses.[8] Medicaid, the government insurance program for low-income people in the United States, does not pay for assisted reproduction; a miniscule number of states make some exceptions for very basic forms of care.[9] Thus, new forms of regulation, whether from the government or professional organizations, that increase costs for treatment will severely impact infertility patients, especially those who do not have insurance to offset the cost of care and/or who are not at least financially secure if not wealthy. Given existing racial disparities among the medically infertile in the United States, with Black women comprising a disproportionate number of people living with infertility and having lower rates of success when able to access fertility services, heightened regulation could also increase this access gap.[10]

Unlike medical infertility, "social infertility" refers to individuals who use assisted reproduction not because they cannot conceive without third-party assistance but because they have a partner of the same sex or perhaps have transmissible diseases or disabilities that they want to avoid passing on to their offspring.[11] The distinction between the two types of infertility—medical versus social—is meaningful because it can serve as a dividing line between those who can access needed care to create pregnancies and those who are shut out of access due to finances, discrimination, or other factors. There are individuals who have same-sex partners who are medically infertile and people who want to screen for disease markers in future children who are also medically infertile. Thus, the two categories are not mutually exclusive, but the impact of the differing diagnoses can be significant, as some fertility providers, often for personal reasons, choose not to treat social infertility.[12] Even in states that mandate insurance coverage for those who use assisted reproduction, plans may exclude the socially infertile because they lack a medical diagnosis.[13]

The expressive consequence of this divide is to create different categories of people who are deemed worthy of accessing the technological tools to create their families of choice and those whose choices (and families) are not worthy of such care and concern. Given the number of single women, same-sex couples, people with disabilities, and others whose families are nontraditional—meaning they do not conform to an increasingly archaic notion of what "real" families look like—rules that impede access to fertility care can be challenging financially and psychologically.

Over time, the line between medical and social infertility has blurred, with the American Society for Reproductive Medicine (ASRM) offering a more inclusive definition of infertility in 2023.[14] The ASRM is the leading professional organization in the United States for those practicing reproductive medicine. The updated definition incorporates social infertility rather than treating it as a separate and potentially less "serious" form of infertility. This blurring of the difference between medical versus social infertility is crucial in the quest to make access to assisted reproduction more equitable in the United States. Even as it dissipates, the persistence of such a line explains some existing forms of legal regulation and lays the groundwork for critique of regulatory proposals that may disparately impact marginalized families.

The inability to become pregnant, create a pregnancy, or successfully carry a pregnancy to term can be devastating and life-altering for many people existing in a reality in which parenthood may be expected and motherhood can still feel mandatory.[15] Whether for biological or social reasons, or a powerful combination of both, many people desire to procreate and to parent children who share their genes. And when they cannot do so coitally, they turn to the fertility industry to achieve their desires.

The Rise of the Baby Business in the United States: Regulating Gametes and the People Who Sell Them

Treating infertility is big business in the United States and globally, and the profit potential is only growing. As far back as 1992, "infertility care in [the United States] was a $2 billion per year business; today [2022], it is about [$8 billion] in gross revenues."[16] On a global scale "the industry is estimated to be worth $25 billion and is predicted to grow to $41 billion by 2026."[17] It is no surprise, then, that there are hundreds of fertility clinics in the United States catering to this booming market[18] that diagnose and treat infertility. Some clinics also recruit egg and sperm sellers and/or gestational surrogates. In addition to the clinics who provide medical care, there are hundreds of banks that sell gametes, which includes recruiting gamete sellers and/or matching gestational carriers with intended parents to facilitate surrogacy arrangements. In all parts of the industry, there is money to be made.

Given the size of the industry in the United States, there is surprisingly little law that specifically targets commerce in sex cells. As discussed below, there are laws and regulations related to testing gametes before sale, laws about insurance coverage for fertility care, and laws related to parentage when children are made using gametes that are sold or donated. However, many laws that impact gamete sales are not specific to the industry, and much of the targeted regulation comes from professional organizations like ASRM and the Society for Assisted Reproductive Technology (SART) that set standards for care and provide ethics opinions among many other services. For decades, the relative scarcity of laws governing the fertility industry sparked debate about whether the industry needed deeper regulation and, if so, what form that regulation should take. The following sections consider and critique six possible forms of regulation.

Regulating the Safety of Gametes

Regulating for safety is the easiest and most justified form of regulating the sale of gametes, meaning whether those gametes are free from communicable disease. The US Food and Drug Administration (FDA) requires that banks selling gametes conduct testing in approved labs, document the results of those tests, mark as ineligible donors who test positive for certain diseases, and keep records of the testing for a designated period of time.[19] Those who wish to sell their gametes must submit to screening that includes "a current donor medical history interview to determine medical history and relevant social behavior, a current physical examination, and treatments related to medical conditions that may suggest the donor is at increased risk for a relevant communicable disease."[20] As required by law, gametes must be tested for sexually transmitted infections like HIV, hepatitis B, hepatitis C, syphilis, chlamydia, and gonorrhea.[21] People buying gametes should feel secure that the gametes they purchase will not give them a sexually transmitted infection. There is no justification for not having this basic form of regulation, which has existed for decades.

A similar but not identical concern about safety is whether the gametes being sold come from sellers who have genetic risks or anomalies that should be shared with those purchasing the gametes. These concerns can be dealt with by creating legal requirements that banks perform more due diligence than just asking questions of the people from whom they are buying gametes. If the law required banks to engage in minimal attempts to confirm more of the information offered by gamete sellers or even required genetic testing along with testing for sexually transmitted infections and sharing the risks they discover, then parents and progeny would have better access to health information. Currently, gamete-selling banks, especially those selling sperm, routinely do basic forms of genetic testing not because of legal requirements but as a response to the desires of their customers. The benefits of creating a new statutory requirement must be weighed against the possibility of higher costs for what is now one of the cheapest forms of intervention for those seeking fertility treatment in a country where many people do not have access to insurance to cover the costs of fertility treatments.

Regulating to Protect the Bodies of Gamete Sellers

A regulatory regime focused on gametes being sold as part of the fertility industry must reckon with the reality that gametes can be sold only after they are extracted from bodies. The exception is traditional surrogates who become pregnant through AI and use their own egg to create a child who will be parented by others.[22] The extraction process is an initial point of considering appropriate legal protection for gamete sellers.

Sperm is necessary for AI and sperm and ova are necessary for IVF, in which fertilization takes place in a petri dish before the fertilized ova are transferred into a uterus. IVF is physically, financially, and emotionally taxing for those who use it. When possible, the people intending to parent use their own gametes to create embryos. When the gametes of the intended parent or parents will not be used to make babies, gametes from known[23] or unknown donors or sellers can be used instead,[24] which requires those individuals to engage in acts that will remove their gametes from their bodies.

In sharp contrast to the many steps involved in egg retrieval, sperm collection typically requires the person providing the sperm to masturbate, obviating the need for medical intervention. Happily, the physical risks of masturbation are miniscule if they exist at all, so the bodies of men who sell their sperm are subjected to less physical intervention than women experience. Therefore, there is no powerful claim to be made that regulation is necessary to protect the bodies of men who sell their sperm.

Selling ova requires that the seller go through egg retrieval, which begins by prescribing hormones for the seller/patient that she must inject to stimulate her ovaries to produce more eggs than would typically be released during a normal menstrual cycle. She may also receive hormones to help the eggs mature or to delay ovulation before the eggs are ready. Harvesting multiple eggs increases the chances of having a sufficient number of healthy embryos to implant and may reduce the number of egg retrievals a woman must undergo. A vaginal ultrasound and/or blood tests determine when the eggs are mature enough to be harvested. If the follicles, the sacs in ovaries that contain immature ova, are not viable, retrieval will be canceled and the woman will need to take a new round of hormones for a subsequent attempt. Once the follicles and the mature ova they contain are ready, they will be removed at the fertility center through a multistep process that involves pain medication and a transvaginal ultrasound through which the physician will insert a thin needle connected to a suction device to collect the follicles. In the alternative, the physician might need to conduct an abdominal ultrasound and insert the needle through the stomach and into the ovaries. Post-procedure impacts can include cramping and feelings of fullness or pressure in the abdomen.[25]

Things can go wrong at numerous points during an IVF cycle, so the time committed, physical discomfort, and exposure to risk that a woman experiences does not guarantee a pregnancy will result, and a pregnancy does not guarantee a successful birth. Further, the hormones involved can cause issues like ovarian hyperstimulation syndrome in which the ovaries swell and become painful. The position can reverse itself in mild cases, and treatment may simply be over-the-counter pain medications and drinking lots of water. More severe cases can cause extreme abdominal pain, blood clots, shortness of breath, a tight or enlarged abdomen, and severe and persistent nausea or vomiting. Acute cases may require hospital admission for monitoring, IV fluids, and other medications to suppress the overstimulation. The direst cases may lead to "surgery for a ruptured ovarian cyst or intensive care for liver or lung complications [and] anticoagulant medications to decrease the risk of blood clots."[26] The long-term medical impact of selling eggs has not been sufficiently studied to offer definitive information on whether women who participate will find themselves with fertility or other medical difficulties if or when they are prepared to have children of their own.[27]

Given the potential for short- or long-term physical harm during the steps that lead to extraction and the extraction itself, some form of regulation that protects the health of a woman selling her eggs is justified. Without making any across-the-board claim about the quality of medical care in the United States, the necessary involvement of health care providers in the process of egg retrieval means that there is a medical standard of care[28] that guides treatment and that, if breached, can result in legal liability and even the loss of one's medical license in sufficiently egregious circumstances. Being a seller does not alter any of the warnings that must be given to any patient undergoing an egg retrieval to ensure that her consent is informed and voluntary.

This obligation to share information is legal and ethical. ASRM recommends that health care providers inform prospective egg sellers of:

- the potential medical and psychological risks of undergoing oocyte retrieval for reproduction or research; [and]
- the potential negative health and psychological effects of oocyte donation.[29]

It is also prudent and appropriate to warn that all medical risks may not yet be known or well understood. Health care providers violate these standards at their own peril because, again, the status of being an egg seller does not make a person any less of a patient with all of the rights that flow from that status.

The sale of gametes falls within the prevailing legal paradigm about bodies in the law, which is that competent adults can make a wide swath of decisions about what is done with their own bodies, including how they choose to monetize those bodies. Certainly, there are glaring exceptions to this paradigm, such as the criminalization of sex work, and the radical reshaping of abortion law after the Supreme Court's 2022 *Dobbs v. Jackson Women's Health Organization* decision overturning *Roe v. Wade*. Perhaps the prohibition on selling organs is akin to regulation of selling gametes, but gametes are different from organs in meaningful ways for the person selling them. For example, selling a kidney leaves a person at a great disadvantage if their remaining kidney fails them. Other organs, like corneas, cannot be sold without immediate detrimental impacts. By contrast, cis women are born with millions of ova, and sperm is embarrassingly easy to come by. Gametes are much more akin to blood plasma, which is routinely sold in the United States without widespread controversy.

Requiring the furnishing of information to gamete sellers beyond the medical standard of care or what is strongly recommended by the leading professional organization is the kind of overreach seen in abortion regulation. Some states, in their zeal to make accessing abortion as onerous as possible, mandate the language of informed consent, including conveying false or misleading information in some cases. If the general understanding is that medical professionals, not government regulators or politicians, determine appropriate standards of care, it is questionable whether in the United States there is any need for specific laws regulating consent when selling gametes.

The question of so-called psychological risk is more complicated than physical risks. Multiple banks that sell gametes claim that their sellers meet with mental health providers to ensure full understanding of the potential ramifications of participating in the gamete-selling process including the potential emotional consequences.[30] In the case of selling ova, ASRM recommends that a dedicated counselor engage with women selling their eggs to ensure that the women:

- [U]nderstand that they could later develop desires to establish contact with their genetically related children, desires that may be difficult to satisfy because of legal or other barriers. Alternatively, donors should be apprised that remaining anonymous to the recipient(s) or resulting offspring may not be possible because of increasingly sophisticated genetic tracing and social-media technologies.
- Donor candidates should be encouraged to explore their possible emotional responses, particularly those that could develop if they experience infertility problems themselves.
- The prospective donor's motivation for participating should be explored . . . with the goal of providing information to allow her to assess her decision to donate her eggs, given the potential consequences of her donation and possible associated risks, and to ensure that she is not unduly influenced by financial hardships that might compel her to participate.[31]

The language ASRM uses here mimics the argument about regret made by proponents of more formal regulation of the gamete-selling industry. That argument posits that gamete sellers may regret the choice to sell their gametes because of concerns about phantom children who share their genes or because they might experience infertility when they seek to have children of their own. One might think of this as the "mini-me" hypothesis in the sense that it posits a seller who comes to believe that a child born from their gametes should not be a stranger to them. Regret may also flow from a belief that they have forfeited their chance to have a child of their own because they sold their gametes to others when they were younger.

Perhaps some gamete sellers will regret their choice to sell gametes for a variety of reasons, and some may even seek to find children made from their gametes. There is no existing legal impediment to that search, though there are no easy legal paths for a person who sold gametes to forge a legal relationship to a genetically related minor child. But the possibility of regret is not itself a weighty reason to regulate the choices a competent adult makes about monetizing her body products. Regret can come from a poorly conceived tattoo, from donating an organ, or from participating in risky activities, but the law must be careful not to conflate possibility with certainty or to presume that people who have regrets should have been saved from making those decisions in the first instance, especially where there is insufficient data to support such a claim. Again, using abortion as an example, in *Gonzales v. Carhart*, in which the United States Supreme Court upheld a ban on a specific abortion procedure, Justice Anthony Kennedy wrote for the majority: "While we find no reliable data to measure the phenomenon, it seems unexceptionable to conclude some women come to regret their choice to abort the infant life they once created and sustained."[32] Regulating on the basis of no reliable data is as bad as regulating based on no data or, even worse, in the face of contrary data. There are risks to subjecting a whole swath of people to rules created based on concerns that may be relevant to very few, thereby leading to undue and unnecessary constraint on the choices that everyone gets to make. It is better to be led by actual knowledge and research lest we convert moral or faith-based preferences into binding law.

It is also patronizing to assume that all people experience genetic ties in the same way. Everyone does not have the same sense of genetic connection or responsibility that others might have. For many gamete sellers, it is possible to disconnect from their gametes without feeling that they have abandoned children who may not even exist or who may have no interest in being contacted by a stranger. In this sense, each body that contributes bits of genetic code to create a child need not have obligations to that child beyond having allowed the child to be created using their genes. In opting to sell their gametes, these individuals choose to procreate without parenting, and their incursion into existing families can be disruptive and potentially destabilizing (discussed later in this chapter). Gamete sellers are not deadbeat or absentee parents who are frequently derided with little concern for the personal circumstances that may impede their ability to parent. In fact, as genetic progenitors, these sellers are parents only in the most technical sense: they have no legal rights or responsibilities and none of the benefits and burdens of parenting. These sellers create opportunities for parenthood for others for several reasons, including financial renumeration, and do so with the specific plan not to be a rearing parent or even necessarily to be known. The choice to sell their sex cells is not a reprehensible one even if it is just for money, but for many the choice also flows from feelings of generosity and empathy for infertile people.

Anyone sufficiently competent to sign the contracts and, in the case of women who have their eggs extracted, the informed consent forms attendant to selling gametes is sufficiently competent to understand how babies get made. Mining their psyches for deeper understanding is likely unnecessary and potentially infantilizing and insulting. If someone later regrets their choices, it will likely be because they have changed with time, not because of what they were told or not told when they sold their gametes. That being said, the industry has already created its own standards around the consent process for selling gametes that does enough without doing too much. New laws would either be redundant or an excuse to create unnecessary requirements.

Regulating Compensation

The differences in extraction for sperm and ova have implications for regulating price in the context of selling gametes. Compensation for women selling their eggs ranges widely based on whether the eggs are to be used fresh or frozen and the clinic, bank, or individual facilitating the purchase. One bank offers recruits up to $9,000 per cycle to compensate for time and effort,[33] while another promises up to $6,000 in reimbursement.[34] Where there is high demand due to scarcity or highly sought-after characteristics, often true for women of color (especially women of Asian descent), the price people will pay for eggs can skyrocket, sometimes into five figures.[35] There are also accounts of wealthy couples hiring brokers to seek out potential egg sellers who may not already be affiliated with an agency. This is done by targeting women at Ivy League or other elite educational institutions who possess desired traits (athletic, specific hair and eye color, etc.) and contacting them, sometimes through social media, to see if they can be convinced to sell. One agency owner claimed to have worked with women who sold their ova for $50,000 and at least one woman who sold her ova for $100,000.

As Kara Swanson describes in her book *Banking on the Body: The Market in Blood, Milk, and Sperm in Modern America*: "Sperm banks, long spurned by a medical profession that preferred fresh semen for artificial insemination, developed a for-profit business model that focused on recruiting patients as customers rather than on serving doctors."[36] Therefore, modern sperm banks recruit and cultivate clients and sell the sperm that they purchase to eager consumers at a markup. To procure sperm, banks seek out young men, often advertising on or near college campuses. Sperm providers will typically be paid approximately $100 for each vial of sperm they produce. One agency informs potential donors that they can consistently make up to $1,500 per month because they can donate several times per week.[37]

To the extent that compensation is not driven simply by the worth of the gamete, which presumes an objective way of pricing sex cells, the price of extraction (physical, psychological, and temporal) justifies the compensation differential between sperm and ova. The market drives the significant gaps in pricing, and there are no laws that cap or set a minimum price. However, two of the professional associations that work with fertility providers created their own soft cap on compensation for ova that faced a legal challenge.

In 2011, Lindsay Kamakahi filed suit against ASRM, SART, and all clinics and banks that chose to abide by the two organizations' long-standing professional guidelines that suggested that compensation for the sale of eggs should be no more than $5,000 in general and no more than $10,000 in exceptional circumstances. Kamakahi argued that the suggested caps violated antitrust laws by engaging in the unfair business practice of price-fixing, which artificially suppressed the price for selling ova. ASRM defended these guidelines as a way to cabin the costs of fertility care thereby increasing access for infertility patients, with the unfortunate consequence of reducing the price women could demand for their ova.[38] The debate about compensation for women who sell their eggs remains contentious. In its most recent postlitigation pronouncement on the subject, ASRM wrote: "Compensation to women providing oocytes should be fair and not used as an undue enticement that will lead prospective donors to discount risks. Monetary compensation should reflect the time, inconvenience, and physical and emotional demands associated with participating in oocyte donation."[39]

Based on the language from ASRM, one could claim that unfairly capping the compensation for gamete sellers, especially ova sellers, is an unwarranted regulation of the bodies of women and men who choose to participate in this market. But others hold that prices that are too high are equally if not more problematic. Professor Michael Sandel argues that paying what the market will bear in cases like this leads to coercion because desperate circumstances, such as deep poverty, drive participation.[40] For reasons described below, the potential for coercion in the U.S. gamete market is far less acute than is true in other markets for body products, like blood plasma, for which there is a thriving market.

There are substantial barriers to entry into the gamete market as compared to markets for blood plasma in which desperation can drive people's participation. This leads to the fear that some individuals eager to make money from selling blood plasma will not be honest about their medical conditions or risk factors. There is "some evidence that paying for plasma does, indeed, lead more people to conceal their disease status or risk behaviors. For instance, the Government Accountability Office looked at California's blood versus plasma supply back in the 1990s and found that the plasma had much higher rates of HIV. There are reports of desperate donors lying about illnesses to donate for cash."[41]

Unlike the market in blood plasma, the gamete market, in part because it is a market driven by those who have the money to pay for its expensive services, is less likely to attract those who are in the direst of straits. For both sperm and ova, banks recruit people who are young, healthy, tall (if they are men), fairly well educated, athletic, slim (or at least not clinically obese), and often conventionally attractive.

For sperm, recruitment often happens on or near college campuses to recruit people who are or will be college educated. This is even more true for the ova market, where the donors are similarly young and often college-educated or in the process of becoming so. Additionally, the months of preparation and physical requirements of being an egg seller create a weighty natural barrier to entry for many people. Further, because of actual or perceived market demands from sellers, the number of people who banks will deem unqualified—some being barred simply by virtue of an initial screening for height and weight—is significant. Becoming a successful sperm or ova seller places a person into an elite club marked by exclusivity, and exclusivity does not come cheap. Certainly, barriers to entry do not mean that these young sellers are impervious to economic coercion, but the requirements and consequences of participation provide an obstacle that allows for time and consideration that might not exist in other markets for body products with a low threshold for entry.

Recognizing the fear of undue inducement into the market as a consequence of overcompensation does not answer the question of what level of compensation is appropriate for sperm or ova sellers. Compensation is impacted by scarcity, a basic rule of economics, but that does not help to fashion a specific number that is fair and equitable without being coercive. Thus, a person who is willing to subject herself to risk in exchange for money may be restrained from engaging in that sale because the price is set artificially low or may be unduly influenced to sell because the price is too high by someone's standard. In such a case, and given the unique nature of the exchange, regulation seems ill-suited to fixing exact dollar amounts versus offering advice about the factors that should properly be considered when setting a price to be paid, as the ASRM chose to do after being sued.

Regulating for Quality and Characteristics

The hunt for gametes often begins with a simple search on easily found websites for an agency that sells gametes. Some medical practices that provide fertility care also sell sperm and eggs, but there are many independent banks that sell gametes to patients who have them sent to their medical providers for their use. Once on a website, gamete purchasers can filter results based on race, ethnicity, height, weight, eye color, hair color, and other physical traits as well as find information about degrees earned, hobbies, occupations, and reasons for selling their gametes. As discussed above, as the price of genetic testing has fallen, banks have increasingly made such testing routine with results available to intended parents.

Beyond safety of the gametes themselves, gamete banks have fairly wide latitude to function as they see fit in terms of how they recruit new gamete sellers, share information about those sellers with purchasers, and set prices for the gametes they buy and sell. While banks offer a significant amount of information about their sperm and egg sellers on their websites, including medical histories for the seller and close family members, as well as likes, dislikes, and potentially appealing habits, they do not guarantee that they have fully vetted and verified the information they are sharing, with the exception of the specific genetic testing and required FDA testing.

No matter how special one believes gametes to be, given where they come from (human bodies) and what they do (make more human bodies), they are arguably still products when placed on the market, and therefore gametes essentially come with an implied warranty of merchantability. This is a contracts concept in which the seller makes a "basic promise that the goods sold will do what they are supposed to do and that there is nothing significantly wrong with them. In other words, it is an implied promise that the goods are fit to be sold."[42] All merchants make this promise, and it cannot be waived.

When selling gametes, merchants (banks procuring and then selling gametes in this case) make various categories of promises to the buyer (the intended parents). The first promise is that the sperm or ova can be used to create a pregnancy or an embryo, which is the purpose for which the gametes are purchased. A sperm bank would violate this part of the warranty if they sold sperm from someone who was himself infertile due to issues with the quality of his sperm. The same is true for selling ova. An egg broker who sold ova from a woman whose eggs cannot be fertilized for some reason, perhaps because the ova did not mature properly because of polycystic ovary syndrome, could also violate this warranty. In both cases, the chances that faulty sperm or immature ova would ever be sold are miniscule given the screening processes conducted before and after egg retrievals and sperm collection.[43] Success as a business also requires that banks sell a good product, meaning gametes that actually create pregnancies. Thus, banks have a natural incentive to sell products that work as expected if they want to stay in business. So while there is a potential remedy for selling a faulty product, the problem is unlikely to occur.

The second promise is that the sperm or egg will not cause physical harm to the person using it (i.e., by transmitting disease). Again, given proper screening procedures, this should never happen.

The third promise is that the gametes purchased come from the specific seller that the buyer chose. If a buyer purchases vials of sperm from Donor 123, the vials sent for her use must all contain sperm from Donor 123. The same should be true of anyone buying ova. Liability for a seller who sends the wrong product—meaning ova or sperm from the incorrect gamete seller—should be relatively straightforward in the same way that, if you bought a new car and the dealer delivered a car other than the one you purchased, the dealer would need to rectify the error or compensate the seller for it. Unfortunately, in the world of gamete-selling, there are heart-wrenching examples of failures to send the correct product.

One such case occurred in 2011 when Jennifer Cramblett and her female partner, both white, purchased sperm from a white sperm seller to use for AI. Due to poor recordkeeping by the sperm bank, the sperm Cramblett used to become pregnant came from a Black man. Cramblett became aware of the error about five months into her pregnancy when she called to purchase more vials of sperm from the same donor so that her partner could later have a child using that sperm, making their children genetic half-siblings. The couple's daughter, Payton, a "beautiful, obviously mixed-race, baby girl,"[44] was born in August 2012. The agency reimbursed Cramblett for the cost of the incorrect sperm they sent to her and apologized for their mistake, but Cramblett was not satisfied with mere reimbursement.[45] In 2014, she sued the sperm bank for wrongful birth and breach of warranty.

The warranty claim is a fairly easy one in terms of establishing liability. Cramblett purchased sperm from Donor 380, but the sperm bank sent sperm from Donor 330 to the physician who performed Cramblett's inseminations. The agency's low-tech, handwritten records made it easy for such a mistake to occur. The special nature of gametes means that mistakes cannot be rectified or compensated for in the same way that might be available for a typical consumer item.[46] If the bank had discovered their error before the insemination, it would have sent Cramblett the proper sperm to fix the error before it became a more intractable problem. However, once she became pregnant, the only fix was pregnancy termination, which would have been possible if she had learned of the mix-up early enough in her pregnancy, if she was willing to have an abortion, and if she could access safe abortion care in a timely manner. Even then, she might still have a claim for the cost of the abortion. Despite being reimbursed for the sperm's cost; Cramblett found this compensation wholly inadequate to redress the harm she claimed to experience because of Payton's existence as a visibly biracial child with white mothers in an almost all-white community. Cramblett sued the sperm bank for damages in excess of $50,000 as compensation because she "suffered personal injuries, medical expense, pain, suffering, emotional distress, and other economic and non-economic losses, and will do so in the future."[47]

The second and more troubling claim in Cramblett's case was for wrongful birth, for which she claimed the same damages of "personal injuries, medical expense, pain, suffering, emotional distress, and other economic and non-economic losses." Wrongful birth claims are typically filed in cases where a child is born with significant disease or disability because of a health care provider's neglectful care. Often, that care involves doing or failing to do something that would have revealed the child's condition at a time when the pregnancy could have been terminated or failing to properly disclose information about the condition when discovered during the pregnancy. In these cases, the claim centers not on harm to the child but the harm to the parent by virtue of being denied the ability to make a choice about whether to continue with a pregnancy. In a wrongful birth case, to prove her claim the parent must indicate that she would have terminated the pregnancy if she had been made aware of the information about the condition of the child at the appropriate time.[48] Usually parents in wrongful birth cases have children who need significant care, often over the course of their life span, and the damage awards help to offset those costs.

In the Cramblett case, the only so-called problem with Payton was that she was identifiably biracial. As Cramblett and her partner lived in an area with little racial diversity, Payton's birth meant that Ms. Cramblett "live[d] each day with fears, anxieties and uncertainty about her future and Payton's future." Her community was "intolerant," and her family was unwilling to deal with differences, including Cramblett's identity as a lesbian. Cramblett had to travel some distance to a Black neighborhood, "where she is obviously different in appearance, and not overtly welcome,"[49] to find someone to do Payton's hair. To protect her child from the mental and emotional harm occasioned by living in an area and within a family where she was likely to feel isolated and unwelcome, Cramblett felt that she must move to a more racially diverse area, and this relocation would come at a significant financial cost.

The viscerally disturbing nature of Cramblett's claim speaks to why purchasing sperm and ova is different from purchasing other commodified products derived from human bodies. First, to the extent that race is a social construct and not a true biological category, Cramblett might not have sued if Payton did not *look* Black or biracial. The phenomenon of passing as white reminds us that Black people, even those who are not biracial or multiracial, come in a wide variety of shades, hair textures, and facial features. Had Payton emerged with skin tone and features that allowed her mother to conceal her racial heritage and raise her as white, the harm Cramblett claimed would presumably dissipate even if concealing her daughter's racial provenance might negatively impact Payton.

Second, much can be made of the fact that Cramblett and her partner were fine with racial homogeneity and intolerance in their chosen community so long as it would not be directed at them or their child. Before having children, they moved from Akron, Ohio, a much more racially diverse area, to their racially homogenous community to take advantage of better schools. What is the appropriateness of awarding damages to people for whom seeking out the comforts of a white community was a priority until their family ceased to be all white? The court initially tasked with resolving Cramblett's claim dismissed the lawsuit. Had she prevailed, the troubling narrative about the undesirability of Blackness and the presence of Blackness in a child as a form of harm for a family would denigrate the worth of a Black child and for a court to legitimize that narrative would be deeply problematic.[50]

Cramblett's story is emblematic of the racial politics of assisted reproduction and gamete-selling because racial hierarchy and white supremacy are so deeply entrenched in the United States. The vast majority of people who purchase gametes in the United States are white, and most of them buy gametes collected from other white people, leading to the birth of white babies.[51] In other words, the market makes it easy to have and pursue preferences for racially homogenous families along with the many other preferences that can be satisfied through a search of what gametes are available from a given agency.

Consciously or subconsciously, many people prefer racial homogeneity in their personal lives, including in choices about marriage and family. Despite its racial diversity, people in the United States largely live in racially segregated communities, which means that they socialize within their own race, marry within their own race, worship within their own race, and give birth to children who share their racial identities.[52] To the extent that whiteness is a form of property,[53] white people who use assisted reproduction and buy gametes as part of that process use money to ensure that they pass the privileges of whiteness to their children. Consequently, the gamete market targets white gamete sellers to satisfy this preference. This is not to say that passing down a legacy of racial privilege is the primary goal of white people purchasing gametes, but it is a predictable outcome. By contrast, and in tension with a narrative that fertility markets care only about whiteness,[54] intended parents of color who purchase gametes will find scant choices within the existing market dominated by gametes from white people.[55] The lack of gamete sellers of color means that those people of color who do choose to sell their gametes may be able to command above market rates, upending the usual way that whiteness works in other markets, including the market for adoption.

The foregoing description of one way in which race operates in gamete markets should not be read as a condemnation of those who use technology to build the racially homogenous family that they would have had without infertility. Rather, it is simply an observation that matters of race remain strongly relevant in many aspects of family-building. That race matters in fertility markets, as it does in almost every aspect of U.S. society, does not in itself make the market corrupt, at least no more so than the millions of people who choose to have babies with partners who are of their same race through coital reproduction.

The market in gametes also creates the potential to fetishize race. Consider a white woman who buys sperm from a Black or brown man because she loves brown skin or thinks that multiracial babies are especially beautiful. Putting aside the fact that Black and brown people have skin tones that run the spectrum from dark to white passing, this kind of behavior is egregious for its frivolity and lack of care for the child's experience. Despite her legal claims of harm, Jennifer Cramblett recognized that she needed to be a culturally competent white parent to a child of color. Someone who picks a sperm provider for the aesthetics of multiracial babies may not be the best person to parent that child. Further, a white person purchasing sperm from a provider of color for aesthetic reasons would be commandeering a scarce resource that could be desperately desired by a person of color seeking gametes in a market dominated by white people. As long as race matters and racialized bodies are perceived and treated differently in the United States, race will remain an integral and challenging part of family-building through third-party reproduction, and it is difficult if not impossible to imagine a constitutionally sound regulatory regime that could alter this status quo.

In a case like Cramblett's, while an agency could be liable for sending the wrong gametes, a category of responsibility for which the agency would not be held liable is where donor characteristics that led the buyer to select a certain sperm or egg provider do not become characteristics shared by a child born from those gametes. As described above, gamete buyers can search for gamete providers by screening for a variety of characteristics, some of which are known to be genetically transmissible and others that are not. For instance, a person who purchased sperm from a red-haired, green-eyed gamete provider who is a disciplined and successful athlete, accomplished pianist, book lover, and world traveler might produce a child with brown hair and brown eyes who has two left feet, never moves past playing a recorder in elementary school, hates to read, and loves nothing more than being at home. In other words, there can be no warranty—from the agency or the gamete provider—that any specific trait—genetically transmissible or not—will manifest in a child simply by virtue of what is known about the egg or sperm seller. Even if it later becomes clear that the gamete seller lied about some of their traits (perhaps they are not a virtuoso pianist and have never owned a passport), the claims that the egg or sperm seller makes about her- or himself are not claims to which they or their banks will be held liable. One could certainly argue that gamete sellers have an ethical obligation to be truthful, but that obligation does not have a legal dimension, and in any case truth does not guarantee transmissibility, which would raise serious issues of causation and harm in any lawsuit.

Thus the promises that banks make to buyers are limited in scope. You will receive what you order, meaning it comes from the body of the person you thought you were buying from, any medical screenings required by law or regulation or that the agency promises will be done will, in fact, have been conducted and the results conveyed to the buyer in an appropriate fashion. Beyond that, the child who emerges cannot be a harm to their parents simply by failing to conform to the hopes, desires, and expectations of the intended parents. Unless the form of reproduction being pursued is human cloning, which remains banned for purposes of reproduction in the United States, the body that makes a child offers no guarantees about the ensuing child's body, habits, or talents.

Regulating Quantity

The question of regulating the bodies of those who sell gametes with no intent to parent or even know those babies is especially acute in the case of serial or mass donors/sellers, which refers to men who are genetic fathers to extremely large numbers of children.[56] One such donor, Jonathan Jacob Meijer, a Dutch musician in his thirties, is suspected to have fathered approximately 550 children in the Netherlands and other countries.[57] In April 2023, a judge at The Hague District Court in the Netherlands, in a case brought by a woman who used Meijer's sperm to have her child, enjoined Meijer from continuing to donate sperm because Dutch law limits donors to a maximum of 25 children with 12 mothers. According to the court, Meijer lied to some parents about how many children he had fathered to get them to use his sperm to make more children. Meijer also fathered children with women who, for assorted reasons (typically expense), did not work with an agency to find sperm. In one case, Meijer met a woman at a train station to exchange his fresh sperm for 165 euros and his travel costs. She later gave birth to a daughter who Meijer claimed was only his eighth genetic child, even though he knew he had fathered many more children by this point.[58]

Another sperm donor in the Netherlands, known as "Louis," has fathered about 200 children. In such a small country, those half siblings are running into each other, sometimes on dating apps.[59] A man in New York, Ari Nagel, nicknamed the "Target Donor" because he sometimes met with women at Target to exchange sperm, believes he has fathered about 76 children. One British unlicensed sperm donor, Simon Watson, told the BBC in 2016 that he had been providing sperm to women for about 16 years and thought he was a genetic father to about 800 children.[60] He told the network: "I've got kids all the way from Spain to Taiwan, so many countries. I'd like to get the world record ever, make sure no-one's going to break it, get as many as possible."[61] Working within the system created by the National Health Service, Watson's ability to donate would end after his sperm was used to successfully create ten families.

In the United States, the FDA has used its authority to crack down on a serial donor by accusing him of being a "firm or establishment . . . that recovers and distributes semen and therefore is a manufacturer of human cells."[62] In this case, Trent Arsenault had already fathered 14 children with several women to whom he gave his sperm for free, but the FDA put a stop to his free service by claiming that he must be held to the same standards as a lab/agency in the business of selling sperm. In this case, the regulatory agency treated Mr. Arsenault differently than a person who was engaging in coital reproduction, with the lesson being that regulating sex cells is fine so long as there is no actual sex involved.

There is much to find distasteful in stories of men who, in many cases, are taking advantage of systems that make it difficult or impossible for women to access sperm within more established, and hopefully safer, channels. If a woman cannot use a formalized system, she is left to place her trust in a man whose fresh sperm may give her an STI. She may have no background information on the seller/donor and no intermediary to track him down in the future if there is an issue—for instance, a genetically transmissible anomaly of which the seller/donor may be unaware. She may be purchasing sperm from a man whose sperm has low motility and is less likely to get her pregnant. In other words, her ability to seek information and later redress a claim if she is wronged by virtue of a faulty product is made significantly more challenging when working with someone whose interest is in creating as many children as possible and who is subject to no oversight.

Serial donors/sellers are outliers who largely work outside the established system because it is the only way that they can produce immense numbers of offspring. If anything, the presence of these serial donors supports the existence of sperm banks that can be subject to regulation and inspection so that women do not find themselves at the mercy of men who are intent on breaking records without regard for the risks they create for the children who share their genes or the women who use their sperm.

Many of the concerns raised about the gamete-selling industry, including the concern about serial donors/sellers, could be drastically reduced with regulation of the industry, not individuals, but of course individuals will feel the sting of being driven away from a potential source of income. For instance, fear of accidental incest can be cut down if banks limit the number of children produced by a single gamete seller. If strictly enforced by banks and regularly checked by regulating agencies charged with enforcement, this change in practice could have an impact on the bottom line of commercial banks due to the need to take popular sperm sellers out of their rotation. If deemed necessary, a hit to industry profits is an insufficient reason not to create and enforce such limits, as has been done in other countries with some measure of success.[63] The question, though, is whether concerns justifying caps on the number of children or families that can be made with a single person's sperm are necessary in a country as large as the United States in which there are thousands of vials of sperm sent across state lines and out of the country each day to be used by customers living hundreds or even thousands of miles away from each other.

Even more crucially, the law does not create caps on procreation for people who do so coitally. A man who wanted to have dozens of babies by having sex with and impregnating dozens of women would not be subject to legal sanction for that choice beyond possible claims for unpaid child support, which seems likely unless the man was incredibly wealthy.[64] By contrast, if you are extracting your sex cells to make money (leading to the birth of dozens of babies), the law may seek to end your baby-making spree. Thus, it is necessary to subject proposed caps on procreation for gamete sellers to an exacting inquiry to justify why they should be treated differently than a person having sex. In other words, why is a man who exchanges sperm through sex leading to the birth of hundreds of babies substantively different from a man who exchanges sperm in a Target bathroom leading to the birth of hundreds of babies? If the only distinction is that sex is harder to regulate or that there are constitutional/human rights involved in one instance and not the other, there may be compelling arguments to support that distinction, but people clamoring for regulation are not necessarily making any of those arguments.

Regulating Relationship

Beyond questions of compensation for extraction, other questions have been raised about what this chapter will refer to as "compensation for relationship." Increasingly, banks are disinclined to sell gametes anonymously. In the not-so-distant past, however, anonymity was the standard such that banks charged a premium for gametes from sellers willing to be identified to any person produced from their gametes once that person reached the age of majority. The obvious impact of sharing identifying information about the gamete sellers is that sellers may be contacted by a genetically related individual, putting sellers in the potentially awkward position of deciding whether their decision to extract and sell their gametes will lead to a connection they did not seek or desire. In the modern age, even without an agreement to be identified, gamete sellers have been discovered through at-home DNA testing companies like 23andMe.[65] Understanding why this is an issue worthy of discussion starts with a foundation of how anonymity has functioned in the world of gamete sales.

The early market for sperm focused on opposite-sex couples, who frequently were committed to hiding their use of a donor through donor matching—that is to say, attempting to find a donor who shared physical characteristics with the intended parent whose genes were not being used to make the child. The modern market for sperm has shifted to single women and same-sex female couples. In one study of a single clinic conducted in 2022, women comprised 70 percent of the people purchasing sperm.[66] Similarly, some ova are now purchased by single men and same-sex male couples who plan to bring children into their lives through gestational surrogacy.[67] In cases involving same-sex couples or single people, hiding the use of assisted reproduction or purchased sperm is much more difficult if not impossible, and thus the question of concealing how a child came to be is answered well before the child could begin to suspect that a parent or parents are hiding information about the child's backstory.

When a person sells their gametes through an agency, they know that a child born from those gametes will have no legal bond with the gamete; child support will not be owed, the seller's name will not appear on the birth certificate, and the child has no entitlement under rules of intestacy. In fact, the gamete seller may not ever know if a child is produced from their gametes. In this sense, the assumption or demand that bodies that share genetic connection must also have a familial connection is severed before a child is even conceived. This is important because critics of gamete-selling condemn this market despite the fact that the transfer of parental rights and responsibilities is ubiquitous in the United States when children are placed for adoption privately or through the foster care system. Thus, eschewing parental rights in the context of gamete sales is not unique. Unfortunately, and unfairly, adoption is frequently described as a second-best alternative to being raised by genetic parents, still often referred to as "natural" parents. This reinforces the notion that genes make a family and that loving connections between children and their genetic progenitors are fated, never forced. Thus, those who sell gametes are accused of upending the natural order of things.

Even more crucially, when a child is born and her biological parents choose not to or cannot parent that child, even as the transaction is described by some as "suboptimal," the person stepping in to parent that child routinely receives much praise for their selfless act. Even if the biological parents may be condemned by some for "abandoning" their children, there is a strong modern narrative that placing a child for adoption when one is not prepared to parent is a profound act of love.[68] The same is true of the thousands of step-families that exist or the thousands of chosen families that become the village to help raise a child when one or both genetic parents are unable or unwilling to do so. Thus, it cannot be persuasively argued that a situation in which a child's parents are not biological parents is always wrong, or even usually wrong, legally or ethically.

Much of the critique of gamete sales centers on the commercial transaction that leads to deliberate severing of the connection between genetics and parental responsibility or accountability. Adoption narratives carefully avoid language that foregrounds the role that money plays in adoptions. Those narratives are about righting an unfortunate wrong—the child whose biological parents are not prepared to parent—by replacing biological parents with, hopefully, eager adoptive parents. Laws make clear that these rights transfers are not done in exchange for money,[69] even though substantial fees often must be paid to adoption agencies and lawyers in private adoptions. Adoptive parents can also legally pay reasonable costs related to a pregnancy, such as the cost of maternity clothes, but birth parents cannot legally be paid to transfer parental rights to an adoptive parent. To do so would be baby-selling, which is legally and ethically anathema.

Unlike in adoption, when gametes are sold, there is no child in existence or even a future child being gestated who is in desperate need of parents. Instead, the sale of sperm and ova is a prelude to a series of commercial transactions that lead to the birth of a child if successful. The person who sells the sperm or ova does so in exchange for money to compensate for their time and effort. The gamete seller's role ends when their body has done its work. The critique is that creating a child as part of a commercial transaction sullies what would otherwise have been a natural, unproblematic process, but this paints far too simplistic a picture. Children are made to save failing marriages, to balance gender ratios in a family, to trap women in abusive relationships, or because of birth control failures or lack of access to accessible abortion care. Families are and always have been messy, and many of these circumstances feel more problematic than selling gametes to eager intended parents.

Selling gametes standing alone is often identified as a problem, but those sales are chiefly fraught when done anonymously, especially in the sperm market, perhaps because of the possibility of large numbers of children being born from one individual sperm seller. As alluded to above, there are sensational stories of men who sold their sperm anonymously only to later be found by their ambitious progeny using tools like 23andMe and Ancestry.com.[70] To have sold sperm in one's twenties, only to discover later in life that dozens of children exist in the world who have half your genes, can be weighty for the person who sold their gametes, the children produced from those gametes, and potentially their rearing parents.

In the end, much of the concern raised about anonymity is less about information than it is about relationships. The argument being made by those objecting to anonymity, especially some very vocal members of the donor-conceived community, is that they feel a deep sense of loss and emotional turmoil because they do not have a connection to their genetic parent or parents. One donor-conceived adult opposed to such conceptions said: "The fact that I have been intentionally separated from my father is the single most important facet of my identity, and the pain this has caused is with me every day of my life."[71] Another donor-conceived person describes the impact of the mode of her conception as follows: "Many donor offspring, I know, frequently say that they would prefer to be conceived from a one night stand rather than from sperm donation[,] which is a clinical, often commercial conception between strangers, who are your genetic parents. This, along with the intentional alienation of all our associated kinship and cultural heritage on the donor's side, is a source of profound identity loss and burden for us."[72]

The feelings of some donor-conceived people about their origins are not invalid and should be part of the discussion about selling gametes and the well-being of children who are produced from those gametes. One can believe deeply in the right to procreate for the infertile and also recognize that, whenever anyone creates new people, one owes them a measure of care and concern. What we cannot predict, however, is how those new people will see or perceive the world as they grow and experience life and, therefore, what exactly expressing care and concern requires. For some people, connection with their genetic progenitors brings enormous satisfaction; for others it is a nightmare. Even so, there are fundamental questions about how to contextualize the fervent and sincere concerns that some donor-conceived people raise about the mode of their conception.

First, it is impossible to say whether those who feel abandoned by their donors are speaking for the whole or only have the loudest megaphone. Undoubtedly, there are many donor-conceived adults who do not feel a deep sense of existential disconnect expressed in the quotes shared above. There are several studies of donor-conceived children in which the children studied do not perceive that they have been harmed by virtue of their mode of conception.[73] And if those children maintain their sense of peace as adults, they will likely spend their time living a happy life rather than trying to change the nature of the gamete-selling industry as a whole. This is not to dismiss or deny the pain of those donor-conceived adults who feel damaged by their mode of conception, but the experience of some may not be the most appropriate standard by which to determine the direction of law and policy in the realm of reproduction—a realm where government interference can often be discriminatory and problematic. One need only reflect on the long history of sterilization abuse, disparate impacts of the family policing system, and prosecutions of pregnant women for behaviors deemed to place their fetuses at risk to recognize that the law is often a clumsy and deeply discriminatory tool when it comes to family formation.

Second, in thinking about selling gametes and what it means for the children born from those gametes, there must be a reconciliation with the reality that parents who reproduce coitally make a myriad of irrevocable decisions about their children's lives before those children are born. Imagine a woman who becomes pregnant by a man who she knows has fathered and abandoned several children. The correct response to this choice is not that she should not have had a child at all or—even more draconian—that she should be legally forbidden from having a child if there is a significant risk that the child would not have a relationship with their biological father. Even if there is an ethical argument that all would-be parents should act in the best interest of their future children, including in their selection of a partner with whom to have that child, it is difficult to frame a plausible argument that would support legislation related to pre-pregnancy partner selection, which in some sense is what calls for eliminating anonymity in the gamete market seek to accomplish. It is well documented that a substantial number of children born in the United States each year are deceived about their genetic origins, but there are no laws that require people to be truthful on birth certificates. People who are donor-conceived are far from being the only people in the world who do not know the totality of their genetic roots, but parents who conceive coitally are under no legal obligation to disclose information that they have chosen to conceal. As this author has argued elsewhere, we must be careful in regulating the procreative lives of those who must or choose to use assisted reproduction in a manner that would be completely abhorrent if focused on coital reproduction.[74] Further, as states begin flexing the newly aggrandized "state interest in potential life," as the Alabama Supreme Court did in declaring frozen embryos to be unborn children,[75] the risk that incursions into family-making and parental choice—even before a child exists—raises the specter of state control of who gets to access the tools of assisted reproduction, which is a frightening prospect.

Forced disclosure could also encourage more deception from parents, especially opposite-sex parents, who would have incentive to lie about their child's origins in the hope of never having to reveal the name of a gamete seller who assisted them in creating their child. Secrecy and deception are forms of psychic harm to children as well, and the risk of being found out is increasingly high in a world of easy access to home-based genetic testing. One category of data available about children conceived through assisted reproduction and gametes from donors or sellers reveals that secrecy about the manner of conception creates distrust and shatters relationships between parents and children.[76] Regulating in ways that might encourage more secrecy is unhelpful and potentially damaging.

Third, the reliance on genetic connection as familial and individual destiny raises a myriad of practical and more philosophical concerns. As a matter of law and practice, the United States has slowly moved toward a much more expansive view of family. It is no longer the case that nuclear families consisting of one man, one woman, and their biological children are the only families worthy of legal recognition and protection. It has long been the case that families come in a wide variety of forms: they can include partners of the same sex, partners who have no interest in having a family with children, and partners whose children are not biologically related to them or who are related to one partner and not the other. Assisted reproduction complicates the landscape even more, with children being brought into families by gestational carriers who have no genetic tie to the children they gestate; married opposite-sex partners who use gametes from others to have children; and same-sex female couples who use IVF so that one partner is the genetic parent and the other the gestating parent of their shared children. The idea that flourishing requires a child to have two opposite-sex married parents to whom the child is genetically linked is a relic.

There are at least two ways of being a parent, and one need not presuppose the other. One can be a genetic progenitor by selling and giving away sperm or ova or by engaging in a sexual act that leads to the creation of a pregnancy, but that person is a parent in its most technical and arguably least useful sense. Being a genetic parent and wanting to parent a child by committing to all that is required to raise a child are distinct desires. The assumption that the genetic tie demands further connection with a child or with a genetic parent is belied by the myriad ways in which people eschew parenting or children reject their parents. Forced parenthood, like most forced relationships, tends not to end well for any of the parties.

Some, of course, argue that having a child without the intent to parent that child is ethically dubious, but it is not clear why that should be true in all cases. The idea that genetic ties should always bind has, in so many cases, led to tragic outcomes. It is telling that the original saying "blood of the covenant is thicker than water of the womb" has been bastardized over time to simply "blood is thicker than water," meaning that we should value the families we are born into as more precious than the relationships we forge based on agency rather than accident. We do a disservice to the project of family formation if we assume that family, at its root and in its most acceptable or laudable form, requires genetic connection or, in the opposite case, that the presence of genetic connection requires that we remain yoked to parents or others whose presence in our lives does not serve us.

The sense of loss and disconnect that some donor-conceived people experience is powerful, but questions about how individual people form a sense of self and community are deep and difficult to answer for all of humanity. How do biology and genetics ground us (or not), and when should the law demand that they permanently attach us to others? What do parents owe to children in terms of connection with genetic progenitors? For instance, do we imagine that parents owe family stories to their children even when those stories are painful or tragic? If genetic understanding can be gleaned through other routes, like for-profit companies that are happy to tell us where our great-great-great-grandparents emerged from, then placing the burden of sharing on individual people, especially people who have made clear that they do not want that responsibility, should be part of determining the proper regulatory path. Even if a thing is right in some theoretical sense, it is not unequivocally clear what is right in these circumstances, and legislating this kind of specific behavior from people, especially people who have waived any rights related to their genetic offspring, is overreach.

Finally, if genetic connection is indeed so deeply prized, it should not cut in only one direction. In a world in which those providing gametes are forced to be known to offspring, perhaps they should also be allowed or encouraged to play a greater role in selecting who gets to use their gametes. The ASRM writes: "Empiric data suggest that some oocyte donors may wish to know whether children are born as a result of their donation. Others may have preferences about how their donated oocytes are used. For example, donors may not want their oocytes to be provided to unmarried persons, same-sex couples, or persons of a different religion or race, or they may not want unused embryos produced with their oocytes to be destroyed or used for research."[77] Where a gamete seller knows that genetic children may one day appear on her doorstep, she may believe that she has viable interests in what happens to those gametes and therefore stake a claim to playing a role in who receives her gametes, just as genetic parents in open adoptions wield the power to choose future parents for their genetic children. A gamete industry that became more like open adoption markets would create its own share of potentially catastrophic complications for all parties.

Conclusion

There is a plethora of concerns in the United States and around the globe about the operation of the gamete-selling industry. One axis by which to discuss whether, and if so how, the sale of gametes should be regulated is by focusing on the categories of persons who may be harmed by their participation in the gamete-selling industry: sellers (meaning the young people who are working with banks or individuals who want to buy their gametes), buyers (meaning intended parents who want to get good building blocks for the babies they wish to create), and the children created from these commodified gametes and the types of regulation that have been proposed to date, as this chapter explores. For each category of person, there are some harms that overlap and others that are distinct. This chapter seeks to respond to some of the many complications while recognizing that the issues here are layered, intensely personal, and not easily subject to regulation.

The constitutional rights involved in baby-making (sex, pregnancy, parenting) fall into a zone of privacy that recognizes that these decisions are some of the most intimate that people can make.[78] So, too, is the decision to sell one's gametes for profit. As such, regulation in this space has been and always will be fraught and will become only more so as technology expands opportunities for manipulating and controlling the procreative process.

None of us had a say in the circumstances of our conception, and that is a fact not subject to change. With exceptions that we should never follow, such as eugenic practices like coerced sterilizations, attempts to control coital reproduction are few and dangerous. Assisted reproduction presents an opportunity for government oversight of procreation that should be pursued only with the utmost care and concern. The goal of protecting gamete sellers, intended parents, or future children from potential future harm is laudable, but those calling for more government oversight should carefully consider the risks inherent in such a practice. Discriminatory practices in the world of assisted reproduction are already challenging and invite greater scrutiny and expansive regulation of with whom and how people choose to make babies will inevitably impact marginalized communities more harshly than others. Some states already differentiate deserving infertility patients (i.e., those under a certain age or those who are using their own gametes) and those who are less deserving. As the project of expanding the definition of legally protected family forms is not yet at its completion, we should be wary of the ways in which people who build their families with the assistance of technology are subject to layers of regulation not placed on people who reproduce coitally. Instead of targeting them, we should consider less intrusive ways of protecting actors in fertility markets that do not involve increasing governmental overreach into what we can do with our bodies and how we build families with children.

NOTES

1 This chapter uses the phrase "donor-conceived people" to refer specifically to people whose parents used purchased or donated gametes to create them. It is a term that is preferred by many in this community, so it is used here to respect that choice even though there is a certain political valence to the term.
2 The arguments in this chapter build in part on the constitutional right to procreate established by case law in the United States. Skinner v. Oklahoma, 316 U.S. 535

(1942). That right is also an established human right, as part of an array of rights related to sexual and reproductive health. As described by the United Nations:

> [R]eproductive rights embrace certain human rights that are already recognized in national laws, international laws and international human rights documents and other consensus documents. These rights rest on the recognition of the basic rights of all couples and individuals to decide freely and responsibly the number, spacing and timing of their children and to have the information and means to do so, and the right to attain the highest standard of sexual and reproductive health. It also includes the right to make decisions concerning reproduction free of discrimination, coercion and violence, as expressed in human rights documents.

The right to procreate in U.S. law and in human rights law is not unfettered, and specifically within the U.S. context the government has no obligation to financially support individuals who want to exercise that right. What it does mean, however, is that prohibitions against discrimination do apply so that, for instance, a fertility provider could not refuse access to his services on the basis of race, religion, or national origin among other categories. Ultimately, the infertile have a right to procreate just as fertile people do, but the necessity of using assisted reproduction to effectuate that right creates a layer of complication for infertile people that those who can reproduce coitally do not experience. Kimberly Mutcherson, "Procreative Pluralism," *Berkeley Journal of Gender, Law & Justice* 30 (2015): 22–75, doi.org/10.7282/T3NZ8C1P.

3   Morgan Snow et al., "Estimates of Infertility in the United States: 1995–2019," *Fertility and Sterility* 118, no. 3 (Sept. 2022): 560–67, doi:10.1016/j.fertnstert.2022.05.018, https://dx.doi.org/10.1016/j.fertnstert.2022.05.018.

4   Cleveland Clinic, "Infertility," Cleveland Clinic, April 19, 2023, https://my.clevelandclinic.org.

5   CDC, "Infertility Frequently Asked Questions," CDC, May 15, 2024, www.cdc.gov/reproductive-health/infertility-faq/index.html.

6   Ibid.

7   According to a 2023 article in *Forbes* magazine, "A single IVF cycle—defined as ovarian stimulation, egg retrieval and embryo transfer— can range from $15,000-$30,000 depending on the center and the patient's individual medication needs." Marissa Conrad, "How Much Does IVF Cost," August 14, 2023, www.forbes.com.

8   RESOLVE, "Insurance Coverage by State," RESOLVE, September 30, 2024, https://resolve.org.

9   As one study indicates, "most state Medicaid programs did not cover infertility diagnosis or treatment services, and even those states that provide some coverage do not cover AI or IVF," Erica L. Eliason, Marie E. Thoma, and Maria W. Steenland, "Differences in Use of Fertility Treatment Between People with Medicaid and Private Health Insurance Coverage in the United States," *Women's Health Issues* 33, no. 4 (July 2023): 367–73, doi:10.1016/j.whi.2023.03.003; Gabriele Weigel et al., "Coverage and Use of Fertility Services in the US," KFF.org, September 15, 2020, www.kff.org.

10 Isabel Galic et al., "Disparities in Access to Fertility Care: Who's in and Who's Out," *F&S Reports (Online)* 2, no. 1 (March 1, 2021): 109–17, doi:10.1016/j.xfre.2020.11.001.
11 Weei Lo and Lisa Campo-Engelstein, "Expanding the Clinical Definition of Infertility to Include Socially Infertile Individuals and Couples," *Reproductive Ethics II*, 71–83, ed. Lisa Campo-Engelstein and Paul Burcher (New York: Springer International Publishing, 2018).
12 Ibid.
13 For instance, the insurance mandate in Texas requires that "the patient's eggs must be fertilized with her spouse's sperm." Tex. Health and Safety Code, section 1, chapter 161 (2023).
14 ASRM revised its definition of infertility as of October 2023 as follows: Infertility is a disease, condition, or status characterized by any of the following:
- The inability to achieve a successful pregnancy based on a patient's medical, sexual, and reproductive history, age, physical findings, diagnostic testing, or any combination of those factors.
- The need for medical intervention, including, but not limited to, the use of donor gametes or donor embryos in order to achieve a successful pregnancy either as an individual or with a partner.
- In patients having regular, unprotected intercourse and without any known etiology for either partner suggestive of impaired reproductive ability, evaluation should be initiated at 12 months when the female partner is under 35 years of age and at six months when the female partner is 35 years of age or older.

    Nothing in this definition shall be used to deny or delay treatment to any individual, regardless of relationship status or sexual orientation.

    American Society for Reproductive Medicine. "ASRM Publishes a New, More Inclusive Definition of Infertility," American Society for Reproductive Medicine, October 14, 2023, www.asrm.org.
15 Hanna Szekeres, Eran Halperin, and Tamar Saguy, "The Mother of Violations: Motherhood as the Primary Expectation of Women," *British Journal of Social Psychology* 62 (2023): 1875–96, https://doi.org/10.1111/bjso.12661.
16 Pasquale Patrizio et al., "The Changing World of IVF: The Pros and Cons of New Business Models Offering Assisted Reproductive Technologies," *Journal of Assisted Reproduction and Genetics* 39, no. 2 (February 2022): 305–13, 307, doi:10.1007/s10815-022-02399-y.
17 Ibid.
18 The Centers for Disease Control estimates that there are approximately 500 fertility clinics in the United States. Centers for Disease Control, "National ART Surveillance," Centers for Disease Control, June 7, 2023, www.cdc.gov/art/nass/index.html.
19 Food and Drug Administration, "What You Should Know About Reproductive Tissue Donation," Food and Drug Administration, November 5, 2010, www.fda.gov/vaccines-blood-biologics/safety-availability-biologics/what-you-should-know-reproductive-tissue-donation.

20 Ibid.
21 Ibid.
22 In traditional surrogacy, in which a woman becomes pregnant through artificial insemination, she is selling her egg at the same time that she is receiving compensation for gestating any child created. In this instance, there are arguably two transactions taking place (gestation and a gamete sale) even though the gamete is not extracted to achieve fertilization.
23 "Known donors" as used in this chapter refers to donors who are known to the intended parents and who donate sperm specifically for the use of those intended parents and not others.
24 The fertility industry typically uses the language of "donor(s)" for people who provide gametes for assisted reproduction, but that language should not be read to mean that the gametes are being given for free. There are certainly many circumstances when a friend or family member will provide gametes for use by a loved one, but many people—whether because they are single, a same-sex couple, or they do not have viable gametes to use—will purchase gametes. For this reason, this chapter uses the terminology of "seller(s)" to refer to these individuals and demarcate them from true donors who do not receive monetary compensation for the use of their gametes.
25 Mayo Clinic, "Infertility," Mayo Clinic, September 13, 2023, www.mayoclinic.org/diseases-conditions/infertility/symptoms-causes/syc-20354317.
26 Mayo Clinic Staff, "Ovarian Hyperstimulation Syndrome," Mayo Clinic, November 9, 2021, www.mayoclinic.org/diseases-conditions/ovarian-hyperstimulation-syndrome-ohss/symptoms-causes/syc-20354697.
27 Emily Woodruff, "'We Simply Don't Know': Egg Donors Face Uncertain Long-Term Risks," STAT.org, January 28, 2017, www.statnews.com.
28 The "medical standard of care" refers to the way that a physician in good standing in the medical community would perform a certain procedure and includes everything from providing appropriate informed consent to using correct equipment and techniques and appropriate after procedure monitoring.
29 The Ethics Committee of the American Society for Reproductive Medicine, "Financial Compensation of Oocyte Donors: An Ethics Committee Opinion," *Fertility and Sterility* 116, no. 2 (August 2021): 319–22, https://doi.org/10.1016/j.fertnstert.2021.03.040.
30 Egg Donor America, "The Psychological Evaluation of Egg Donors: Why It's Important and What It Entails," Egg Donor America, www.eggdonoramerica.com/blog/the-psychological-evaluation-of-egg-donors-why-its-important-and-what-it-entails.
31 The Ethics Committee of the American Society for Reproductive Medicine, "Financial Compensation of Oocyte Donors: An Ethics Committee Opinion," *Fertility and Sterility* 116, no. 2 (August 2021): 319–22, doi.org/10.1016/j.fertnstert.2021.03.040.
32 Gonzales v. Carhart, 550 U.S. 124 (2007).

33 Advanced Fertility Center of Chicago, "Become an Egg Donor in Chicago," Advanced Fertility Center of Chicago, https://advancedfertility.com/fertility-treatment/donor-eggs/donate-your-eggs-at-afcc.
34 The World Egg and Sperm Bank, "The Egg Donation Process," The World Egg and Sperm Bank, www.theworldeggandspermbank.com/donors-egg/the-egg-donation-process.
35 The Fertility Institute of Hawaii advertises that payment can be up to $30,000 for women who participate in their egg-donor program. Fertility Institute of Hawaii, "Become an Egg Donor," Fertility Institute of Hawaii, www.ivfcenterhawaii.com/3rd-party/become-an-egg-donor.
36 Kara W. Swanson, *Banking on the Body, The Market in Blood, Milk, and Sperm in Modern American* (Cambridge, MA: Harvard University Press 2014), 199.
37 San Diego Sperm Bank, "Increase Your Income as a Sperm Dono," San Diego Sperm Bank, www.sandiegospermbank.com/blog/increase-your-income-as-a-sperm-donor/#:~:text=If%20you're%20a%20healthy,up%20to%20%241%2C500%20per%20mont.
38 Kimberly D. Krawiec, "Egg-Donor Price Fixing and *Kamakahi v. American Society For Reproductive Medicine*," *The Virtual Mentor: VM* 16, no. 1 (January 1, 2014): 57–62, doi:10.1001/virtualmentor.2014.16.01.pfor1-1401.
39 Ethics Committee of the American Society for Reproductive Medicine, "Financial Compensation Of Oocyte Donors: An Ethics Committee Opinion," *Fertility and Sterility* 116, no. 2 (August 2021), https://doi.org/10.1016/j.fertnstert.2021.03.040.
40 Michael J. Sandel, *What Money Can't Buy: The Moral Limits of Markets* (New York: Farrar, Strauss and Giroux, 2012).
41 Elizabeth Preston, "Why You Get Paid To Donate Plasma and Not Blood," *STAT*, January 20, 2016, www.statnews.com.
42 Federal Trade Commission, "Business Persons's Guide to Federal Warranty Law," Federal Trade Commission, www.ftc.gov/business-guidance/resources/business-persons-guide-federal-warranty-law.
43 21 CFR Part 1271.150(c)(1).
44 Complaint, Jennifer Cramblett v. Midwest Sperm Bank, LLC (on file with author).
45 "Black Donor Sperm Mistakenly Sent to White Mom Jennifer Cramblett: Suit," NBCnews.com, October 1, 2014, www.nbcnews.com.
46 Because there are often multiple actors involved—the agency that sells the gamete and the provider who uses those gametes to try to create a baby for the patient—these cases could become even more legally complicated. For instance, if the health care provider receiving the sperm had a protocol for ensuring that the right patients get the right sperm and failed to follow that protocol in a certain case, which led to the mistake, the agency that provided the sperm would certainly claim that the negligence of the health care provider either totally shifted blame from the agency or at least partially did so such that liability and compensation to the plaintiff would be split between both parties.

47 Complaint, Jennifer Cramblett v. Midwest Sperm Bank, LLC (on file with author).
48 Smith v. Cote, 513 A.2d 341 (1986).
49 Complaint, Jennifer Cramblett v. Midwest Sperm Bank, LLC (on file with author).
50 In *Palmore v. Sidoti*, 466 U.S. 429, 433 (1984), a case in which a Florida court deprived a white mother of custody of her daughter when her former husband sought custody because the mother began cohabiting with a Black man, the U.S. Supreme Court wrote: "Private biases may be outside the reach of the law, but the law cannot, directly or indirectly, give them effect."
51 The racial and socioeconomic disparities in accessing fertility treatment are "widely acknowledged," and even insurance mandates do not close the gap between white women and women of color. The disparity is such that the ASRM prioritized access to care in its 2014–2019 strategic plan. Galic et al., "Disparities in Access to Fertility Care".
52 One study revealed that "out of every metropolitan region in the United States with more than 200,000 residents, 81 percent (169 out of 209) were more segregated in 2019 than they were in 1990." Stephen Menendian, Samir Gambhir, and Arthur Gailes, "Twenty-First Century Racial Residential Segregation in the United States," June 21, 2021, https://belonging.berkeley.edu/roots-structural-racism.
53 Cheryl I. Harris "Whiteness as Property," *Harvard Law Review* 106, no. 8 (1993), 1707–91, https://doi.org/10.2307/1341787.
54 Dorothy E. Roberts, "Race, Gender, and Genetic Technologies: A New Reproductive Dystopia?" *Signs* 34, no. 4 (2009): 783–804, https://doi.org/10.1086/597132.
55 Rachel Robertson, "Sperm Banks Lack Diverse Donors for Diverse Recipients," *MedPage Today*, October 20, 2023, www.medpagetoday.com.
56 It is more difficult as a matter of biology for women to become mass/serial donors because the process of extracting eggs is more cumbersome and requires medical assistance.
57 Associated Press, "Dutch Court Bans Sperm Donor Who Fathered At Least 550 Children," April 28, 2023, www.nbcnews.com.
58 Jacqueline Mroz, "The Case of the Serial Sperm Donor," *New York Times*, February 1, 2021, https://nytimes.com.
59 Ibid.
60 "Man Claims He Fathered '800 Kids' by Donating Sperm," *Financial Express*, January 15, 2016, https://search.proquest.com/docview/1756943355.
61 Ibid.
62 CBS News, "FDA Cracks Down in Fremont Man's Sperm Donations," CBS News Bay Area, December 7, 2011, www.cbsnews.com.
63 The United Kingdom, the Netherlands, Australia, Denmark, and South Africa, among other countries, limit how many families or children can be created by a single donor.

64 There have been court cases in the United States where judges have used bans on procreation as a means of punishment, but those cases are very controversial and of questionable constitutionality. One example of such as case is *State v. Oakley*, 629 N.W.2d 200 (2001).
65 Brett Molina, "Woman Discovers She Has 29 Siblings After Taking DNA Test. And Counting," *USA Today*, April 8, 2019, www.usatoday.com.
66 Emily Bazelon, "Why Anonymous Sperm Donation Is Over, and Why That Matters," *New York Times Magazine*, December 3, 2023.
67 Ibid.
68 A google search will reveal adoption agencies called An Act of Love, numerous pages on adoption websites that use the word "love" to describe the choice to place a child for adoption or adopt a child, and even more articles and opinion pieces that characterize adoption as fundamentally about "love."
69 Most states have laws related to compensation and adoption that allow only for money exchanges from adoptive parents to birth parents for "medical, living, legal, and other expenses for the biological mother." Cullen T. Wallace, "Permitting the Compensation of Birth Mothers for Adoption Expenses and its Impact on Adoptions," *B.E. Journal of Economic Analysis & Policy* 22, no. 3 (2022): 573–600, https://doi.org/10.1515/bejeap-2022-0010.
70 Meghana Keshavan, "Consumer DNA Tests Negate Sperm-Bank-Donor Anonymity," *STAT*, September 11, 2019, www.statnews.com.
71 Margaret Somerville, "Donor Conception and Children's Rights: 'First, Do No Harm,'" *CMAJ: Canadian Medical Association journal = journal de l'Association medicale canadienne* 183, no. 2 (2011): 280, doi:10.1503/cmaj.101388.
72 Ibid.
73 Dorothy A. Greenfeld, "The Impact of Disclosure on Donor Gamete Participants: Donors, Intended Parents and Offspring," *Current Opinion in Obstetrics and Gynecology* 20 , no. 3 (June 2008): 265–68; Susan Golombok et al., "Families with Children Conceived by Donor Insemination: A Follow-up at Age Twelve," *Child Development* 73, no. 3 (2002): 952–68, http://www.jstor.org/stable/3696261; G. Pennings, "Disclosure of Donor Conception, Age of Disclosure and the Well-Being of Donor Offspring," Human Reproduction 32, no. 5 (May 1, 2017: 969–73, doi:10.1093/humrep/dex056; Ingrid Torjesen, "Donor Conceived Children Shouldn't Have Right to Be Told of Their Origins, Says Nuffield Council," *BMJ: British Medical Journal (Online)* 346 (April 17, 2013), doi:https://doi.org/10.1136/bmj.f2475; Jennifer Readings et al., "Secrecy, Disclosure and Everything In-Between: Decisions of Parents of Children Conceived by Donor Insemination, Egg Donation and Surrogacy," Reproductive BioMedicine Online 22 (2011): 485–95.
74 Kimberly Mutcherson, "Procreative Pluralism," *Berkeley Journal of Gender, Law & Justice* 30, no. 1 (Winter 2015): 22–75.
75 LePage et. al, v. Center for Reproductive Medicine, SC-2022–0579 (Supreme Ct. of Alabama 2024).

76 Ken Daniels and Letitia Meadows, "Sharing Information with Adults Conceived as a Result of Donor Insemination," *Human Reproduction* 16, no. 9 (September 1, 2001): 1792–96, https://doi.org/10.1093/humrep/16.9.1792.
77 Ethics Committee of the American Society for Reproductive Medicine, "Financial Compensation of Oocyte Donors.
78 Skinner v. Oklahoma, 316 U.S. 535 (1942); Griswold v. Connecticut, 381 U.S. 479 (1965).

2

My Genetics, My Choice?

Parents, Children, and Pediatric Genetic Testing

ALLISON M. WHELAN

From the moment of conception, if not before, our lives and our bodies are regulated by others. This chapter explores one area in which the decisions and actions of others often preclude us from writing and telling our own stories. More specifically, this chapter explores parental regulation of a child's future privacy, autonomy, and bodily integrity through the use of new innovations in genetic testing. The results of the genetic testing discussed in this chapter may reveal information that directly or indirectly alters the course of a person's life. Importantly, once learned, the information cannot be unlearned.

This chapter focuses on this phenomenon in the United States. American law and jurisprudence recognize and support a substantial role for parents in making decisions about many aspects of their children's lives: education, religion, health care, home life, and much more. Strengthening this tradition is the United States Supreme Court's long-standing recognition that parents have a constitutional right to direct the care, custody, and control of their children. These rights, however, are not absolute, and the line between permissible and impermissible parental control over decisions for their children remains murky and much contested.

The phrase "pediatric predisposition genetic testing" (PPGT) will be used to describe genetic testing done on a minor, at the request/with the consent of their parent(s), for the purpose of: (1) determining whether the minor has genetic mutations that will result in an adult-onset disease that lacks a known cure or method of prevention, such as Huntington's disease or amyotrophic lateral sclerosis (ALS); or (2) assessing the risk that the minor could develop an adult-onset disease, including those with known curative treatment options, such as various types of cancer.

An important disclaimer: PPGT is used to refer to genetic testing performed on children after birth for the two specific purposes just listed. It therefore represents a technology distinct from preimplantation genetic testing (PGT) and preimplantation genetic diagnosis (PGD), which are performed in conjunction with various artificial reproductive technologies such as in vitro fertilization prior to implantation or performed on an embryo or fetus in utero.[1]

Since the 1990s, there have been significant advancements and increasing interest in genetics and genomics throughout society: scientists working in labs; policymakers and legislators drafting rules and regulations; health care providers and patients in clinics; and individuals in their homes using direct-to-consumer (DTC) genetic tests from companies like 23andMe.[2] To illustrate this growth, consider that from 2012 to 2022 a total of 51,803 new genetic tests were made available in the United States, an increase from the 607 new genetic tests in 2012.[3]

The growth of genetic-testing capabilities owes a great deal to the completion of the Human Genome Project, an international effort that began in 1990 and culminated with the first sequence of the human genome in 2003.[4] At the time of the Human Genome Project's completion in 2003, scientists had sequenced about 92 percent of the total human genome. The remaining 8 percent was completed in early 2022.[5] Human genome sequencing has facilitated tremendous innovation in health care, including the development of genetic tests to diagnose disease (diagnostic testing) or to determine the risk or susceptibility of future disease (predisposition testing).[6]

The march continues toward a day when genetic testing becomes part of mainstream medicine, providing us with countless new ways to control our health and our bodies. That said, new ways to control our *own* bodies also create new ways for *others* to control our bodies. Indeed, the future of genetic medicine raises a myriad of legal, ethical, and sociopolitical questions and controversies: issues of privacy, informed consent, discrimination, eugenics, accessibility, affordability, and health disparities, to name just a few. Moreover, advancements in biotechnology and medicine provide parents with increasing power over their children's current and future health in unprecedented ways. Specifically, PPGT raises particularly complicated questions including when, or even if, PPGT should be used; who can access test results; how the data may be collected, retained, and shared; and whether the child being tested must have the capacity to both want and consent to the testing and the receipt of results.

The challenging questions raised by emerging medical technologies affect all members of society, but the burdens are often heightened for vulnerable populations. Minors, defined as individuals under the age of majority as set by applicable state law, represent one such vulnerable population that has been subject to mistreatment throughout history in the areas of science, medicine, and beyond.[7] The mistreatment of vulnerable populations may even be reinforced by law, which has long been used as a tool to establish patterns of discrimination based on race, sex, disability, sexual orientation, gender identity, age, and other identities.[8]

Minors, especially preadolescents, represent a particularly vulnerable population with respect to PPGT because they are considered by law to be incapable of providing their own consent and thus may remain voiceless in decision-making, precluded from writing and telling their own stories. Instead, parents or legal guardians possess the authority to consent to medical care and services for their children, sometimes even over the child's own objections. Parents also act as the primary recipients of information about their children's health. In so many ways, parents regulate their children's bodies, minds, and much more. These practices are deeply entrenched in American law, society, and jurisprudence. Yet despite general acceptance and understanding of broad parental rights, guidance as to how those rights apply—or should apply—to decisions involving minors, their futures, and emerging medical technologies remains underdeveloped, unsatisfactory, ad hoc, or unworkable.

Moreover, children too often become pawns in political and culture wars fought between parents and the state. On the one hand, there has been a recent resurgence of the parental rights movement, largely among political conservatives with respect to school curriculum.[9] On the other hand, there has also been a troubling trend of states policing decisions—parental and otherwise—that historically were left to the private sphere, such as decisions about reproduction and gender-affirming medical care.[10] The inconsistencies in these trends are obvious. For example, the conservative push to restrict access to abortion and to prohibit parents from obtaining gender-affirming care for their children are in tension with the conservative-led parental rights movement, which is grounded largely in notions about the privacy of the family.[11]

The controversies are often depicted as pitting parents against the state. Yet the children suffer the most. By failing to consider the rights of the child, American law and jurisprudence fail to consider the parent–state–child "rights triad" in ways that adequately protect the current and future rights of the child.[12] Relatedly, the "best interests" standard,[13] used often by courts, the medical profession, and others when making determinations about children, often fails to achieve its child-centered goals. This standard, which purports to center on children's rights and interests, is nevertheless often interpreted in ways that prioritize parental rights and interests above those of the child.[14]

Despite some medical and bioethical scholarship and debate on PPGT and related issues, the law and legal discourse have not kept pace with new developments in genetic technologies, which creates gaps and vulnerabilities. To address the gaps, it is necessary to revisit the parental rights jurisprudence and analyze whether and how the jurisprudence answers questions about PPGT.[15]

This chapter engages with these issues in three sections. First, it provides a descriptive account, exploring health care decision-making for minors generally and with respect to PPGT specifically. Second, it canvases the risks and benefits of PPGT. Finally, it turns to normative considerations, arguing that law and society should recognize greater authority for children to control and regulate their own genetic futures.

Minors and Health Care Decisions

Parents typically provide the consent required for their children's medical care, a practice with deep roots in common law.[16] Buttressing this tradition is a long-standing recognition by the United States Supreme Court that parents have a constitutional right to direct the care, custody, and control of their children.

Parental rights, however, are not absolute. Today, many state laws provide exceptions to the general requirement of parental consent for medical care in specific situations. For example, many states allow adolescents over a specific age to consent to health care services such as drug and alcohol treatment, reproductive health services, treatment for sexually transmitted infections, outpatient mental health services, emergency services, and other general health care services including certain vaccines.[17]

Furthermore, American law and society have increasingly emphasized that parental decision-making should be guided by the "best interests" of the child.[18] Decisions that are not clearly in a child's best interest can—and should—be challenged. The best interest standard, however, has its faults. The standard is vague, is nonpredictive, and can permit the law to justify custody and other decisions that actually harm children. At times, courts have gone further, recognizing that children do, in fact, have their own cognizable constitutional rights in a variety of circumstances that are separate and apart from the rights of their parents or another third party.[19]

This long-standing tradition and general societal and legal acceptance of parents' control over their children raise questions about whether decisions about PPGT might deserve a unique approach. This section provides additional grounding, describing common scenarios and controversies that arise in the medical care of children, both historically and because of emerging technologies.

Type One Decisions: The Routine—Preventative Care and Treatment of the Sick

There is no question that parents can and must make many medical decisions for their children. Indeed, children would not survive to adulthood to have a future if their parents lacked this right. Consider the following two examples of routine and generally uncontroversial decisions parents make for their children:

1. A five-year-old child has strep throat. Strep throat is easily diagnosable and highly treatable with a course of routine antibiotics. Left untreated, strep can lead to inflammation of the kidneys, scarlet fever, rheumatic fever, and abscesses of the tonsils.[20]
2. At their child's two-month checkup, the pediatrician informs the parents about starting the recommended four-dose series of the polio vaccine. The four-dose series is 99 percent effective in preventing polio.[21] Without the vaccine, the child remains at risk of

contracting polio, which is a disabling and potentially deadly virus that can spread from person to person and infect a person's spinal cord, causing paralysis.[22]

Many would agree that these children's parents can—or even must—consent to potentially lifesaving treatment or routine and recommended preventative care such as vaccines. Given the children's young age in these examples, the medical services would be provided without the child's consent or even assent. In fact, controversies involving these routine scenarios more typically arise when parents refuse to consent to medical intervention or decide to use alternative or unproven treatments for religious or other reasons.

The case of thirteen-year-old Daniel Hauser exemplifies such a controversy. Daniel's story made international news in 2009 when his mother refused to consent to chemotherapy to treat Daniel's Hodgkin's lymphoma, based on her belief in natural healing. Daniel also did not want chemotherapy, even though it was proving to be successful. At the time, the survival rate for people under age 20 treated for Hodgkin's lymphoma was 91 percent, whereas those untreated often died. After a court ordered Daniel's treatment, Daniel and his mother fled their home in Minnesota. Ultimately, Daniel returned to Minnesota and completed chemotherapy.[23]

In scenarios like Daniel's or the two hypothetical scenarios above, where the disease or condition has the potential to cause death or significant harm, and a known and effective method of treatment or prevention exists, the best interest standard looms large: parents have the authority to make decisions about the care of their child until such decisions harm the child's best interests. In these scenarios, given the anticipated benefits of treatment and the risks of nontreatment, standard treatment generally represents the course of action deemed in the child's best interest.[24] In fact, state intervention may result if parents refuse such effective interventions, under the doctrine of parens patriae, which recognizes that a state may act as a "surrogate parent" when necessary to protect the health and wellbeing of children.[25]

Where treatments do not exist, are unproven, are unlikely to be successful, or when the risks of forgoing treatment are low, the state is less inclined to intervene.[26] The child's age may also influence the state's involvement and the outcome of any judicial decisions on the matter. For example, when an adolescent agrees with their parent's decision and appears sufficiently mature and capable of consent, courts may let that decision stand.[27]

A crucial factor influencing the outcome of Type One decisions is that generally these decisions cannot be postponed until the child "possess[es] adequate capacity, cognitive ability, and judgment to engage effectively in the informed consent or refusal process for proposed care."[28] Instead, Type One decisions are those that must be made quickly (e.g., treatment for an *existing* disease or condition) to avoid potentially fatal or life-altering consequences.

Type One decisions prompt additional controversy when the parents' decision to forego standard treatment is grounded in religious beliefs that the child may or may not share. As discussed further in the second section, the U.S. Supreme Court has long upheld the rights of parents to make decisions for their children based on religion, particularly in the realm of education. Lower federal and state courts have extended these rights to medical decisions,[29] and some states have codified them into law.[30] Yet at the same time, the Supreme Court has made clear in persuasive dicta that "[t]he right to practice religion freely does not include liberty to expose the community or the child to communicable disease or the latter to ill health or death."[31] These and other cases demonstrate that little is black and white when it comes to medical decision-making for minors. Emerging medical technologies have only added to the shades of gray.

Type Two Decisions: Pediatric Predisposition Genetic Testing

Along with standard and relatively routine health care decisions that parents must make for their children to ensure their health and survival, emerging medical technologies provide new options and raise new questions, particularly in the realm of genetics, future health risks, and elective genetic testing. The scenarios described in this section represent the main focus of this chapter and involve parental consent to PPGT for adult-onset diseases in two main categories:

1. Category One—Definitive, Unpreventable, and Uncurable: tests for adult-onset diseases that have no known cure or reliable/effective method of prevention. This could include tests for conditions such as Huntington's disease, for which genetic testing can show definitively whether a person will develop the disease, but the disease lacks a known cure or method of prevention. This could also include diseases for which tests can only show susceptibility to a disease that lacks a known cure or method of prevention, such as ALS.
2. Category Two—Susceptibility/Risk: tests that show possible susceptibility to a disease and are generally performed on an otherwise asymptomatic person. Although many diseases are influenced by genetics to some degree, most are not like Huntington's, which is caused by a variant/mutation in a single gene. Rather, most diseases are a complex mix of both genetic and environmental factors. Therefore, a genetic test can show susceptibility but cannot definitively say a person will develop a specific disease.[32] Testing for BRCA1 and BRCA2 mutations, which are correlated with the development of breast and ovarian cancers, represent an example of a Category Two test.

Future developments will likely result in changes to the types of tests and diseases found within each category.

As genetic testing capabilities emerged during the late twentieth and early twenty-first centuries, the medical and bioethical communities largely agreed that children should not be tested for adult-onset disorders that lacked any known cure or treatment.[33] Today, "[t]he emerging position is one of greater flexibility," with decisions made on a case-by-case basis.[34] The extent to which PPGT occurs in the clinical setting is unknown, but as availability and affordability improves, requests from parents will likely increase.[35] Moreover, easily accessible and relatively affordable at-home genetic testing options raise the possibility of parents testing their children at home without the benefit of consultation with a pediatrician and/or genetic counselor. Misunderstanding and misinterpreting the results of a genetic test can have long-term consequences.[36] As positions on this issue and professional guidance continue to evolve, further discussion and debate—grounded squarely in both the present and future rights and interests of the child—remain necessary.

PPGT: Risks, Benefits, and Rights

Once it is acknowledged that parents must make certain decisions for their children, including medical decisions, it must be asked: Should PPGT be treated differently? If so, why? Despite some similarities between Type One and Type Two decisions discussed above, a number of important differences must be considered.

PPGT: The Potential Benefits

A key difference between Type One and Type Two decisions is that with Type Two decisions the child is not currently sick, symptomatic, or in need of immediate treatment to prevent serious harm or death; nor is there a well child receiving standard and effective preventative medical care to maintain their current well-being (e.g., annual physicals) or effectively prevent harmful diseases (e.g., routine child vaccinations).

Proponents of PPGT commonly put forth a number of arguments, including:

1. PPGT aligns with the rationales of preventative care because it can provide parents and children with an opportunity to mitigate the risk of an adult-onset disease, such as through lifestyle changes (e.g., diet and exercise), more frequent health screenings, or other interventions.
2. For diseases that cannot be prevented, early knowledge of a disease that will later develop allows the person to make appropriate life plans in light of the forthcoming disease, to learn coping skills before the disease develops, and to create systems of future medical, social, and emotional support.
3. Knowledge of genetic risks can inform a child's future decision about whether to have children. Relatedly, a parent's knowledge of their existing child's genetic risks could inform their own decision about whether to have additional children. That said, this later "benefit" provides a relatively weak argument in favor of PPGT because parents can already gain such information through their own genetic testing or through PGT or PGD. As noted, PGT and

PGD are separate and distinct from PPGT and raise their own issues that are outside the scope of this chapter.

As always, these potential benefits must be weighed against potential risks and harms.

PPGT: The Potential Risks

The harms that may transpire from PPGT include: (1) subjecting children to unnecessary and excessive testing or invasive procedures; (2) causing overconfidence, complacency, or inaction when test results are negative (i.e., show no increased risk); and (3) imposing socioemotional burdens on children who receive positive results and may experience unwarranted anxiety and differential treatment.

From a physical perspective, even though PPGT is minimally invasive and low-risk—typically requiring a blood test or cheek swab—the child's physical health can still be affected if certain actions are taken based on the results. As noted, a parent might incorporate various lifestyle changes in an attempt to reduce the child's risk of the specific disease. Yet there is no guarantee that preventative actions will ultimately influence whether the disease develops. More importantly, people may lack the resources to obtain the testing or to engage in the preventative measures most likely to be effective. Indeed, even if PPGT itself becomes routine and widely affordable and accessible, some individuals may be able to access the tests but then lack the resources to act on those results. Moreover, PPGT is not necessary to induce such general preventative behaviors. On the contrary, these types of lifestyle modifications should be undertaken regardless of the results of a genetic test.

Problematically, test results that suggest an increased risk for disease may compel parents to seek more radical interventions or excessive testing. These consequences can result in financial, physical, and emotional costs for the family and child. For example, some parents may seek out various imaging tests to try to discover early physical changes or presence of disease. These might include things like X-rays, CT scans, or other radiological imaging. Such imaging tests are noninvasive and relatively low-risk, but they can be expensive, and overexposure to radiation may increase the risk of certain cancers.[37] Moreover, they use limited health care resources, can cost thousands of dollars, and may not be covered by insurance if not considered medically necessary.

In many cases, the most effective methods of prevention or risk reduction—if they exist—will be unavailable or inadvisable during childhood. For example, consider a mother who learns that her child has the BRCA1 or BRCA2 mutation and is told that her child has a significantly increased risk of cancer. It is unlikely that any health care provider would recommend or agree to perform a prophylactic double mastectomy or oophorectomy on a child.[38] At the other end of the spectrum, where testing finds no increased risk (i.e., a "negative" result), false reassurance and overconfidence in the negative result could have the opposite effect, causing parents, and later the child as an adult, to decline care and various risk-reducing, potentially lifesaving interventions, screenings, and other measures.[39] Genetic predispositions, or lack thereof, are not guarantees. Yet they are too often treated as such, which risks serious consequences.

Of perhaps greater concern are the possible consequences for the child's socioemotional well-being, autonomy, and privacy. Broader and more affordable access to genetic testing increases the risk that PPGT will be used without taking adequate pause to consider the consequences of having the information that may result. The results of PPGT may reveal information that directly or indirectly alters the course of a person's life. Notably, once learned, the information cannot be unlearned. The parents, and importantly the child—who may not have had a say in whether to seek out this information—must live with that knowledge for the rest of their lives. The burdens of this knowledge are highly individualized and immeasurable.

Information from PPGT can be both a blessing and a curse. Studies correlate deleterious genetic testing results with poor body image and self-esteem, as well as feelings of unworthiness and/or shame. Other possible harms include social stigmatization and damage to familial relationships.[40] As one genetic counselor explains:

> The underlying premise is that if a parent knows that his or her child is at risk for a genetic disease, how the parent treats the child[,] and his or her expectations/hopes for the child's future will change. The concern is that parents will potentially change how they support their children, specifi-

cally by withdrawing or limiting resources—emotionally, financially, and physically—from a child who is at risk for developing a disease.[41]

Some professionals believe that genetic testing can trigger unnecessary anxiety, especially when results are ambiguous or of unclear significance.[42] This is particularly likely if testing is done without proper genetic counseling, which may not be accessible or even offered in the case of DTC tests.

Along with the potential harms imposed on the individual child, broader societal harms may transpire. This includes "clogging" already overburdened hospitals and health care providers unnecessary testing and follow-ups that may result from false positives.[43] There are also equity concerns. Many of these tests remain costly and not covered by insurance, meaning that only the wealthiest will have access. This will further the deep health disparities that exist in the United States. Moreover, even if the tests themselves are affordable, a person with sufficient resources may be able to reduce their nongenetic risks of disease, such as through diet, exercise, and routine preventative care. Yet historic and ongoing racism, discrimination, and other structural barriers often mean that members of historically marginalized and vulnerable populations—who may already be at higher risk for disease—cannot avail themselves of these preventive measures, increasing their risks of myriad diseases and poor health outcomes and exacerbating health disparities throughout the United States. Perniciously, genetic testing may be used to pressure certain people or groups not to have children.

The relative novelty and infrequent use of PPGT results in a current dearth of evidence-based literature on the short- and long-term consequences of PPGT. With time, data may support or refute the existence of long-term harms. Empirical work must continue to ensure that law and policy reflect reality rather than assumptions.

Regardless of what future research discovers about the socioemotional harms and benefits of PPGT, other important and perhaps paramount considerations remain relating to the rights to bodily autonomy, privacy, and, more generally, the power to write and tell one's own story.

Autonomy concerns are much discussed in bioethics literature. In short, PPGT disregards children's future decision-making capacity and forces information upon them that they may not want to know now or in the future. The philosopher Joel Feinberg's concept of the "right to an open future" informs these arguments.[44] Feinberg developed the concept of "rights-in-trust," which he describes as follows:

> When sophisticated autonomy rights are attributed to children who are clearly not yet capable of exercising them, [rights-in-trust] refer to rights that are to be saved for the child until he is an adult, but which can be violated "in advance," so to speak, before the child is even in a position to exercise them. . . . His right while he is still a child is to have these future options kept open until he is a fully formed, self-determining adult capable of deciding among them.[45]

Those concerned about PPGT thus assert that delaying decisions about PPGT ensures that the child retains the ability to make their own determinations in the future about the risks and benefits associated with genetic testing. Importantly, this includes the person's right to not know at all. Indeed, a primary harm of PPGT is that once the results are learned they cannot be unlearned—Pandora's box cannot be closed. These types of autonomy-based concerns and the right to an open future ground the historical consensus against the use of PPGT, but that consensus may be changing. And while many Americans may want to know their genetic predispositions, others do not.[46] In a space as important and personal as genetics, law and policy must avoid ascribing the views of the majority to all members of society, particularly those who have not yet attained the capacity to consent and make autonomous decisions.

The autonomy harms relate closely to another issue that often corresponds with genetic testing: privacy. Privacy concerns often arise from fears about genetic discrimination. Some concerns have been assuaged by the passage of laws such as the Genetic Information Nondiscrimination Act of 2008 (GINA), a federal law that prohibits discrimination on the basis of genetic information with respect to health insurance and employment. Specifically, GINA: (1) prohibits health insurers from using genetic information to determine a person's eligibility for insurance or to make decisions about coverage, underwriting, or premiums; and (2) prohibits employers from using genetic information in employment decisions such as hiring, firing, promotions, pay, and job assignments.[47]

Additional protections against genetic discrimination can be found in: (1) the Health Insurance Portability and Accountability Act (HIPAA), which limits the release of a patient's health information (including genetic information) and prohibits the use of health information by insurers to determine health insurance benefits and premiums;[48] (2) the Patient Protection and Affordable Care Act (ACA), which prohibits health insurers from discriminating against patients because of preexisting conditions and limits criteria upon which premiums may be based;[49] and (3) a patchwork of state laws that vary in scope and applicability and may provide protections beyond those found in federal laws.[50]

All these protections have critical limitations:

- GINA's protections do not apply to long-term care insurance, life insurance, or disability insurance.
- GINA's employment protections do not extend to the U.S. military, thus allowing the military to use genetic information in employment decisions.
- GINA does not apply to employers with fewer than fifteen employees, an important gap given that approximately twenty million Americans work for employers with fewer than twenty employees.[51]
- Many conservative politicians continue to call for the repeal of the ACA, which would eliminate the current protections for those with preexisting conditions.[52]

As to HIPAA, many assume that the law protects more health information than it does in reality. For example, HIPAA contains exceptions that allow prosecutors to compel businesses to relinquish information relevant to various kinds of legal action. Moreover, HIPAA applies to results from genetic tests administered by health care providers, but it does not apply to DTC genetic testing. In fact, no federal law directly addresses privacy and DTC genetic testing. Databases holding genetic information, such as electronic health records and those of DTC testing companies, are vulnerable and have suffered data breaches.[53] And although most companies have policies against sharing data, the companies are not immune from being hacked or receiving law enforcement requests. In fact, in 2018 California police used GEDmatch to identify a man they believed to be the Golden State Killer, Joseph James DeAngelo. Since then, investigators have used genetic genealogy to identify suspects and victims in hundreds of cases.[54]

Privacy concerns are not unique to genetic testing, although they have been magnified in the current digital age. We live in a digital society, and our personal data are everywhere, as are threats to the privacy of that data. Comprehensive legal and policy improvements remain necessary to safeguard our personal information. Protections for genetic privacy and prohibitions against genetic discrimination remain particularly underdeveloped and inconsistent, leaving important gaps that render our most intimate data vulnerable to misuse.[55] Wide swaths of this intimate data are merely clicks away, housed in electronic health records, digital databases, mobile apps, and more. As Professor Danielle Citron presciently warns, "[o]ur fertility, dating, and health apps, digital assistants, and cellphones track our every move, doctor visit, health condition, prescription, and search; the details of our intimate lives are sold to advertisers, marketers, and data brokers. Law enforcers can purchase or subpoena [that data]."[56] Without additional protections, "[e]veryone's life opportunities are on the line."[57]

Privacy concerns compound for minors because decisions to collect, store, and share their genetic information are generally made by their parents. In many cases, particularly for young children, the minor—the person to whom that information truly belongs—is left out of the discussion and decision.

The legal protections discussed above also do not address a primary privacy concern raised by PPGT: a child's right to bodily autonomy and privacy from their parents. Whereas adults may have the power and ability to limit their parents' access to their genetic information—at least to some degree—that is not true for minors. For minors, their parents represent the primary recipients of PPGT results. Thus, the minor's most personal information is outside their control from the start:

> Testing a minor for a genetic disorder violates his or her confidentiality because the test result will be shared with the parents without the child's consent. The child also has no control over with whom the parents share the genetic test results. Disclosure of these results by a healthcare provider to the parents, or by the parents with other indi-

viduals, without express consent of the minor violates the minor's autonomous right to privacy.[58]

Moreover, minors lack adequate power to prevent the disclosure of their genetic information, and they also lack an adequate avenue for recourse when it occurs. Dr. Ellen Wright Clayton explains:

> Unemancipated minors have virtually no access to the courts to enjoin parental behavior and so have little independent legal basis to obtain an injunction to stop genetic or genomic testing for which their parents have given permission. They are not even able individually to seek damages from their parents after the fact, as parents are generally immune from liability for actions that are deemed to be within their latitude to discipline or control, a concept that courts have interpreted very broadly to protect parents.[59]

Some may challenge the idea that a minor has a right to privacy from their parents. Parents, by necessity, have access to a host of confidential information about their children, including health information, which can affect their children's futures. American law and jurisprudence generally support such access.

This chapter does not contest that parents should, and often must, know intimate information about their children. Indeed, as discussed below, such information is often necessary to ensure children's safety, well-being, and continued survival. Yet important distinctions should be acknowledged when considering PPGT. In brief: There is no long-standing tradition of parents having access to information about a child's genetic predisposition to future disease; nor is there any pressing need for them to have such access. Historically, this type of information would be learned only after children reached adulthood and could make their own decisions, including whether to share that information with their parents. Indeed, federal laws like HIPAA, in conjunction with state laws, provide some privacy protections for adults.[60] But prior to adulthood, a child's right to privacy from their parents remains limited. The advent of PPGT continues to expand the breadth of information available to parents, potentially violating a child's right to future privacy of their medical information, as well as their right not to know this information in the first place. In an era of "sharenting," where parents increasingly use social media to share content, intimate information, and photos about their children, there is reason for pause and more robust consideration of whether and when parents may access and share certain information about their children.[61]

PPGT: The Law's Limits and Future Directions

According to U.S. Supreme Court Justice Sandra Day O'Connor, "the interest of parents in the care, custody, and control of their children is perhaps the oldest of the fundamental liberty interests recognized by this Court."[62] For more than a century, the Supreme Court has consistently held that parents have a constitutional right to make decisions about their children's care and upbringing. Nevertheless, the jurisprudence does not adequately inform whether these rights include the right to consent to PPGT and thrust that information upon a nonconsenting child. Moreover, because the jurisprudence often focuses on parent–state conflicts, it generally does not provide guidance about how to resolve direct conflicts between children and parents.[63]

We no longer live in an era where parents only make decisions for their children that must be made only during childhood (e.g., decisions about primary education, consent to surgery or treatment for existing conditions, consent to childhood vaccinations). With PPGT, parents can now also make decisions and access information that historically was left to the control of the child upon reaching adulthood. Long-standing jurisprudence and traditional legal and policy frameworks do not necessarily translate well to addressing emerging technologies, such as those that now allow parents to essentially make medical decisions and learn health information that will affect the child only during adulthood. This illustrates a common theme observed in the legal, ethical, and medical literature: the law often fails to keep pace with medical and other technological advancements. The uncertainty that transpires sets the stage for legal, political, and ethical battles, which too often results in harm, particularly to vulnerable populations.

The Limits of Supreme Court Law and Jurisprudence

In 1923, Arthur F. Mullen, arguing for the plaintiffs in *Meyer v. Nebraska* (1923),[64] told the U.S. Supreme Court that a state law prohibiting the teaching of modern foreign languages in public and private schools would "change the history of the entire human race" by allowing the state to "take the child from the parent and prescribe the mental bill of fare that child shall follow in its education."[65] Seven Supreme Court justices, in apparent agreement with Mullen, struck down the Nebraska law. Justice James Clark McReynolds's short opinion for the Court remains the foundational case for parental rights, establishing that the liberties protected by the Fourteenth Amendment include the right to "bring up children."[66] Many subsequent cases reaffirm and expound upon the breadth of parental authority over the care, custody, and control of their children. In addition to *Meyer*, other foundational cases include:

1. *Pierce v. Society of Sisters* (1925), which struck down an Oregon statute requiring children to attend public schools, reasoning it interfered with a parent's right to select private or parochial schools;[67]
2. *Wisconsin v. Yoder* (1972), which held that Wisconsin's compulsory education law violated an Amish father's right to remove his fifteen-year-old children from school to complete their education in Amish ways at home;[68] and
3. *Troxel v. Granville* (2000), which concluded that a Washington law allowing any person to petition for a court-ordered right to see a child over a custodial parent's objection, even if visitation is in the child's best interest, interferes with the parent's fundamental right to direct the care, custody, and control of their children.[69]

A common theme emerges in the Supreme Court's early parental rights jurisprudence: the Court tends to ignore or disregard the child's point of view or the child's right as an individual separate from their parents, even as the Court claims to apply the best interests of the child standard.[70] Instead, the Court concentrates primarily on an overarching conflict between the parents and the state, spilling little ink on whether the laws at issue implicate the current or future rights of children. Little thought is given as to how these parental powers influence a child's ability to determine their own destinies and tell their own life stories. The language of *Pierce* is illustrative, suggesting that children do not direct or influence their own destinies; that right instead belonged to the parents, "who nurture [their children] *and direct [their] destin[ies]*."[71]

In an illuminating revisionist history of *Meyer* and *Pierce*, Professor Barbara Bennett explains that although we tend to think of the rights to establish a home and bring up children "as the good personal liberty gold of substantive due process," a "dark side" emerges upon closer examination: the establishment of a "dangerous form of liberty, the right to control another human being."[72] Professor Bennett explains: "Stamped on the reverse side of the coinage of family privacy and parental rights are the child's voicelessness, objectification, and isolation from the community."[73] In short, the rights of children remain secondary to the rights of their parents, if they are acknowledged at all. These cases thus "serve as a reminder that substantive due process can be a conservative as well as a liberating force. . . . Especially in family law, which deals with collective organisms, liberty is a difficult concept: one individual's liberty can spell another's suppression or defeat."[74] That warning has salience for PPGT, which risks prioritizing the parent's immediate rights over the child's right to future privacy.

The general lack of consideration given to children in the early jurisprudence slowly gave way to greater concern for child welfare and the recognition of children as free individuals who are "merely entrusted to their parent for nurture."[75] To align with this evolution, courts began addressing the welfare and interests of children more directly. In *Prince v. Massachusetts* (1944), for example, the Court clarified that parental rights are broad but not absolute and that they may be subject to state intervention to "protect the welfare of children."[76]

Yet even while *Prince* began to establish important boundaries on the rights of parents, those boundaries largely represent the point where *parental* rights end and the *state's* right to intervene begins. That is, *Prince* did not consider the interests of the child *as represented by the child*; nor did it describe children as having rights of their own separate from their parents or the state.

The early parental rights jurisprudence also reflects how societal and cultural views influence judicial thinking. By the early twentieth century, although many no longer viewed children solely as "paternal property subject to paternal whim," "obstinate counter-trends" remained: "Patriarchal ideals and structures that treated the child as property of the parent continued to exist side-by-side with Lockeian theories of individual liberty, in which the child was essentially free, merely entrusted to the parent for nurture."[77] It thus comes as little surprise that courts failed to meaningfully consider the rights and desires of children.

Despite increasing attention to child welfare and the "best interests of the child" throughout the latter part of the twentieth century, courts often interpreted those interests as represented by the parents or the state rather than by the child. In that way, children's rights "belonged" either to their parents or the state; the recognition and protection of their rights depended largely on others.[78]

Judicial language reflects this, framing the issues as involving children's "interests" rather than "rights."[79] Although often conflated, *rights* and *interests* represent distinct concepts.[80] According to Joseph Raz's theory of rights, *interests* inform and provide grounds for *rights*. Essentially, *rights* are stronger than *interests* and exist when an aspect of a person's well-being (i.e., an interest) is of sufficient importance to ground duties in others. Scholars have long debated whether and to what extent children can be "rights-holders."[81]

Yet by denying children their own voice, identity, and distinct rights, their purpose is reduced to being a mere conduit for the interests and rights of their parents. This becomes particularly problematic when the rights and interests of children and their parents conflict. Existing jurisprudence provides far less guidance on how to approach such situations. Indeed, "in most cases in which bold declarations about children's rights are made, children's interests and views are indistinguishable from those of their parents."[82] And although the Supreme Court has concluded that the child's interest may prevail in the face of a parent–child conflict,[83] many court decisions reach the opposite conclusion, finding that the child has no protectable interest or a lesser liberty interest than their parent.[84] In the context of PPGT—where the parent's authority to consent to health care for their child and the parent's interest in knowing genetic information about their child conflict with the child's right to future privacy and right to decide *not* to know—existing jurisprudential frameworks are unsatisfactory and ill-equipped to adequately protect the rights of minors.

Limited Supreme Court jurisprudence addresses the medical decision-making rights of minors directly. And the existing jurisprudence involves fairly unique situations such as abortion and commitment to mental hospitals. Moreover, because the foundational jurisprudence discussed above generally did not consider the potential for conflicts between parents and children, transposing the principles espoused by cases like *Meyer, Pierce*, and *Yoder* proves difficult. The Court's considerations in select cases, viewed alongside increasing judicial and societal attention to children's rights as individuals, are nevertheless informative when scrutinizing parental consent to PPGT.

In *Parham v. J.R.* (1979), minors challenged a Georgia law that allowed parents and guardians to request that their child be admitted to a state mental hospital. The minors alleged that Georgia's procedures violated the Due Process Clause of the Fourteenth Amendment. The Court upheld the law, but it also held that the risk of error inherent in a parent's decision to have their child institutionalized was of sufficient magnitude to require an inquiry by a "neutral factfinder" to determine whether the law's requirements for admission were satisfied.[85] Even still, the Court makes clear that when parent–child conflicts occur, parents do not necessarily lose their decision-making authority: "Simply because the decision of a parent is not agreeable to a child . . . does not automatically transfer the power to make that decision from the parents to some agency or officer of the state."[86] One reading of the Court's language is that it viewed a child's choice as irrelevant if those views are contrary to a parent's choice: "The fact that a child may balk at hospitalization or complain about a parental refusal to provide cosmetic surgery does not diminish the parents' authority to decide what is best for the child."[87]

Furthermore, although the decision recognizes that minors have protectable due process rights, the Court suggests that those rights are not wholly separate from their parents. Instead, a child's interest in not being committed "is inextricably linked with the parents' interest in and obligation for the welfare and health of the child."[88] Thus, the private interest at stake in *Parham* was "a *combination* of the child's and parent's concerns."[89] Relatedly, the Court followed its common practice of focusing on whether decisions should be made by the parent or transferred to the state, giving little attention to the voice of the child or whether the child should play a role in the decision-making process.

During the same term as *Parham*, the Court issued another seminal decision involving health care decisions and minors: *Bellotti v. Baird (1979)*. *Bellotti* involved a challenge to a Massachusetts law that required pregnant minors seeking abortions to obtain either the consent of their parents or judicial approval following parental notification.[90] At the time of the decision in 1979, abortion remained a constitutionally protected right, including for minors.[91] In keeping with *In re Gault* (1967), the Court noted that "[a] child, merely on account of his minority, is not beyond the protection of the Constitution" and held that the Massachusetts law unconstitutionally burdened the right of pregnant minors to obtain an abortion.[92] As a result of this decision, states typically include a judicial bypass procedure, which allows minors to obtain court approval for abortions without parental consent or notification.[93]

Bellotti established more assertively that parents do not have unfettered rights to dictate decisions for their children, particularly when the minor's constitutional rights are at stake. At the same time, *Bellotti* failed to recognize that minors may be capable of making autonomous decisions *on their own*. On the one hand, *Bellotti* liberated adolescents from parental involvement in decisions about abortion. On the other, it required the state—through a judicial bypass procedure—to approve their choices. In short, the state stepped into the role of the parent. Moreover, the Court makes clear that although minors generally deserve the same constitutional protections as adults, "the State is entitled to adjust its legal system to account for children's vulnerability and their needs for 'concern, . . . sympathy, and . . . paternal attention.'"[94]

State and Lower Federal Courts: Ongoing and Forthcoming Battles

State and lower federal courts have had greater occasion to consider the triad of parent–state–child rights in health care decisions for minors, and many state laws allow adolescents over a certain age to consent to certain types of health care services without parental involvement or a need to use a judicial bypass procedure. These include drug and alcohol treatment, reproductive health services, treatment for sexually transmitted infections, outpatient mental health services, emergency services, and some vaccinations.[95] None of these laws address genetic testing directly, and publicly available sources suggest that no court has considered the issues of PPGT addressed by this chapter.

Many courts are now tasked with considering state laws that protect or restrict access to gender-affirming health care services. All of these cases involve the parent–state–child triad, and initial orders from various courts emphasize different parts of that triad. At one end of the spectrum are cases where parents and health care providers sue the state over laws that ban or restrict minors' access to gender-affirming health care services. Many of these cases were ongoing at the time this volume went to publication. Thus far, court decisions have relied on a complex mixture of considerations, including an emphasis on the parental rights established by the Supreme Court's jurisprudence discussed above. The same theme discussed above reemerges, with courts often focusing on conflicts between the parents and state rather than conflicts between the parent and child or state and child.[96] Nevertheless, some court decisions suggest a greater acknowledgement and consideration of a minor's rights and desires in the decision-making process. The Supreme Court will consider the issue of gender-affirming care for minors during the Court's October 2024 term.[97] This case may prove enlightening to broader considerations about the roles of the parent, state, and child in health care decision-making for minors, particularly the types of decisions that have large implications for the child's future, such as gender transition and genetic testing.

American law and jurisprudence make the strength and breadth of parental rights clear. Yet the lack of case law addressing the unique concerns of PPGT, particularly direct and indirect parent–child conflicts, raises concern that the traditional jurisprudence cannot provide a workable framework for PPGT. The next section considers possible pathways forward.

The Right to Future Privacy

This chapter makes clear that children's minds and bodies are constantly regulated and influenced by the choices of others, especially their parents and the state. It furthermore shows that such control is not barred by the United States Constitution; on the contrary, it is largely accepted. Existing Supreme Court jurisprudence does not provide a clear answer as to whether minors have—or should have—control over PPGT and how that right should be exercised and protected. This chapter argues that each individual—not parents or the state—should possess the primary right to control: (1) whether they receive PPGT; (2) whether and how they act on the results; and (3) whether they share the results and with whom. The lack of case law, statutory framework, or consistent institutional policies addressing PPGT results in gaps and vulnerabilities, creating the potential for significant harms. The issue deserves attention now, before PPGT becomes part of routine medical care.

The Right to Future Privacy

The rights and harms implicated by PPGT justify a privacy-based intervention, specifically a "right to future privacy." This right draws upon existing doctrines, including: (1) the right against intrusion upon seclusion and (2) the right to autonomy and bodily privacy.

The first privacy right originates from tort law: intrusion upon a person's seclusion, solitude, or private affairs.[98] The intrusion must be more than mundane; it must "be offensive or objectionable to a reasonable man" and must target something that is "entitled" to be private.[99] As explained by Professor William Prosser: a person "has no right to be alone" in a public place, "and it is no invasion of his privacy to do more than follow him about."[100] Yet "prying" into a person's genetic makeup and genetic future should without doubt fall within the realm of information that is "entitled" to privacy and that a reasonable person would find offensive or objectionable if disclosed without consent.[101]

A second important privacy right of possible relevance is the right to privacy of one's body, sometimes described as a right to bodily autonomy or integrity.[102] As Justice John Paul Stevens once proclaimed: "The sanctity, and *individual privacy*, of the human body is obviously fundamental to liberty."[103] This sentiment dates back to the late nineteenth century, when the Supreme Court expounded: "No right is held more sacred, or is more carefully guarded by the common law, than the right of every individual to the possession and control of *his own person*, free from all restraint or interference of others, unless by clear and unquestionable authority of law."[104]

It is helpful to discuss the right to bodily privacy alongside a related and broader privacy right, which exists within what courts have called "zones of privacy."[105] Frequently discussed "zones" include decisions relating to marriage, procreation, contraception, family relationships, childrearing, and education.[106] Courts have also recognized that certain tangible information, such as medical information, can fall within a zone of privacy.[107] Within these zones, individuals should have "a concomitant right to prevent unlimited disclosure of information"[108] and an expectation of privacy against unreasonable search and seizure or intrusion into their private matters.

As the Supreme Court described in *Griswold v. Connecticut* (1965), these zones of privacy can be derived from multiple sources, including from: (1) various "penumbras" of specific guarantees of the Bill of Rights; (2) the First Amendment right of association; (3) the Third Amendment's prohibition against quartering soldiers; (4) the Fourth Amendment's prohibition against unreasonable searches and seizures; (5) the Fifth Amendment's protection against self-incrimination; (6) in the Ninth Amendment;[109] and (7) the Fourteenth Amendment's guarantee of personal liberty. The drafters of the Fourteenth Amendment described that amendment's guarantee as "personal security," which includes a "person's legal and uninterrupted enjoyment of his life, his limbs, his *body*, his *health*, and his reputation."[110] In *Griswold*, the Court explained the right, its constitutional groundings, and how the right to privacy is a "legitimate" right, despite "many controversies over these penumbral rights of 'privacy and repose.'"[111]

PPGT implicates these strands of privacy in important ways. It violates minors' right to bodily privacy by intruding into their bodies through the test itself (e.g., a blood draw) and through the collection, discovery, and disclosure of their genetic futures. As stated by one U.S. district court, even if genetic information is not disclosed, "there is an invasion of privacy in the information having been gathered, and harm in the information simply existing."[112] Indeed, as consistently reiterated in this chapter, once the information from PPGT is known, it cannot be unknown, thereby violating an individual's right not to know. For many, the knowledge may be a blessing, but for others it is a curse.[113]

Genetic information represents an individual's most sensitive and private information, unknowable by sight and requiring intrusive prying into one's innermost biology. PPGT therefore intrudes into one of the most intimate zones of privacy without the minor's consent. In *Norman-*

Bloodsaw v. Lawrence Berkeley Laboratory (1998), the U.S. Court of Appeals for the Ninth Circuit asserted "that the *most basic* violation [of privacy] possible involves... the non-consensual retrieval of previously unrevealed medical information that may be unknown even to plaintiffs."[114] Not only will the minor likely not provide their own consent to PPGT, the youngest of children may not even be aware that the information is being collected, retained, and disclosed. Importantly, the disclosure of highly personal and genetic information risks "injury, embarrassment, or stigma" if handled inappropriately.[115] As astutely stated by Professor Citron, "self-development... [is] impossible without the ability to decide who has access to our bodies... and intimate data."[116]

Unlike other privacy violations, which may be temporary (e.g., non-consensual surgery or eavesdropping on private conversations), the violation caused by PPGT is everlasting: once the test is performed and the information disclosed, it cannot be unknown. Children, their parents, and others who receive the results cannot "unknow" that information. Children must carry that "badge" on them for life, whether good or bad. If we believe that certain information falls within a protected zone of privacy, genetic information must certainly be included in that zone. As observed by the Ninth Circuit: "One can think of few subject areas more personal and more likely to implicate privacy interests than that of one's health or genetic make-up."[117]

Troublingly, despite the importance of bodily privacy and maintaining zones of privacy, privacy is increasingly threatened and under attack by technological advancements and recent judicial decisions. Because the Constitution does not mention a right to privacy explicitly, courts have relied on that absence to question privacy rights and protections. *Dobbs v. Jackson Women's Health Organization* (2022) exemplifies this judicial line of thought. In that case, the Court implied that for the Due Process Clause of the Fourteenth Amendment to guarantee a substantive right not mentioned in the Constitution such a right must be "deeply rooted in this Nation's history and tradition" and "implicit in the concept of ordered liberty."[118] In *Dobbs*, the Court engaged in what many scholars and other commentators argue was a weak, flawed, and incoherent analysis to strike down the right to abortion.[119] Justice Clarence Thomas's concurring opinion went further and was even more explicit, stating that "the Due Process Clause does not secure any substantive rights."[120] Such judicial assertions render tenuous any and all substantive due process rights, including the one advanced in this chapter, which are not explicitly articulated in the text of the Constitution.

Yet *Dobbs* and other cases that threaten privacy rights need not spell the death of privacy as we know it. In *Dobbs*, the Court primarily attacked the right to privacy that involves "the right to make and implement important personal decisions without government interference."[121] Essentially, this describes a right of personal autonomy and "decisional privacy." Importantly, the Court distinguishes this form of privacy from "the right to shield information from disclosure,"[122] which is essentially "information privacy." Thus, even while the consequences of "*Dobbs* and its implications for autonomy rights in the name of privacy are seismic," the case does not "spell the end of legal protection for other forms of privacy, both under the Constitution and other laws."[123] This distinction drawn by the Court makes clear the importance of considering carefully how we ground a right to future privacy as it is developed further.

Additional Considerations

New and innovative legal and policy frameworks engender controversy and debate. Recognizing new rights or reinforcing existing rights requires consideration of broader consequences, both positive and negative. Each consideration listed below will require further discussion as the right to future privacy develops.

First, critics will contend that parents already have—and must have—the authority to consent to health care services for their children and that this right should include PPGT. Parents' existing authorities also require them to have access to records containing private information about their children. Furthermore, parents cannot avoid making "future-effecting [decisions] for their children every day,"[124] and "[w]e cannot just leave the child's *entire* future open for him to decide later according to his settled adult values."[125] In fact, adopting that approach would be futile and could even result in the child having no future at all, or at least not one that could be described as "open." Take education as one example. If decisions about childhood education are not made by parents and instead postponed until the child reaches the age of consent, that delay would certainly foreclose, or at least delay significantly, a person's ability to enter the workforce, support themselves, gain independence from their parents, and more.

Nevertheless, important distinctions can be made, and there must be limits to a parent's regulation of their children's minds, bodies, and futures. Framing the right as the right to *future* privacy helps distinguish between: (1) decisions that *must* be made for children by others *during childhood*, which cannot be postponed until the child reaches adulthood (e.g., immediate medical care, decisions about primary education); and (2) decisions that are not urgent, necessary, or appropriate to make during childhood. PPGT should fall into this second group of decisions. Other decisions in this second group might include decisions about marriage, occupation, and sexual intimacy.

A second and related consideration is that parents must—within reason—be able to intrude on their child's privacy for reasons of health and safety. A parent who enters and searches their child's room without consent because they believe their child is using illicit or dangerous drugs, or contemplating suicide or other self-harm, is arguably justified in that intrusion. The same would be true for parents concerned that their child may be contemplating violence. One need only consider tragic school shootings in which evidence has emerged of warning signs.[126] A fine line exists between trust and privacy, particularly for adolescents. Any recognition of a minor's right to privacy must draw a proper balance.

PPGT goes beyond these necessary and justifiable privacy intrusions. The right and need of parents to know certain information about their child, even in the face of objections by the child, does not mean that parents have a right to know *everything* about their child. This includes genetic information that will not be of consequence until adulthood, if ever. The adult-onset nature of the information sets it apart in important ways from other information relevant to minors during childhood. American history and jurisprudence make clear that the parents' authority to direct the care, custody, and control of their children is "deeply rooted in this Nation's history and tradition." Yet even if we agree with that method of analysis, it does not follow that parents have the right to consent to PPGT and access the results. There is simply no deep history or tradition of parents having the right to know or demand information about their *adult* children's health or genetic destinies.

To that end, boundaries on a minor's right to future privacy must be considered and delineated. Priority should be given to the right to *future* privacy, withholding from disclosure information that need not, and traditionally would not, be learned until adulthood and thus controlled by the individual to whom that information belonged. As noted above, there are valid reasons for minors to possess less extensive privacy rights than adults, and parents must have the authority to consent to myriad health care services for their children.

A third consideration is the need to craft the right carefully to prevent it from being abused by abortion opponents and those who support fetal personhood laws. For example, proponents of fetal personhood laws could argue that fetuses, if deemed "persons" under the law, should have a right to privacy of their genetic information, which would therefore prohibit various uses of PGD and PGT. Of course, in states where fetal personhood laws are enacted, most if not all abortions will be banned, including for reasons relating to fetal diagnosis. As a result, any such arguments about fetal personhood laws and their impact on PGT may become moot, given that obtaining an abortion after receiving PGT results would be prohibited. These and related issues raise myriad questions requiring much further consideration as the right to future privacy develops to ensure that appropriate distinctions and guardrails are created so that abortion opponents do not co-opt the right to limit the rights of pregnant persons.

Fourth, the right to make decisions about PPGT must not simply be shifted to the state. As described above, parental rights jurisprudence typically pits parents against the state, taking rights from the parents and giving them to the state or vice versa. The right to future privacy, in contrast, must not follow that path by giving states the right to control access to and use of PPGT for minors. Rather, the right to future privacy aims to save the right for the *child* to exercise in the future. Too often, the state inserts itself into private decisions in ways that harm rather than protect individual rights. Relatedly, states should also not get involved by enacting judicial bypass procedures like those used for abortion—procedures that allow minors to obtain an abortion without parental notification or consent but only if they receive judicial authorization. Specifically, a judicial bypass procedure should not be required or available to either the child or the parent. The child should not have to seek judicial approval to undergo or prevent PPGT, and the parents should not be able to seek a judicial order to allow them to obtain PPGT for their child. Succinctly put: the state should not be involved. Transferring decision-making authority to the state raises risks that the decisions will be weaponized or politicized, harming rather than protecting minors in the process.[127]

Fifth, the issues addressed in this chapter expose the need to further consider capacity and consent. This chapter argues that the individual should consent to their own genetic testing. But what does that mean for minors, whom the law may not recognize as capable of consent? At what point should a minor have the right to consent to PPGT? The age of consent can vary significantly by state and by issue. For example, a resident of New York cannot marry until the age of eighteen,[128] but minors in New York can consent to treatment for a sexually transmitted infection.[129] If, as this chapter argues, decisions about PPGT should be postponed until the child is capable of making the decision, serious consideration must be given to consent and to when the right to future privacy becomes a current right that the child can act upon.

Finally, the right must be firm yet flexible enough to evolve with technological and medical innovations. For example, if innovations discover how to definitively prevent certain adult-onset diseases during childhood, then we must reconsider whether parental consent for those tests, and ensuing treatments, should be allowed. Indeed, that is what brought us here in the first place: the failure of law and policy to keep pace with changing technology and medical innovations. The legal and ethical status quo cannot provide answers to these new questions.

Conclusion

Similar to other technological and medical innovations, genetic testing has outpaced advancements in law and policy. There remains a lack of workable frameworks for deciding to whom testing should be offered, whether and when to test, who can consent to testing, and to whom results should be made available. Furthermore, genetic testing has outpaced regulation of the tests themselves.

The questions and potential consequences of genetic testing are magnified when children are involved. Existing law and jurisprudence do not clearly answer whether minors have—or should have—control over PPGT. Moreover, a long line of cases establishing and reaffirming broad parental rights raises significant doubt that a court would side with a minor if a case were to arise involving a child–parent conflict over PPGT. There are many legal and ethical issues implicated by parental consent for PPGT, including the right to future privacy introduced in this chapter.

Diminishing privacy brought about by technological advancements represents a common problem extending well beyond PPGT. Privacy rights continue to be eroded, threatened, or maligned. They are in urgent need of reaffirmation and reinvigoration. This chapter proposes one avenue for doing so, giving a name to the right to future privacy. Our genetic makeup represents perhaps the most intimate data we possess. This chapter does not intend to propose a precise solution but instead names the issue and provides the initial groundwork for a right to future privacy. Protecting privacy during an era when private information is everywhere, available at the touch of a button, requires ambitious and creative thinking. These conversations are worth having and there exists no better time to start that discussion than now. Indeed, "technological change is at the heart of much information privacy law."[130] The law needs updating to combat the unwarranted invasions of future privacy facilitated by PPGT. Important work remains, and this chapter lays the groundwork for important legal and policy innovations in this space.

NOTES

1. University of California San Francisco, "Pre-Implantation Genetic Diagnosis," University of California San Francisco, www.ucsfhealth.org, accessed November 1, 2022; American College of Obstetricians and Gynecologists, "Prenatal Genetic Screening Tests," American College of Obstetricians and Gynecologists, October 2020, www.acog.org.
2. 23andMe, www.23andme.com.
3. Alyssa L. Halbisen and Christine Y. Lu, "Trends in Availability of Genetic Tests in the United States, 2012–2022," *Journal of Personalized Medicine* 13 (April 2023): 638.
4. National Human Genome Research Project, "Fact Sheet: Human Genome Project," National Human Genome Research Project, www.genome.gov, accessed September 12, 2023.
5. National Institutes of Health, "First Complete Sequence of a Human Genome," National Institutes of Health, April 12, 2022, www.nih.gov.

6 Catherine M. Bove, Sara T. Fry, and Deborah J. MacDonald, "Presymptomatic and Predisposition Genetic Testing: Ethical and Social Considerations," *Seminars in Oncology Nursing* 13, no. 2 (1997): 135–36; Simon Tripp and Martin Grueber, "The Economic Impact and Functional Applications of Human Genetics and Genomics" 34, May 2021, www.ashg.org; Stanford Medicine Children's Health, "Medical Genetics; How Genetic Testing is Used," Stanford Medicine Children's Health, www.stanfordchildrens.org, accessed September 12, 2023; Stanford Medicine Children's Health, "Genetic Testing," Stanford Medicine Children's Health, www.ama-assn.org, accessed September 12, 2023.

7 Harriet Washington, *Medical Apartheid* (Doubleday, 2006), 271–98, 333–37; Douglas S. Diekema, "Conducting Ethical Research in Pediatrics: A Brief Historical Overview and Review of Pediatric Regulations," *Journal of Pediatrics* 149 (2006): S3–11; Jascha Hoffman, "New York City Foster Home Accused of Unethical AIDS Drug Trials," *Nature Medicine* 11, no. 5 (January 1, 2005).

8 Benjamin Moore, "The Supreme Court's Entire Term Was an Exercise in Reactionary Rollback of Basic Rights," *Jacobin*, July 6, 2022, https://jacobin.com.

9 Catherine Caruso, "The Parental Rights Movement is History Repeating Itself," *Dame*, March 9, 2022, www.damemagazine.com; Human Rights Campaign, "Maps: Attacks on Gender Affirming Care by State," Human Rights Campaign, August 22, 2023, www.hrc.org.

10 Lara Friedenfelds, "When the Constitution Was Drafted, Abortion Was a Choice Left to Women," *Washington Post*, May 23, 2022, www.washingtonpost.com; Peter Hayes, "Alabama Claims Primacy Over Parents on Treating Transgender Kids," *Bloomberg Law*, June 28, 2022, https://news.bloomberglaw.com; American Medical Association, "AMA to States: Stop Interfering in Health Care of Transgender Children," American Medical Association, April 26, 2021, www.ama-assn.org.

11 Julia Bowes, "Overturning Roe Could Threaten Rights Conservatives Hold Dear," *Washington Post*, June 24, 2022, www.washingtonpost.com.

12 The term "parent–state–child rights triad" is used to describe the different and sometimes incompatible rights at issue in conflicts involving parental rights, state interests, and children's rights.

13 Loretta M. Kopelman, "Children and Bioethics: Uses and Abuses of the Best-Interests Standard," *Journal of Medicine and Philosophy* 22 (1997): 213; Children's Bureau & Child Welfare Information, "Determining the Best Interests of the Child," Children's Bureau & Child Welfare Information, June 2020, www.childwelfare.gov.

14 Janet L. Dolgin, "Why Has the Best-Interest Standard Survived? The Historic and Social Context," *Children's Legal Rights Journal* 16, no. 2 (1996).

15 This chapter focuses primarily on U.S. Supreme Court jurisprudence addressing the rights of parents, children, and the state. It is beyond the scope of this chapter to address every approach taken by the myriad federal and state courts.

16 Bonner v. Moran, 126 F.2d 121, 122 (D.C. Cir. 1941); Zoski v. Gaines, 260 N.W. 99 (Mich. 1935).

17 Lisa Klee Mihaly, Naomi A. Schapiro, and Abigail English, "From Human Papillomavirus to COVID-19: Adolescent Autonomy and Minor Consent for Vaccines," *Journal of Pediatric Health Care* 36, no. 6 (2022), https://doi.org/10.1016/j.pedhc.2022.06.007; Robert S. Olick, Y. Tony Yang, and Jana Shaw, "Adolescent Consent to COVID-19 Vaccination: The Need for Law Reform," *Public Health Reports* 137 (2021):163–64; Centers for Disease Control and Prevention, "State Laws that Enable a Minor to Provide Informed Consent to Receive HIV and STD Services," Centers for Disease Control and Prevention, www.cdc.gov, last reviewed October 25, 2022.

18 Douglas S. Diekema, "Revisiting the Best Interest Standard: Uses and Misuses," *Journal of Clinical Ethics* 22, no. 2 (2011): 128.

19 In re Gault, 387 U.S. 1, 13 (1967); J.D.B. v. North Carolina, 564 U.S. 261 (2011); Planned Parenthood v. Danforth, 428 U.S. 52, 74 (1974); Tinker v. Des Moines Ind. Cmty. Sch. Dist., 393 U.S. 503, 506 (1969).

20 Yale Medicine, "Strep Throat," Yale Medicine, www.yalemedicine.org, accessed August 26, 2023.

21 Centers for Disease Control and Prevention, "Polio Vaccination: What Everyone Should Know," Centers for Disease Control and Prevention, www.cdc.gov, last reviewed October 12, 2022.

22 Centers for Disease Control and Prevention, "Polio Vaccination," Centers for Disease Control and Prevention, www.cdc.gov, last reviewed August 11, 2022.

23 Amy Forliti, "Daniel Hauser Done with Chemotherapy," *MPR News*, September 4, 2009, www.mprnews.org; Ben Jones and Carolyn Pesce, "Medicine, Religion Collide in Chemo Refusal," *USA Today*, May 21, 2009, https://usatoday30.usatoday.com.

24 Lee Black, "Limiting Parents' Rights in Medical Decision Making," *American Medical Association Journal of Ethics* 8, no. 10 (2006):6 76, https://doi.org/10.1001/virtualmentor.2006.8.10.hlaw1-0610.

25 Prince v. Massachusetts, 321 U.S. 158, 166 (1944); Jehovah's Witnesses in State of Wash. v. King Cnty. Hosp. Unit No. 1 (Harborview), 278 F. Supp. 488 (W.D. Wash. 1967), *affirmed* 398 U.S. 598 (1968).

26 Black, "Limiting Parents' Rights in Medical Decision Making," 676.

27 In re E.G., 549 N.E.2d 322 (Ill. 1989); Arthur L. Caplan, "Challenging Teenagers' Right to Refuse Treatment," *American Medical Association Journal of Ethics* 9 (2007): 56, https://doi.org/10.1001/virtualmentor.2007.9.1.oped1-0701.

28 Kathryn L. Weise et al., "Guidance on Forgoing Life-Sustaining Medical Treatment," *Pediatrics* 140, no. 1 (2017).

29 Bendiburg v. Dempsey, 909 F.2d 463, 470 (11th Cir. 1990); Nassau Cnty. Dep't of Soc. Servs. ex rel. A.Y. v. R.B., 870 N.Y.S.2d 874 (Fam. Ct, Nassau Cnty., N.Y. 2008); Appeal in Cochise Cnty, Juvenile Action No. 5666-J, 650 P.2d 459, 465 (Ariz. 1982) (en banc).

30 325 Ill. Comp. Stat. Ann. § 5/3; Aleksandra Sandstrom, "Most States Allow Religious Exemptions from Child Abuse and Neglect Laws," Pew Research Center, August 12, 2016, www.pewresearch.org.

31 Prince v. Massachusetts, 321 U.S. 158, 166 (1944).
32 MedlinePlus, "What Are Complex or Multifactorial Disorders?," National Library of Medicine, May 14, 2021, https://medlineplus.gov.
33 Jeffrey R. Botkin, "Ethical Issues in Pediatric Genetic Testing and Screening," *Current Opinion in Pediatrics* 28, no. 6 (2016): 700, https://doi.org/10.1097/MOP.0000000000000418.
34 Ibid.
35 Angela Fenwick et al., "Predictive Genetic Testing of Children for Adult-Onset Conditions: Negotiating Requests with Parents," *Journal of Genetic Counseling* 26, no. 2 (2017): 244–45, https://doi.org/10.1007/s10897-016-0018-y.
36 Scott M. Weissman, Brianne Kirkpatrick, and Erica Ramos, "At-Home Genetic Testing in Pediatrics," *Current Opinion in Pediatrics* 31, no. 6 (2019): 723–24; Salma Abdalla, "At-Home Genetic Testing Leads to Misinterpretations of Results," Boston University School of Public Health, February 20, 2018, www.bu.edu.
37 Martha S. Linet et al., "Cancer Risks Associated with External Radiation from Diagnostic Imaging Procedures," *CA: Cancer Journal for Clinicians* 62 (2012): 75, https://doi.org/10.3322/caac.21132; American Cancer Society, "Do X-Rays and Gamma Rays Cause Cancer?," American Cancer Society, February 24, 2015, www.cancer.org; Jeffrey R. Botkin et al., "Outcomes of Interest in Evidence-Based Evaluations of Genetic Tests," *Genetics in Medicine* 12, no. 4 (2010): 228–31; Weissman, "At-Home Genetic Testing in Pediatric," 725; Mohana Ravindranath and Lizzy Lawrence, "Kim Kardashian Sparks Debate on the Benefits of Full-Body MRI Scans," *STAT*, August 11, 2023, www.statnews.com.
38 Anne-Marie Laberge and Wylie Burke, "Testing Minors for Breast Cancer," *American Medical Association Journal of Ethics* 9, no. 6 (2007): 7, https://doi.org/10.1001/virtualmentor.2007.9.1.ccas1-0701; F. M. Hodges, J. Svoboda, and R.S. Van Howe, "Prophylactic Interventions on Children: Balancing Human Rights with Public Health," 28 *Journal of Medical Ethics* 28, no. 10 (2002):11; Ying L. Liu, "Risk-Reducing Bilateral Salpingo-Oophorectomy for Ovarian Cancer: A Review and Clinical Guide for Hereditary Predisposition Genes," *JCO Oncology Practice* 18, no. 3 (2021): 202–04.
39 Botkin, "Outcomes of Interest in Evidence-Based Evaluations of Genetic Tests," 231."Consumer Testing for Disease Risk," 137 *Obstetrics & Gynecology* 137 (2021): e1-e4, www.acog.org.
40 Dawn C. Allain, "Testing Children for Adult-Onset Disorders," in *Ethical Dilemmas in Genetics & Genetic Counseling* 96, 102 (Janice L. Berliner ed., 2014); Laberge, "Testing Minors for Breast Cancer," 7.
41 Allain, "Testing Children for Adult-Onset Disorders," 102.
42 Roger Collier, "The Downside of Genetic Screening," *Canadian Medical Journal* 184 (2012): 862, https://doi.org/10.1503/cmaj.109-4169.
43 Ravindranath and Lawrence, "Kim Kardashian Sparks Debate on the Benefits of Full-Body MRI Scans."

44 Joel Feinberg, *Freedom and Fulfillment: Philosophical Essays* (Princeton University Press, 1992).
45 Ibid., 76–77.
46 The Associated Press–NORC Center for Public Affairs Research, "Genetic Testing: Ancestry Interest, But Privacy Concerns," The Associated Press–NORC Center for Public Affairs Research, July 2018, www.norc.org; University of Michigan, National Poll on Healthy Aging, "Older Adults' Views on Genetic Testing," University of Michigan, National Poll on Healthy Aging, October 2018, https://deepblue.lib.umich.edu; Karen E. Anderson et al., "The Choice Not to Undergo Genetic Testing for Huntington Disease: Results from the PHAROS Study," *Clinical Genetics* 96 (2019): 28; Karen E. Anderson et al., "The Choice Not to Undergo Genetic Testing for Huntington Disease: Results from the PHAROS Study," *Clinical Genetics* 96 (2019): 28; University of Utah Health, "National Poll Shows Public Divided on Genetic Testing to Predict Risk," University of Utah Health, February 4, 2014, https://healthcare.utah.edu.
47 Pub. L. No. 110-233, 122 Stat. 881 (May 21, 2008).
48 Health insurance Portability and Accountability Act of 1996, Pub. L. No. 104-191, 100 Stat. 2548 (1996), as amended by the Health Information Technology for Economic and Clinical Health Act of 2009, Pub. L. No. 111–5, 123 Stat. 112 (2009).
49 Patient Protection and Affordable Care Act, Pub. L. No. 111-148, 124 Stat. 119 (2010).
50 National Human Genome Research Institute, "Genetic Discrimination," National Human Genome Research Institute, January 6, 2022, www.genome.gov.
51 U.S. Small Business Administration Office of Advocacy, "2020 Small Business Profile (2020)," U.S. Small Business Administration Office of Advocacy, May 20, 2020, https://advocacy.sba.gov.
52 Steven Benen, "Why It Matters When Republican Senate Hopefuls Endorse ACA Repeal," *MSNBC*, April 6, 2022, www.msnbc.com.
53 Consumer Reports, "The Privacy Risks of At-Home DNA Tests," *Washington Post*, September 14, 2020, www.washingtonpost.com; Eric Rosenbaum, "5 Biggest Risks of Sharing Your DNA With Consumer Genetic-Testing Companies," *CNBC*, June 16, 2018, www.cnbc.com.
54 Kashmir Hill and Heather Murphy, "Your DNA Profile is Private? A Florida Judge Just Said Otherwise," *New York Times*, November 5, 2019, www.nytimes.com; Oliver M. Tuazon et al., "Law Enforcement Use of Genetic genealogy Databases in Criminal Investigations: Nomenclature, Definition and Scope," *Forensic Science International: Synergy* 8 (2024), https://doi.org/10.1016/j.fsisyn.2024.100460.
55 Samantha Cook, "Genes Talk: The Current State of DNA Privacy Law," *Juris Magazine*, May 5, 2019, https://sites.law.duq.edu.
56 Danielle Keats Citron, "The End of *Roe* Means We Need a New Civil Right to Privacy," *Slate*, June 27, 2022, https://slate.com.
57 Citron, "The End of *Roe* Means We Need a New Civil Right to Privacy."

58 Allain, "Testing Children for Adult-Onset Disorders," 104.
59 Ellen Wright Clayton, "How Much Control Do Children and Adolescents Have Over Genomic Testing, Parental Access to their Results, and Parental Communication of Those Results to Others?," *Journal of Law, Medicine, and Ethics* 43, no. 3 (2015): 538–40, https://doi.org/10.1111/jlme.12296.
60 Michelle Andrews, "States Offer Privacy Protections to Young Adults on their Parents' Health Plan," Kaiser Health Network, June 28, 2016, https://kffhealthnews.org.
61 L. Lin Ong et al., "Sharenting in an Evolving Digital World: Increasing Online Connection and Consumer Vulnerability," *Journal of Consumer Affairs* 56 (2022): 1106; Nila Bala, "Why Are You Publicly Sharing Your Child's DNA Information?," *New York Times*, January 2, 2020, www.nytimes.com.
62 Troxel v. Granville, 530 U.S. 57, 65 (2000).
63 It must be acknowledged that in many parental rights cases, the Court either was not confronted with the issue directly or no such conflict existed because the child and parents did not disagree with each other. When the desires of parents and children align, courts are, understandably, unlikely to consider the potential conflict.
64 Meyer v. Nebraska, 262 U.S. 390 (1923).
65 Jeffrey Shulman, "Meyer, Pierce, and the History of the Entire Human Race: Barbarism, Social Progress, and (The Fall and Rise of) Parental Rights," *Hastings Constitutional law Quarterly* 43 (2016): 337–38.
66 *Meyer*, 262 U.S. at 399.
67 Pierce v. Society of Sisters, 268 U.S. 510 (1925).
68 Wisconsin v. Yoder, 406 U.S. 205 (1972).
69 Troxel v. Granville, 530 U.S. 57 (2000).
70 Emily Buss, "What Does Frieda Yoder Believe?," *University of Pennsylvania Journal of Constitutional Law* 53 (1999): 60.
71 *Pierce*, 268 U.S. at 535 (emphasis added).
72 Barbara Bennett Woodhouse, "'Who Owns the Child?': Meyer and Pierce and the Child as Property," *William & Mary Law Review* 33 (1992): 995–97.
73 Ibid., 1000–01.
74 Ibid., 1110.
75 Ibid., 1040–41; John E. B. Myers, "A Short History of Child Protection in America," *Family Law Quarterly* 42 (2008): 449.
76 Prince v. Massachusetts, 321 U.S. 158 (1944).
77 Woodhouse, "Who Owns the Child?," 1039–40.
78 Ibid., 1048, 1055; In re Clark, 185 N.E.2d 128, 132 (Ct. Comm. Pleas Ohio 1962); Heaton v. Jackson, 171 N.E. 364, 365 (Ohio Ct. App. 1930); In re Riff, 205 F. 406, 407–08 (E.D. Ark. 1913).
79 Woodhouse, "Who Owns the Child?," 1057; In re Clausen, 502 N.W.2d 649, 686 (Mich. 1993) (recognizing that children have a due process liberty interest in their family life, but stating that "those interests are not independent of the [] parents").

80 J. Raz, "On the Nature of Rights," *Mind* 93 (1984): 195–96. Aleardro Zanghellini, "Raz on Rights: Human Rights, Fundamental Rights, and Balancing," *Ratio Juris* 30 (2017): 25–26.
81 Raz, "On the Nature of Rights," 195–96.Zanghellini, "Raz on Rights," 26.
82 Buss, "What Does Frieda Yoder Believe?," 59.
83 Elk Grove Unified Sch. Dist. v. Newdow, 542 U.S. 1 (2002); Samantha Williams and Lior Haas, "Child Custody, Visitation & Termination of Parental Rights," *Georgetown Journal of Gender and the Law* 15 (2014): 365–72; Elizabeth S. Scott, N. Dickon Reppucci, Mark Aber, "Children's Preference in Adjudicated Custody Decisions," *Georgia Law Review* 22 (1988):1035.
84 Michael H. v. Gerald D., 491 U.S. 110, 130–31 (1998); In re Kirchner, 649 N.E.2d 324, 339 (Ill. 1995).
85 Parham v. J.R., 442 U.S. 584, 588–92, 606 (1979).
86 Ibid., 603.
87 Ibid., 603–04.
88 Ibid., 600.
89 Ibid., 600 (emphasis added).
90 Bellotti v. Baird, 443 U.S. 622, 625–26 (1979).
91 Planned Parenthood of Cent. Mo. v. Danforth, 428 U.S. 52, 72–76 (1976).
92 *Bellotti*, 443 U.S. at 633.
93 Guttmacher Institute, "Parental Involvement in Minors' Abortions," Guttmacher Institute, September 1, 2023, www.guttmacher.org.
94 *Bellotti*, 443 U.S. at 635.
95 Mihaly, "From Human Papillomavirus to COVID-19: Adolescent Autonomy and Minor Consent for Vaccines"; Robert S. Olick, Y. Tony Yang, and Jana Shaw, "Adolescent Consent to COVID-19 Vaccination: The Need for Law Reform," *Public Health Reports* 137 (2021): 163–64; Centers for Disease Control and Prevention, "State Laws that Enable a Minor to Provide Informed Consent to Receive HIV and STD Services," Centers for Disease Control and Prevention, www.cdc.gov, last reviewed October 25, 2022.
96 Brandt v. Rutledge, Case No. 4:21-cv-00450-JM (E.D. Ark. June 20, 2023); Eknes-Tucker v. Marshall, Case No. 2:22-cv-00184-LCB-SRW, 2021 WL 1521889 (M.D. Ala. May 13, 2022), *appeal filed* Case No. 22–11707 (11th Cir. May 18, 2022); Am. Civ. Lib. Union, *Doe v. Abbott* (October 5, 2022), www.aclu.org; Complaint, Doe v. Abbott, No. D-1-GN-22-000977 at ¶ 120 (Dist. Ct. Travis Cnty. Tex. Mar. 1, 2022).
97 United States v. Skrmetti, No. 23-477.
98 William L. Prosser, "Privacy," *California Law Review* 48, no. 3 (1960): 383–89, https://doi.org/10.15779/Z383J3C; Danielle Citron, *The Fight for Privacy: Protecting Dignity, Identity, and Love in the Digital Age* (W. W. Norton & Company, 2022), 102.
99 Prosser, "Privacy," 390–91.
100 Ibid.
101 United States v. Westinghouse Elec. Corp., 638 F.2d 570, 577 (3d Cir. 1980).

102 Vacco v. Quill, 521 U.S. 793, 807 (1997).Washington v. Glucksberg, 521 U.S. 702, 727 (1997).Cruzan v. Director, Mo. Dep't of Health, 497 U.S. 261, 269 (1990).
103 Cruzan v. Dir., Mo. Dep't of Health, 497 U.S. 261, 342 (1990) (Stevens, J., dissenting) (emphasis added).
104 Union Pac. R. Co. v. Botsford, 141 U.S. 250, 251 (1891) (emphasis added).
105 Griswold v. Connecticut, 381 U.S. 479, 484, 485 (1965).
106 Roe v. Wade, 410 U.S. 113, 152 (1973), *overruled* Dobbs v. Jackson Women's Health Org., 142 S. Ct. 2228 (2022).
107 Hancock v. Cnty. of Rensselaer, 882 F.2d 58, 65 (2d Cir. 2018); Norman-Bloodsaw v. Lawrence Berkely Lab., 135 F.2d 1260, 1269 (9th Cir. 1998); Doe v. City of N.Y., 15 F.3d 264, 267 (2d Cir. 1994); U.S. v. Westinghouse Corp., 658 F.2d 570, 577 (3d Cir. 1980); Haw. Psychiatric Soc. v. Ariyoshi, 481 F. Supp. 1028, 1043 (D. Haw. 1979); In re Lifschutz, 467 P.2d 557, 567 (Cal. 1970).
108 Indus. Found. of the South v. Tex. Indus. Acc. Bd. 540 S.W. 668, 679 (Tex. 1976).
109 Griswold v. Connecticut, 381 U.S. 479, 484 (1965); Winston v. Lee, 470 U.S. 753, 762 (1985).
110 Cong. Globe, 39th Cong., 1st Sess. 1118 (1866) (emphasis added).
111 Griswold, 381 U.S. at 484–85.
112 Fisher for X.S.F. v. Winding Waters Clinic, PC, No. 2:15-cv-01957-SU, 2017 WL 574383, *9 (D. Ore. Feb. 13, 2017).
113 Denise Grady, "Haunted by a Gene," *New York Times*, March 10, 2020, www.nytimes.com; Jessica L. Easton, "Self-Understanding and Identity: The Experience of Adolescents at Risk for Huntington's Disease" (Ph.D. thesis, University of British Columbia, 2003), 301.
114 *Norman-Bloodsaw* (emphasis in original).
115 In re Crawford, 194 F.3d 954, 960 (9th Cir. 1999).
116 Citron, "The Fight for Privacy," 113.
117 *Norman-Bloodsaw*.
118 Dobbs v. Jackson Women's Health Organization, 142 S. Ct. 2228, 2243 (2022).
119 Saralyn Cruickshank, "Inside the 'Dobbs' Decision," *Johns Hopkins University: Hub*, July 1, 2022, https://hub.jhu.edu; Aziz Huk, "Alito's Case for Overturning Roe Is Weak for a Reason," *Politico*, May 3, 2022, www.politico.com; Lawrence H. Tribe, "Deconstructing Dobbs," *The New York Review*, September 22, 2022, www.nybooks.com; American Historical Association and Organization of American Historians, "History, the Supreme Court, and *Dobbs v. Jackson*: Joint Statement from the American Historical Association and the Organization of American Historians (2022)," American Historical Association and Organization of American Historians., www.historians.org.
120 *Dobbs*, 142 S. Ct. at 2301 (Thomas, J., concurring).
121 *Dobbs*, 142 S. Ct. at 2237.
122 Ibid.
123 Amy Gajada, "How Dobbs Threatens to Torpedo Privacy Rights in the US," *Wired*, June 29, 2022, www.wired.com.

124 Jeremy R. Garrett et al., "Rethinking the 'Open Future' Argument Against Predictive Genetic Testing of Children," *Genetics in Medicine* 21 (2019): 2190–92.
125 Feinberg, "Freedom & Fulfillment," 94–95 (emphasis added).
126 Colleen Long, "Secret Service Study Explores School Shooter Warning Signs," *PBS*, November 7, 2019, www.pbs.org.
127 Sophia Naide, "'Parental Involvement' Mandates for Abortion Harm Young People, but Policymakers Can Fight Back," Guttmacher Institute, February 19, 2020, www.guttmacher.org.
128 N.Y. Dom. Rel. L. § 15-a.
129 N.Y. Pub. Health L. § 2305(2).
130 Danielle Citron, "Protecting Sexual Privacy in the Information Age," in *Privacy in the Modern Age: The Search for Solutions*, ed. Marc Rosenberg, Julia Horwitz & Jeramie Scott 46–54, 46 (New York: The New Press, 2015).

3

Mask-Shaming

On Private Enforcement and Disability Politics

DORON DORFMAN

During the COVID-19 pandemic, face masks quickly became a hot-button political issue across party lines. The seemingly simple act of wearing a mask to mitigate the spread of a novel pathogen became laden with questions, value, and meaning. And regardless of whether wearing a mask was mandated from the top down through Centers for Disease Control and Prevention (CDC) recommendations and executive orders from the White House, or merely encouraged from the bottom up due to social norms, ordinary citizens became the primary enforcers.

In this chapter, I argue that the de facto regulation and enforcement of mask-wearing by laypeople can largely be understood through the sociolegal phenomenon of shaming. Shaming involves stigmatizing and disgracing a norm violator and can take many forms, from physical or verbal violence to online bullying. This chapter discusses shaming of people *wearing* masks as well as those *not wearing* masks, thereby exposing for the first time the full scope of mask-shaming.

Specifically I engage with the interests of individuals with disabilities—those who are immunocompromised or have comorbidities that make them particularly vulnerable to complications from COVID-19 and therefore for whom masking is even more crucial to maintain their health. While paying close attention to how norms about mask-wearing intersect with gender and race, I explain how shaming operates as a mechanism of private enforcement of disability rights, and I highlight the dichotomous challenges associated with private, ideologically driven enforcement of public health policy.

Masking as a Preventive Measure During the COVID-19 Pandemic

Masks have probably been the most common and visible symbol of the COVID-19 pandemic.[1] As the disability studies scholar Mel Chen observed almost a decade before the pandemic, "masks both symbolize and effect security; by both representing and doing, they are performative technologies of sort."[2] More than being symbolic of one of the most significant global public health emergencies in recent history, one that arguably has not ended, masking is also a prime example of regulating the body.

Before the COVID-19 pandemic, wearing a mask would signal a person's disability and "out" a person with nonvisible or less apparent disabilities,[3] someone who would otherwise pass as nondisabled (think people with allergies, those with multiple chemical sensitivity, or people who are immunocompromised).[4] Masks, specifically surgical masks, were associated with hospitals and health care professionals. It may be this pre-pandemic unconscious association that the public had between masks, sickness, and disability that evokes the engrained evolutionary fear of becoming disabled that immediately caused resistance to masking.[5] One also needs to bear in mind that masks can be cumbersome and uncomfortable and take time to get used to. They may also create barriers to effective communication and quality social engagement.[6] However, the need to endure at least some level of inconvenience and limits on personal liberty to prevent the spread of a dangerous virus should have been more effectively communicated, especially considering the amount of misinformation online on the severity of the coronavirus and the effectiveness of preventive measures.[7]

Masks as a preventive health measure aimed at the general public were first formally introduced in the United States, at least on the federal level,[8] one month into the pandemic. On April 3, 2020, the CDC first made recommendations that every person over the age of two wear face coverings while in public.[9] This recommendation came with a caveat: an exemption from masking if a person "has trouble breathing, or is unconscious, incapacitated, or otherwise unable to remove the cover without assistance."[10]

While the exemptions were meant to apply to a specific group of people with disabilities (those with sensory processing disorders like autism, with developmental disabilities, and with facial deformities), misinformation concerning mask exemption eligibility, bolstered by ideals around personal liberties and skepticism about the existence or severity of the coronavirus, started spreading online. Nondisabled individuals, specifically right-wing "anti-maskers," started claiming mask exemptions.[11] They wrongly insisted they are not required to present any information about their impairment according to the Americans with Disabilities Act (ADA) and the Health Insurance Portability and Accountability Act.[12] This mayhem around mask exemptions in mid-2020 was therefore a clear, strong, social reaction to efforts to contain the global public health emergency through masking. The bitter irony is that these people falsely claiming mask exemptions were causing *harm* to people with disabilities through the misuse of a law that was designed to *protect* them.

On January 20, 2021, his first day in office, then-President Joseph R. Biden signed an executive order mandating masks on federal property and during interstate travel.[13] Although the politicization of masking had occurred throughout the entirety of the pandemic,[14] Biden's move was received by many as another indication of politicization, especially as President Donald J. Trump openly disregarded the need to wear masks or engage in social distancing.[15]

This process of politicization created a view among many that masks are unnecessary, ineffective, and even a way for the government and states to restrict personal freedom and increase social control through the regulation of the body.[16] This is despite the mounting evidence of the effectiveness of masks in mitigating the spread of COVID-19.[17] In later stages of the pandemic, starting in 2021 and continuing into 2023, suspicion against masking—combined with the desire to declare the pandemic over—yielded a unique phenomenon of shaming and harassing those wearing masks in public.

The use of face masks transformed during the pandemic and after its formal conclusion (on May 11, 2023, per the CDC). During the height of the pandemic, shaming of those not wearing masks was very prevalent. At some point in the pandemic, solidarity eroded. Gone was the understanding that "my mask protects you, your mask protects me."[18] Individuals attempting to avoid COVID-19 infection were left with so-called one-way masking in its place. Discussions of masking as disability accommodations surfaced in practice, in the literature, and in courts, specifically in response to state executive orders prohibiting state governmental agencies, schools, and universities from implementing mask requirements.[19] At this point, shaming became a tactic to enforce masking as a disability accommodation.

Situating Shaming Within Legal Discourse

In 1996, the legal scholar Dan Kahan asserted that shaming penalties—which stigmatize and publicly disgrace the offender or norm violator—are a feasible alternative to imprisonment in criminal law.[20] Many scholars criticized Kahan's position. James Q. Whitman, for example, argued that shaming penalties are ethically wrong because they "involve . . . a species of lynch justice" and "involve an ugly, and politically dangerous, complicity between the state and the [public]."[21] Eric Posner similarly claimed shaming to be an unreliable means of deterring individuals from committing norm violations and that its effects could negatively impact innocent third parties.[22]

Toni M. Massaro noted that "modern shaming methods" do not properly promote the rehabilitation of the shamed nor do they successfully reinforce societal norms.[23] She highlights the fact that offenders of public norms are often shameless; therefore "shaming ends are flatly inconsistent with any rehabilitative purpose" directed at offenders.[24] She also points out that, even if the offender feels shame, "the behavioral consequences of [shame] are unpredictable, and [they] may include anger and a desire to retaliate against the one inflicting the shame."[25] Martha Nussbaum also points out that "shaming penalties are horrifically stigmatizing [and] inconsistent with individual dignity."[26]

In a later article responding to these critiques, Kahan addressed the shortfalls of criminal shaming penalties.[27] Specifically, he stated the following:

> What's *really* wrong with shaming penalties . . . is that they are deeply partisan: when society picks them, it picks sides, aligning itself with those who subscribe to norms that give pride of place to community and social differentiation rather than to individuality and equality.[28]

Since the early debate over Kahan's concept of shaming, other scholars discussed shaming in a variety of legal contexts including corporate law,[29] administrative law,[30] and intellectual property.[31] Public health law scholars mostly rejected shaming as an effective legal and policy tool. In their article on shaming those who refuse to take or give their children vaccines, Ross Silverman and Lindsey Wiley warn that "[t]actics that leverage social capital and connections, shame, and sharpen rhetoric addressed toward vaccine-refusing parents could alienate vaccine-hesitant parents in ways that are counterproductive."[32] Wiley also argued against the use of shaming to combat obesity, showing how it had the opposite of the desired effect: it actually caused obese women to forego health care (including routine gynecological exams, screenings for blood pressure, and care for diabetes).[33] This is unlike successful strategies to de-normalize the use of tobacco and portray smoking as a "deviant social behavior."[34]

The internet and social media have had a great impact on how shaming strategies are used by the public to deter certain behaviors. Online shaming has become a common phenomenon. Yet as Kate Klonick has shown, while the practice of online shaming comes with a low cost to the perpetuator, shaming has severe emotional consequences for its victims.[35]

This chapter demonstrates how shaming and its counterparts—politization, inconsistency, and unpredictability—manifest with regard to the practice of wearing masks in the wake of the COVID-19 pandemic and how social media plays a key role in perpetuating this sociolegal phenomenon.

Shamed for Wearing a Mask

Since the April 2022 Florida federal district court decision in *Health Freedom Defense Fund, Inc. v. Biden* that struck down the CDC's transit mask order and entered a nationwide injunction against it,[36] not only did common carriers and transportation hubs stop requiring masks; other places of public accommodation did, too. Almost overnight, masking largely became an optional, voluntary practice (even if only formally, as many states, localities, and private institutions had practically abandoned their mask policies by that point). Even before the abandonment of mask mandates, but certainly since then, there have been a growing number of incidents of harassment, shaming, and ridicule for wearing a mask in public. It is as if masking in public has become stigmatized and penalized, as evidenced by increasing negative comments and aggression.[37] This type of aggression joins the rank of other upticks in violent phenomena during the pandemic, namely an increase in domestic violence incidents, violence and harassment incidents occurring on airplanes, and violence against people of Asian descent.[38]

The decision not to mask in public has the potential to affect all members of society, but this decision has a disproportional impact on disabled people who are immunocompromised or live with comorbidities. Disabled individuals may not have a strong immune response to COVID-19 vaccination,[39] and they also may be more susceptible to complications from COVID-19 infections due to underlying conditions.[40] Therefore, disabled individuals (and their caregivers) who choose to wear masks in public have become a minority.

While it is hard to assess exactly how common the phenomenon is, anecdotal evidence shows that people who mask in public pay a price for their action. Admittedly, much of the evidence presented in this chapter is based on social media posts by people with disabilities. However, despite its limitations, using social media stories is an important source of information and evidence of the lived disability experiences in the twenty-first century. Disability and media scholars have shown how members of the disability community find social media to be a place for fostering community. Katie Ellis and Gerard Goggin have written about how disabled people use social media as "citizen media"—a tool to encourage other democratic practices of mutual social responsibility.[41] Beth Heller and Susan Cumings have documented how people with disabilities use social media platforms to showcase their lived experiences in a way that disrupts ableist narratives in mainstream media.[42] A number of the following examples highlight these uses.

In June 2021, a man living with lupus was harassed for wearing a mask when going out to New York City Pride and was told that "COVID is over" and that he should "[g]et on with [his] life."[43] A year earlier, in May 2020, at least two women harassed a mask-wearing news reporter by chanting "Take it off!" at him. Video footage of the incident shows that, as the reporter walked away from the scene, people followed him and coughed.⁴⁴ Another 25-year-old man was sucker-punched because he wore a mask at a bar in Long Island. His twin sister, also in attendance, was harassed for masking.⁴⁵ While at a press conference at the University of South Florida, Governor Ron DeSantis said to masked students he saw: "You do not have to wear those masks, please take them off. Honestly, it's not doing anything. We've gotta stop with this COVID theater. So if you wanna wear it, fine, but this is ridiculous."⁴⁶ In 2020, Charlotte-based ESPN senior writer Ryan McGee went out with six other patrons—while masked—to pick up food.⁴⁷ An unmasked man came into the restaurant around the same time, walked up to McGee, pointed a finger at him, and said "what a pretty mask, you sissy!"⁴⁸ A few weeks later, while McGee was exiting his truck, a taunter called him out by name and yelled "snowflake" and "sheep."⁴⁹ Another shocking statement directly connecting masks with shame was made by the former CDC director Rochelle Walensky in a podcast interview in 2022: "I just know people are tired. The scarlet letter of this pandemic is the mask." A scarlet letter is an act of penance, done out of repentance and public shaming for sins. The phrase references a nineteenth-century novel of the same name by Nathaniel Hawthorne, in which the protagonist Hester Prynne is forced to wear an embroidered "A" on her clothing to shame her for committing adultery.⁵⁰ Framing masks as a symbol of shame, even if the intention is to garner sympathy while acknowledging that they are inconvenient and annoying, has the power to give excuses to others to shame others for wearing them. It is a bad way of communicating public health messages.⁵¹

Accounts on social media also demonstrate that mask-shaming is very real. One person tweeted in June 2021: "My friend is immunocompromised and locked down alone. Fully vaccinated—Pfizer—and now has zero antibodies. And when he walks the puppy he got that [sic] keeping him sane, people yell at him to take off his mask. He's just trying to stay alive."⁵² One year later, in September 2022, a person with chronic illness tweeted that they "[w]ent down to the harvest food trucks . . . with a friend who takes immunosuppressants [and they] [g]ot heckled by a car full of men for wearing a mask and 'being scared.'"⁵³ In August 2023, another person tweeted that they "[h]ave several physician friends who've admitted they've been harassed [and] mocked for wearing a mask in healthcare [settings]. This [doctor] works with transplant patients [and] had a relative die of [long COVID]. . . . I don't recognize my profession anymore."[54]

The real problem with shaming and stigmatization of those who wear masks is the possible chilling effect that could result. The legal scholar Lawrence Lessig discussed how, despite the "cost-minimizing effect" of hockey players wearing helmets that are effective in protecting from injury, leading to savings on health care costs, "for much of the history of professional hockey . . . most hockey players did not wear helmets."[55] This is because "helmets were not consistent with the macho self-image of hockey players" and the "stigmatic cost [of a player who dares to wear a helmet] relative to other players, since their and others' vision of his 'machoness' is impaired."[56] In previous research, I explored how stigmatization of preventive medicine can cause a chilling or deterrent effect on their use.[57] Among some of the specific examples I discussed, one evoked Lessig's discussion as it relates to gender stereotypes: the unwillingness of young straight men to undergo colonoscopies because "they view medical intervention as a threat to male sexuality, [and] they associate this body part with homosexuality and gay sex."[58] Like colonoscopies, masks are a preventive measure. By stigmatizing masking, there is a danger that people will not be willing to wear masks to protect themselves or others from COVID-19 or from future pandemics.

What is striking is how the stigmatization of masks has also evoked gender stereotypes during the pandemic, just like other penalized preventive health measures. Men's resistance to showing weakness and vulnerability to disease manifested itself through President Trump's avoidance of wearing a mask in public; Trump's stance was later called out by then-President Biden as "macho" and "falsely masculine."[59] It is therefore critically important to continue to disentangle how the patriarchy—the social system in which positions of power, privilege, and dominance are held mostly by men—contributes to health stigma and jeopardizes wellness and well-being.

Racial prejudice also connects to the stigma surrounding mask-wearing. In the summer of 2020, thousands of individuals took to the streets to protest police violence against Black people following the murder of George Floyd, Breonna Taylor, and others. The massive Black Lives Matter protests that took place during the height of the pandemic raised concerns about spreading coronavirus due to the difficulty of maintaining physical distance during the gatherings.[60] Related concerns included whether "protesters in the Black Lives Matter movement . . . get a free pass on not wearing [masks]"[61] and whether it is hypocritical to support the Black Lives Matter demonstrations and oppose anti-lockdown ones by the right.[62] Those accusations of mostly Black protesters spreading coronavirus through protesting without sufficient protections (including masking) have turned out to be false.[63] Yet they demonstrate the interplay between prejudices toward masking and toward people of color.

To demonstrate this point further, in early summer 2020 Nikita Blakeney-Williams noted that, while her daughters and her youngest son would wear masks in public, her three older sons would not "because of their image and their desire to avoid unnecessary confrontations."[64] Additionally, Williams's husband chose not to wear a mask, and she could not "help but wonder if he too shares a small hidden fear of 'being masked while black' and the possible negative outcome that can accompany it." Similar to the tactic adopted by the Black social psychologist Claude Steele of whistling classical musical while walking down the street at night so to not be perceived as a threat,[65] Enoch Glover, a Black resident of North Carolina, chose to wear a mask but "did so while taking precautions." For example, he avoided using bandanas as a mask because "he felt it could carry a negative connotation," and he made sure the outfit he wore with the mask would not trigger any "racially-motivated suspicions." Lastly, Glover noted the following: "I have two sons, and I've always had discussions with them about wearing hoodies and not putting their hoods up until they are in a safe environment. . . . Masks are really the new hoodie."

This statement comparing face masks to hoodies in the context of stereotypes of criminality connected with Blackness has manifested in policy. In March 2023, the mayor of New York City, Eric Adams, instructed owners of bodegas and delis in the city to require customers coming into the businesses to take off their masks as part of the effort to prevent robberies and shoplifting. The idea is that removing the mask would allow security cameras to capture the potential criminal hiding behind it. According to Adams: "When you see these mask-wearing people, oftentimes it's not about being fearful of the pandemic, it's fearful of the police catching them for their deeds."[66] Obvious concerns about requiring immunocompromised individuals to take off their masks when coming into businesses have been raised, yet the guidelines still stand.[67]

The stereotyping of face masks, coupled with their politicization, which intersects with gender and race, have led to shaming of those who wear masks. Such a phenomenon is dangerous because it can cause a deterrent, chilling effect on mask-wearing, putting immunocompromised individuals at heightened risk. It also jeopardizes public cooperation and preparedness for future public health emergencies.

The next section highlights another, less prominent form of mask-shaming and attempting to regulate others' bodies that has recently emerged: shaming for *not* wearing a mask.

Shamed for Not Wearing a Mask

Historically, people with disabilities have been segregated from society due to U.S. public policy's heavy reliance on large-scale, isolated institutions—such as nursing homes, asylums, boarding homes, psychiatric hospitals, prisons, and group homes—that dates back to the late eighteenth century and early nineteenth century.[68] In the late twentieth century, however, the independent living movement that started in Berkeley, California, in the late 1960s,[69] the introduction of the Medicaid program in 1965,[70] and the enactment of the ADA and its interpretation in the 1999 United States Supreme Court case *Olmstead v. L.C. ex rel. Zimring*[71] contributed to a process of deinstitutionalization that allowed many (though not all) people with disabilities to live in the community.[72]

Nevertheless, the integration of people with disabilities into society, in accordance with disability rights law, has met challenges. As I have written before: "The ADA successfully raised public awareness of the topic [of disability], and now laypeople at least seem familiar with the general issues and basic concepts of reasonable accommodations. However, the statute and movement failed to change perceptions toward disability in courtrooms and the public sphere," with many seeing disability as a status conferring "special rights" that allow unfair advantages.[73] When people with disabilities are in public, they are met with harassment, suspicion, and questioning about their perceived deservingness[74] to use disability rights and accommodations.[75] This type of scrutiny, which I termed "fear of the disability con," has been documented in parking lots,[76] at theme parks,[77] in airports,[78] on college campuses,[79] and anywhere with a no-pet policy where people with disabilities bring their service animals.[80]

As discussed above, exemptions from mask-wearing, though limited, do exist under CDC guidelines and could be given to those with sensory processing disorders like autism, people with developmental disabilities, and people with facial deformities.[81] And yet disabled people who tried to use their exemptions have been misunderstood, suspected, and harassed.

In June 2020, at the height of the pandemic, Israel Del Toro, a disabled veteran from Colorado, went into a credit union unmasked. He consequently was turned away and was told to use the drive-through. Del Toro, however, could not use the drive-through, as he lost his fingers in an explosion in Afghanistan. He also could not wear a mask, as he lost his ears in the same explosion, so he could not secure a mask to his face. Moreover, another medical condition made it hard for him to breathe, and the mask would worsen the condition. After the story went viral, the credit union issued an apology for its employees' failure to use good judgment.[82] In addition to the issue of disbelief, another important insight can be uncovered from Del Toro's incident. A disability studies analysis of the story surfaces a tacit hierarchy in disability deservingness within disability communities, with disabled veterans perceived as most deserving, as highlighted by the disability law scholar Sagit Mor.[83] Here, a story about a clearly deserving veteran was used to raise awareness of the mask exemption issue that could affect other disabled individuals.

A similar incident occurred in the suburbs of Chicago a month earlier in May 2020: a Target employee threatened to call the police on a father and his 22-year-old daughter with cerebral palsy and autism who took her mask off in the store (she had an exemption).[84]

In March 2021, Cheri Fleming, one of her friends, and Fleming's son Bryan Crisp—all of whom have disabilities—attempted to fly from Chicago to Los Angeles with Southwest Airlines.[85] Because of Crisp's developmental disabilities, he had an exemption from wearing masks. Crisp had two doctor's notes confirming this, along with his negative COVID-19 test and proof of his COVID-19 vaccinations.[86] Nevertheless, the flight attendant demanded that Crisp wear a mask on the plane, because Southwest was not yet allowing passengers to apply for federal exemptions.[87] So even though there allegedly were 40 open seats on the plane, allowing Crisp to socially distance from masked passengers and diminish the risk of infection, Crisp, Fleming, and Fleming's friend were all forced off the plane.[88]

A student at Lancaster University in the United Kingdom with a less apparent disability reported suspicion and harassment by student workers and university staff who simply did not believe her exemption and did not allow her a chance to explain herself. The student was forced to leave university buildings on some occasions due to the suspicion that she did not really deserve or have a mask exemption.[89] The university responded to the incident with the following statement: "To support our students we are engaging with the national Sunflower Lanyard Scheme [a British initiative to identify people with less apparent disabilities] and developing our own e-exemption card which will be optional to those who find it useful."[90] Although this story is from the United Kingdom, the university's response reflects dilemmas regarding disability identification that also exists in the United States. Due to the fear of the disability con, individuals are subject to bureaucratic burdens and privacy invasions. Indeed, the Target employee who threatened to call the police on the father and his unmasked disabled daughter asked to see documentation proving the mask exemption (despite the fact that those type of formal documents did not exist).[91] The disability studies scholar Ellen Samuels has referred to this issue as "biocertification," which "materializes the modern belief that only science can reliably determine the truths of identity and generally claims to offer a simple, verifiable, and concrete solution to questions of identity. Yet in practice, biocertification tends to produce not straightforward answers but documentary sprawl, increased uncertainty, and bureaucratic stagnation."[92] These dilemmas have existed in the United States in multiple contexts, specifically with regard to disabled parking and the use of service dogs, and this chapter shows how they exist with respect to mask polices.[93]

This issue of suspecting people of faking disabilities to escape mask requirements might seem anecdotal or marginal, but it has been recognized as an issue by the New Zealand government in 2021. The Ministry of Health issued an official response regarding people with disabilities who were exempted from wearing a mask and yet were "'confronted and harassed' when accessing essential services" to the point that some were "too scared to go out in public for fear of the response of over-zealous Kiwis."[94]

Not long after, however, not wearing a mask became the "new normal," particularly with the widespread availability of COVID-19 vaccines. Masks have become less and less visible since 2021, and in the United States the CDC ended the pandemic "state of emergency" on May 11, 2023. From then on, and to this day, many immunocompromised and disabled individuals feel they have been left behind. Many individuals who are immunocompromised or disabled try to emphasize, mostly on social media—which has become an even more important outlet for the disability community during the pandemic—that COVID-19 is not over for them.

For disabled and immunocompromised individuals, masking has become a symbol of solidarity and inclusion. The gesture of masking to accommodate a person with disabilities can be described in terms of "access intimacy," a term coined by the disability studies scholar Mia Mingus.[95] For Mingus, a gesture that allows for disability inclusion creates solidarity between disabled and nondisabled individuals. It is about "knowing that someone else is willing to be with me in the never-ending and ever-changing daily obstacle course that is navigating an inaccessible world."[96]

In this new situation, the regulation and policing of those not wearing masks in large events or enclosed spaces seems to have shifted: it is now members of the disability community who are shaming others. An event that has unfolded online via X (formerly Twitter) particularly exemplifies the complexities of how mask-shaming and private enforcement of disability-related issues have evolved with time.

The American Association of People with Disabilities (AAPD) is a well-regarded disability rights organization led by individuals with disabilities, and many established disability rights and justice activists are associated with it. On July 26, 2023, AAPD held its annual celebration to recognize the anniversary of the ADA at the Salamander Hotel in Washington, D.C.[97] In the two days following the event, prominent disability activists who attended the event posted photos of themselves at the party. One caption said: "What a day! I love an after party selfie. @AAPD #ADA33 anniversary event did not disappoint. It was a reunion of friends, [a] celebration, and recommitment to the work that need[s] to be done. Cheers and let's go!"[98] Yet when those seemingly generic posts appeared on social media feeds, they created quite a stir. This is because most of the activists in the photo were not wearing masks. One response to the photos stated: "One mask at an ADA celebration event. Setting a great example for disabled, immunocompromised [people], and all people during an ongoing pandemic. Covid is airborne. Wear a mask. Make events accessible to all disabled people."[99] When many more accusatory and shaming tweets appeared, the activists tried to explain their position. Mia Ives-Rublee, the director of the Disability Justice Initiative at the Center for American Progress, wrote:

> Dear humans, I am going to explain one more time and I know I'll still get heat for it. I wear my mask as often as I can. But there are times I don't because: 1) I'm talking to someone who is HOH [hard of hearing] or deaf 2) People [are] racists against Asians and I need to mitigate that. . . . I know I am an imperfect human being and I'm trying to live in a world that is imperfect and I live at an intersection that leaves me vulnerable no matter what I do. I try to live my life truthfully and navigate the systems to advocate forcefully. I know I often fall short.[100]

In her explanation and apology, Ives-Rublee is evoking the concept of competing access needs for people with different disabilities.[101] Early in the pandemic, a clash arose with regard to the need to mask to protect immunocompromised individuals and the need to allow people with hearing impairments to be able to read lips.[102] Reactions to this explanation on social media were mixed. While some accepted the apology, one user added a screenshot of a group photo from the same event that Ives-Rublee uploaded on another social media platform and wrote:

> I noticed some others who were at the event choosing masks that help those who are HOH. These masks with a clear section have been around since 2020. They allow those who are HOH to lip read but still include those immune compromised to events (or the workplace, etc.)[103]

The other disability activists who appeared unmasked in the photo also posted apologies. The activist and writer Emily Ladau, for example, wrote:

About the photo: My choice to be unmasked made the event inaccessible, no excuses. I value the labor done to call me on it. I'm sorry for contributing to an unsafe environment, but more importantly for causing pain and not being in solidarity as I should have been. . . . I am fully aware that a single tweet does not equal repairing harm or undoing a choice, but know that I am listening, you are heard, and I own my actions.[104]

Ladau's apology seems to have been better accepted. Yet the backlash against the well-regarded disability activists by members of their own community symbolizes a deeper issue that highlights the risks of private enforcement of norms, laws, and policies, which I examine in the next section.

On Private Enforcement and Disability Politics

Mask-shaming can be conceptualized as part of a bigger phenomenon of private enforcement of laws and policies by laypeople (as opposed to formal enforcers by the state, federal, or local government). Private enforcement in the United States can be traced back to the nineteenth century with roots in the bleak history of slavery and the Fugitive Slave Acts of 1793 and 1850 that deputized bounty hunters to capture enslaved individuals who were on the run.[105] Since then, private enforcement mechanisms have spread to other areas of the law, such as the environment, securities and banking, housing, elections, and national security.[106] More recent controversies surrounding state laws relying on private enforcement include ones that allow laypersons to bring actions against anyone who aids or abets the performance or inducement of an abortion after approximately six weeks of pregnancy and those allowing one to sue school districts that teach critical race theory or gender- and LGBTQ-related issues.[107] Legal scholars have criticized such laws on the ground of creating "a new form of legal vigilantism."[108]

Disability law in the United States is another area that primarily depends on private enforcement via members of society,[109] from the enforcement of accessibility in the built environment that is done through a "private attorney general model"[110] to business owners who enforce federal regulations regarding the use of service animals in public.[111] In previous work, I and other scholars discussed the zealous enforcement of disabled parking placards.[112] The surveillance and enforcement of those who are suspected to be abusing a disabled parking permit have been done using technological means such as designated websites or apps, as well as through individual interactions in parking lots.[113] Reactions to a suspected violation of disabled parking rules range from friendly advice to confrontation (whether done face-to-face or by leaving a note on the car) and even retribution (by damaging the alleged violator's vehicle, blocking their car, or even engaging in physical violence).[114] As a public administrator said in an interview in my previous research: "[W]e have some very zealous people, for a lack of a better term, who would just literally sit in the Walmart parking lot all day long and do nothing but take down license plates of individuals who park in the disabled parking spots and don't have a placard . . . and I would say 70% of the time, these are people who do have placards who just forgot to hang them up."[115]

Indeed, private enforcement of disability law has harmed many disabled people, mainly through mistaken identification and rushed judgments by zealous private enforcers. The disability community is incredibly diverse. Just to name a few, people with mobility, mental, sensory, and intellectual impairments have various needs that require different degrees of care and support.[116] Intersectionality with gender, class, race, and ethnicity adds another layer to the complexity of lived experiences of people with disabilities.[117] What is also unique about the disability experience is how fluid it is: disability can not only take visible or less apparent forms, but it also can also come and go in waves over time periods as short as one day or as long as a life course.[118] The complexity of disability makes private enforcement very tricky. The identification process is fraught with stereotypes (of how a disabled person should look and act and where they should be) and deservingness bias.[119]

Although masking is a public health policy that aims to mitigate the spread of coronavirus, because of the disproportionate effects of the pandemic on people with disabilities, one can think of it as a disability policy. This is particularly true after the height of the pandemic, when masking is usually used to accommodate a disabled person (and not as a universal policy). In short, masking has become a new arena for private enforcement of disability law. The byproduct of such private enforcement has been mask-shaming on both sides (for wearing a mask and for not wearing one).

Final Thoughts

What can mask-shaming from either side tell us about private enforcement, the social psychology of in-groups and out-groups, public health, and disability rights?

Public health law scholars have pushed for the understanding of the field through a population perspective that includes the concept of communal responsibility for health.[120] Yet leaving enforcement of such measures to the public can have a price, especially in a society that seems to be more polarized than ever. This is because a whole set of political meanings and values may be attached to public health measures.[121] Identification with a certain goal and way of life can create a strong urge to zealously enforce norms and policies in ways that could alienate and further polarize social groups.

Indeed, mask-shaming shows how the politicization of an issue is bidirectional: as the right doubled down on shaming people for wearing masks, people in the disability community reacted by zealously enforcing masks in public spaces and holding people who they see as members of the in-group (activists and allies) accountable. Nevertheless, such a move by the disability community can be seen as emulating patterns that harm people with disabilities in terms of surveillance, shaming, and strong language. Indeed, some disability activists called out that type of mask-shaming.[122]

This chapter contributes to the legal debate on shaming by showing how this strategy can be used by multiple groups advocating for opposite sides of the debate. As other legal scholars have demonstrated, shaming is an ethically contentious practice for regulating behavior that can lead to unwanted results. While it may be too early to determine the exact consequences of mask-shaming, exposing this phenomenon is helpful in further reflecting on the relationship between private enforcement, public health, and disability law and politics.

NOTES

For helpful feedback and fruitful engagement with this chapter, I would like to thank John Blume, Susanna Lee, Kat Macfarlane, Kim Mutcherson, Wendy Parmet, Chloe Reichel, Austin Sarat, and Allison Whelan. Maura Quinn provided excellent research assistance. I am also grateful for feedback by the participants of the "Pulling Back the Veil: Issues Revealed by the COVID-19 Pandemic" panel at 2024 Health Law Professors Conference hosted by the American Association of Law & Medicine and Temple University Beasley School of Law.

1. Doron Dorfman, "Pandemic 'Disability Cons,'" *Journal of Law Medicine & Ethics* 49 (2021): 402–03.
2. Mel Y. Chen, "Masked States and the 'Screen' Between Security and Disability," *WSQ: Women's Studies Quarterly* 40 (2012): 79.
3. As I have discussed in previous work, due to the fluid nature of disability, the line between visible and invisible disabilities is not as clear cut as one would assume: a person could use a mobility device one day and not use it the next. In addition, the concept of visibility can be considered subjective. See Doron Dorfman, "Fear of the Disability Con: Perceptions of Fraud and Special Rights Discourse," *Law & Society Review* 54 (2019): 1067; Doron Dorfman, "[Un]Usual Suspects: Deservingness, Scarcity, and Disability Rights," *UC Irvine Law Review* (2020): 568; Doron Dorfman, "Suspicious Species," *University of Illinois Law Review* 2021 (2021): 1401.
4. Chen, "Mask States," 82.
5. As the disability psychologist Michelle Nario-Redmond summarizes it: "[E]volutionary sources of disability prejudice propose that our avoidance of certain people reflects an unconscious bias that overreacts by automatically triggering fears of contagion when faced with certain observable impairments." See Michelle Nario-Redmond, *Ableism: The Cause and Consequences of Disability Prejudice* (Hoboken, NJ: John Wiley & Sons, 2019), 40.
6. Dorfman, "Pandemic 'Disability Cons,'" 404; Shana Kushner Gadarian, Sara Wallace Goodman, and Thomas Pepinsky, *Pandemic Politics: The Deadly Toll of Partisanship in the Age of COVID* (Princeton: Princeton University Press 2022): 110; Anya Kamenetz, "After 2 Years, Growing Calls to Take Masks Off Children in School," *NPR* (January 28, 2022), www.npr.org.
7. As Francis Collins, the former director of the National Institutes of Health (NIH), admitted in a December 2021 television interview, albeit using vaccine hesitancy as an example: "Maybe we [NIH] underinvested in research on human behavior. I never imagined a year ago, when those vaccines were just proving to be fantastically safe and effective, that we will still have 60 million people who have not taken advantage of that [did not vaccinate] because of misinformation and disinformation that somehow dominated all of the ways in which people were getting their answers." See PBS News Hour, "What Could NIH Have Done Differently During the Pandemic?" *Twitter (X)* (December 20, 2021), https://twitter.com/NewsHour/status/1473082652181807106.
8. This is while, in response to the 1918 influenza pandemic, "many local governments ordered the general public to wear face masks. Legal challenges were largely rejected by the courts, which described the flu pandemic orders as 'reasonable measures to slow the spread of disease.'" See Lindsay F. Wiley, "Democratizing the Laws of Social Distancing," *Yale Journal of Health Policy, Law, and Ethics* 19 (2020): 63.
9. Gadarian, Goodman, and Pepinsky, *Pandemic Politics*, 100; Wiley, *Democratizing the Laws*, 75.

10. Dorfman, "Pandemic 'Disability Cons,'" 403; Doron Dorfman and Mical Raz, "Mask Exemptions During the COVID-19 Pandemic—A New Frontier for Clinicians" *JAMA Health Forum* (July 10, 2020).
11. Dorfman, "Pandemic 'Disability Cons,'" 403; Elizabeth Pendo, Robert Gatter, and Seema Mohapatra, "Resolving Tensions Between Disability Rights Law and COVID-19 Mask Policies," *Maryland Law Review Online* 80 (2020): 5; Doron Dorfman, "Being Anti-Mask Doesn't Make You Disabled," *Newsday* (May 21, 2020), www.newsday.com.
12. Dorfman, "Pandemic 'Disability Cons,'" 403.
13. The White House, *Executive Order on Protecting the Federal Workforce and Requiring Mask-Wearing* (January20, 2021), www.whitehouse.gov.
14. Gadarian, Goodman, and Pepinsky, *Pandemic Politics*, 100.
15. Wiley, "Democratizing the Laws," 80; Wendy E. Parmet, *Constitutional Contagion: Covid, the Courts, and Public Health* (New York: Cambridge University Press 2023), 2–3.
16. Gadarian, Goodman, and Pepinsky, *Pandemic Politics*, 110. Admittedly, one could assume that the politicization of masking also pushed some on the left to embrace masking to show they were not on Trump's side. Thus, in effect, masking became for some a type of political signaling. The use of masking on the left is beyond the scope of this chapter but could be a fascinating topic for future research.
17. Gadarian, Goodman, and Pepinsky, *Pandemic Politics*, 103.
18. Wayne J. Franklin, "Your Mask Protects Me, My Mask Protects You," *Phoenix Children's* (December 18, 2020), https://phoenixchildrens.org.
19. Mical Raz and Doron Dorfman, "Bans on COVID-19 Mask Requirements vs Disability Accommodations A New Conundrum," *JAMA Health Forum* (August 6, 2021); Michelle M. Mello & David M. Studdert, "The Political and Judicial Battles Over Mask Mandates for Schools," *JAMA Health Forum* (October 28, 2021); Doron Dorfman, "Third-Party Accommodations" (forthcoming, unpublished manuscript with the author).
20. Dan M. Kahan, "What Do Alternative Sanctions Mean?," *University of Chicago Law Review* 69 (1996): 594, 650.
21. James Q. Whitman, "What's Wrong with Inflicting Shame Sanctions," *Yale Law Journal* 107 (1998): 1059.
22. Eric A. Posner, *Law and Social Norms* (Cambridge, MA: Harvard University Press, 2000), 92–93, 109.
23. Toni M. Massaro, "The Meanings of Shame: Implications for Legal Reform," *Psychology, Public Policy, and Law* 3 (1997): 648.
24. Massaro, "The Meanings of Shame," 648.
25. Massaro, "The Meanings of Shame," 648.
26. Martha C. Nussbaum, *Hiding from Humanity: Disgust, Shame, and the Law* (Princeton: Princeton University Press 2006), 230–33.
27. Dan M. Kahan, "What's Really Wrong with Shaming Sanctions," *Texas Law Review* 84 (2006): 2075.

28 Kahan, "What's Really Wrong," 2076.
29 David A. Skeel, Jr., "Shaming in Corporate Law," *University of Pennsylvania Law Review* 149 (2001): 1812.
30 Sharon Yadin, "Regulatory Shaming," *Environmental Law* 49 (2019): 419.
31 Elizabeth L. Rosenblatt, "Fear and Loathing: Shame, Shaming, and Intellectual Property," *DePaul Law Review* 63 (2013): 47.
32 Ross D. Silverman and Lindsey F. Wiley, "Shaming Vaccine Refusal," *Journal of Law Medicine & Ethics* 45 (2017): 578.
33 Lindsay F. Wiley, "Shame, Blame, and the Emerging Law of Obesity Control," *U.C. Davis Law Review* 121 (2013): 133–34.
34 Wiley, "Shame," 130.
35 Kate Klonick, "Re-Shaming the Debate: Social Norms, Shame, and Regulation in an Internet Age," *Maryland Law Review* 75 (2016): 1031; Kristine L. Gallardo, "Taming the Internet Pitchfork Mob: Online Public Shaming, the Viral Media Age, and the Communications Decency Act," *Vanderbilt Journal of Entertainment and Technology Law* 19 (2020): 729.
36 Health Freedom Def. Fund, Inc. v. Biden, No. 21-cv-1693-AEP, 2022 WL 1134138, at *20–22 (M.D. Fla. Apr. 18, 2022).
37 Jason Vermes, "Called Out for Wearing a Mask? You're Not Alone. What May be Driving This Kind of Pandemic Aggression," *CBC Radio* (July 16, 2022), www.cbc.ca.
38 Gadarian, Goodman, and Pepinsky, *Pandemic Politics*, 106–08.
39 CDC, "COVID-19 Vaccines for People Who Are Moderately or Severely Immunocompromised," www.cdc.gov, updated May 31, 2023.
40 Robyn M. Powell, "Applying the Health Justice Framework to Address Health and Health Care Inequities Experienced by People with Disabilities During and After COVID-19," *Washington Law Review* 96 (2021): 108; Jordan Grunawalt, "The Villain Unmasked: COVID-19 and the Necropolitics of the Anti-Mask Movement," *Disability Studies Quarterly* 41 (2021).
41 Katie Ellis and Gerald Goggin, "Disability Media Participation: opportunities, obstacles and Politics," *Media International Australia* 154 (2015): 79.
42 Susan G. Cumings, "Making Invisible Disability Visible," in *The Image of Disability: Essays on Media Representations*, ed. J. L. Schatz and Amber E. George (Jefferson, NC: McFarland and Company, 2018), 138; Beth A. Heller, *Disabled People Transforming Media Culture for a More Inclusive World* (New York: Rutledge, 2024), 18. On the vast use of social media by the neurodiversity community in particular, see Anne McGuire, *War on Autism: On the Cultural Logic of Normative Violence* (Ann Arbor: University of Michigan Press, 2016), 62–64.
43 Kiara Alfonseca, "Mask Shaming Ignores COVID-19 Fears Of Immunocompromised People," *ABC News* (July 14, 2021), https://abcnews.go.com.
44 Kaelan Deese, "Reporter Harassed for Wearing a Mask While Covering a Restaurant Reopening-Turned-Protest," *The Hill* (May 23, 2020), https://thehill.com.

45 Carolyn Gusoff, "Family: Brother with Asperger's Punched, Sister Harassed for Wearing Masks at Long Island Bar," *CBS New York* (November 14, 2022), www.cbsnews.com.
46 Zac Anderson, "Florida Gov. DeSantis Asks High School Students to Remove Masks at Event: 'This is Ridiculous,'" *USA Today* (March 2, 2022), www.usatoday.com.
47 Laurie Larsh, "Mask Shaming: America's New favorite Pastime During COVID-19—Including in Charlotte," *Charlotte Observer* (May 19, 2020), www.charlotteobserver.com.
48 Larsh, "Mask Shaming."
49 Larsh, "Mask Shaming."
50 Alexander Nazaryan, "Are We Done with Masking?," *Yahoo News* (March 1, 2022), https://news.yahoo.com.
51 Artie Vierkant and Beatrice Adler-Bolton, "The Year the Pandemic 'Ended' (Part II)," *The New Inquiry* (December 22, 2022), https://thenewinquiry.com.
52 Soo Youn, "My friend is immunocompromised . . . ," *X* (June 23, 2021), https://twitter.com/lalasoo/status/1407578279368822785.
53 Amber Chisolm, "Went down to the harvest food trucks . . . ," *X* (Sep. 18, 2022), https://twitter.com/Weakshine/status/1571469970202050562.
54 Dr. Alice, "Have several physician friends . . . ," *X* (August 18, 2023), https://twitter.com/calirunnerdoc/status/1692589080524083665.
55 Lawrence Lessig, "The Regulation of Social Meaning," *University of Chicago Law Review* 62 (1995): 67.
56 Lessig, "The Regulation," 67.
57 Doron Dorfman, "Penalizing Prevention: The Paradoxical Legal Treatment of Preventive Medicine," *Cornell Law Review* 108 (2024): 326, 350, 363.
58 Dorfman, "Penalizing Prevention," 370.
59 James R. Mahalik, Michael Di Bianca, and Michael P. Harris, "Conformity to Masculine Norms and Men's Responses to the COVID-19 Pandemic," *Psychology of Men & Masculinities*, 23 (2022): 445; Daniel Victor, "Coronavirus Safety Runs Into a Stubborn Barrier: Masculinity," *New York Times* (October 10, 2020), www.nytimes.com; Julia Marcus, "The Dudes Who Won't Wear Masks," *The Atlantic* (June 20, 2020), www.theatlantic.com.
60 Ashley Quigley et al., "Estimated Use and Temporal Relationship to COVID-19 Epidemiology of Black Lives Matter Protests in 12 Cities," *Journal of Racial and Ethnic Health Disparities* 10 (2023): 1213; Evelyn Arana-Chicas et al., "'I Felt What Was Happening in Our Country [USA] with Race was So Much Scarier than the [COVID-19] Virus.' Black Lives Matter Protesters' Beliefs and Practices During the COVID-19 Pandemic," *Journal of Health Ethics* 17 (2021): 1.
61 Philip Galanes, "Shoppers Should Wear Masks. Shouldn't Protesters, Too?" *New York Times* (July 9, 2020), www.nytimes.com.
62 Bjorg Thorsteinsdottir et al., "Are Physicians Hypocrites for Supporting Black Lives Matter Protests and Opposing Anti-Lockdown Protests? An Ethical Analysis," *Hastings Center* (August 27, 2020), www.thehastingscenter.org.

63 Ashley Quigley et al., 1218; Leah Asmelash, *Black Lives Matter Protests Have Not Led to a Spike in Coronavirus Cases, Research Says*, CNN (June 24, 2020), www.cnn.com.
64 Larsh, "Mask Shaming."
65 Claude M. Steele, *Whistling Vivaldi: And Other Clues to How Stereotypes Affect Us and What We Can Do* (New York: W. W. Norton & Company, 2010), 7.
66 Bill Chappell, "NYC Mayor Eric Adams is Telling Stores to Have Customers Remove Their Face Masks," NPR (March 7, 2023), www.npr.org.
67 Chappell, "NYC Mayor."
68 Laura I. Appleman, "Deviancy, Dependency, and Disability: The Forgotten History of Eugenics and Mass Incarceration," *Duke Law Journal* 68: 427 (2018); Liat Ben-Moshe, *Decarcerating Disability: Deinstitutionalization and Prison Abolition* (Minneapolis: University of Minnesota Press, 2020), 11–15.
69 Joseph P. Shapiro, *No Pity: People with Disabilities Forging a New Civil Rights Movement* (Portland, OR: Broadway Books, 1993), 41–49; Rabia Belt and Doron Dorfman, "Disability, Law, and the Humanities: The Rise of Disability Legal Studies," in *Oxford Handbook of Law & Humanities*, ed. Simon Stern, Maksymilian Del Mar, and Bernadette Meyler (New York: Oxford University Press 2019), 148.
70 Doron Dorfman, "Commentary on Olmstead v. L.C ex rel. Zimring," in *Feminist Judgments: Rewritten Health Law Opinions*, ed. Seema Mohapatra and Lindsey F. Wiley (New York: Cambridge University Press, 2022), 181.
71 527 U.S. 581 (1999). Due to its emancipatory impact and desegregation message, *Olmstead* has been known as the *Brown v. Board of Education* for the disability community; see Dorfman, "Commentary on Olmstead," 179.
72 See generally Ben Moshe, *Decarcerating Disability*.
73 Dorfman, "Fear of the Disability Con," 1060; Michael E. Waterstone "The Costs of Easy Victory," *William & Mary Law Review* 57 (2015): 609.
74 I borrow the term "deservingness" from the field of social policy studies and more specifically from research on the welfare state. "Deservingness" refers to general public support for services. I expand the use of this term to also include accommodations and rights in places of public accommodations, outside the realm of social benefits. See Dorfman, [Un]Usual Suspects, 652–53.
75 Dorfman, "[Un]Usual Suspects," 562.
76 Dorfman, "[Un]Usual Suspects," 599–603; Dorfman, "Fear of the Disability Con," 1080–82; Ellen Samuels, *Fantasies of Identification: Disability, Gender, Race* (New York: New York University Press, 2014), 132–36.
77 Dorfman, "[Un]Usual Suspects," 585.
78 Dorfman, "Fear of the Disability Con," 1062.
79 Dorfman, "Fear of the Disability Con," 1083.
80 See generally Dorfman, "Suspicious Species."
81 Dorfman and Raz, "Mask Exemptions."
82 CBS Colorado, "Injured Veteran Denied Service At Credit Union Says He Can't Wear A Face Mask," *CBS News Colorado* (June 18, 2020), www.cbsnews.com.

83 Mor discussed this hierarchy in the context of the Israeli public benefits system, yet her underlying idea can be extrapolated into the U.S. context more generally. Sagit Mor, "Between Charity, Welfare, and Warfare: A Disability Legal Studies Analysis of Privilege and Neglect in Israeli Disability Policy," *Yale Journal of Law & the Humanities* 18 (2006): 65.
84 NBC Chicago, "Father Speaks Out After Store Worker Threatened to Call Police When His Daughter Removed Her Mask," *NBC Chicago* (May 5, 2020), www.nbcchicago.com.
85 Matthew Klint, "Southwest Kicks Off Disabled Man for not Wearing Mask, Despite Federal Exemption," *Live and Let Fly* (March 11, 2021), https://liveandletsfly.com; Rebecca Speare-Cole, "Disabled Man Kicked Off Southwest Flight Over Mask Despite Doctor's Notes," *Newsweek* (March 10, 2021), www.newsweek.com.
86 Klint, "Southwest Kicks Off Disabled Man."
87 Speare-Cole, "Disabled Man Kicked Off Southwest."
88 Klint, "Southwest Kicks Off Disabled Man"; Speare-Cole, "Disabled Man Kicked Off Southwest Flight."
89 Victoria Bromley, "Exempt 'Harassed' and 'Discriminated' Against by Uni Staff for Not Wearing Mask," *The Tab* (April 28, 2021), https://thetab.com.
90 Victoria Bromley, "Exempt Student."
91 NBC Chicago, "Father Speaks Out."
92 Samuels, Fantasies of Identification, 122. For criticism of excessive documentation to receive accommodations under the ADA, see Katherine A. Macfarlane, "Disability Without Documentation," *Fordham Law Review* 90 (2021).
93 Dorfman, "Suspicious Species," 1411–13; On the bureaucratic burden of living with disabilities, see Elizabeth F. Emens, "Disability Admin: The Invisible Costs of Being Disabled," 105 *Minnesota Law Review* 2329, 2342–44 (2021).
94 Matt Burrows, "COVID-19: Kiwis with Disabilities 'Confronted, Harassed' for Not Wearing Mask Now Scared to Access Essential Services—Ministry of Health," *NewsHub* (May 9, 2021), www.newshub.co.nz.
95 Mia Mingus, "Access Intimacy, Interdependence, and Disability Justice, Leaving Evidence" (April 12, 2017), https://leavingevidence.wordpress.com.
96 Mingus, "Access Intimacy."
97 2023 AAPD ADA Celebration, www.eventbrite.com/e/2023-aapd-ada-celebration-tickets-638128638937.
98 Persephone, Just in case here's a screenshot . . . X (July 28, 2023), https://x.com/citrusdriad/status/1685075057121320960?s=20.
99 Ellen Lee Schwartz, One mask at an ADA celebration event . . . X (July 28, 2023), https://x.com/Ellen_Lee3/status/1685091657484582912?s=20.
100 See Mia Roll, Dear humans, I am going to explain . . . X (July 28, 2023), https://x.com/SeeMiaRoll/status/1684933452418699264?s=20; see Mia Roll, I know I am an imperfect human being . . . X (July 28, 2023), https://x.com/SeeMiaRoll/status/1684934795820683264?s=20.

101 Another example of competing access needs involves the use of service dogs, and people living with allergies. In a federal case on this issue, a Ohio district court sided with the service dog handler after it was convinced that other students' "allergies are not so severe as to outweigh the presumption favoring the use of service animals under the ADA." See Entine v. Lissner, No. 17-CV-946, 2017 WL 5507619, at *10 (S.D. Ohio Nov. 17, 2017). For further discussions on clashes involving the rights to use a service dog and others' allergies see Dorfman, "Suspicious Species," 1381–82.

102 Rachel Kolb, "How Masking Changed My Experience of Being Deaf," *The Atlantic* (September 11, 2022), www.theatlantic.com, Jennifer Finney Boylan, "I'm a Lip Reader in a Masked World," *New York Times* (July 22, 2020), www.nytimes.com.

103 Stacey Alexander, I noticed some others who we at the event . . . , X (July 29, 2023), https://x.com/Stace_Alexander/status/1685247910152130560?s=20.

104 Emily Ladau, About the photo . . . X (July 28, 2023), https://x.com/emily_ladau/status/1685022283755130880?s=20; Emily Ladau, I am fully aware that . . . X (July 28, 2023), https://x.com/emily_ladau/status/1685022285743235074?s=20.

105 Luke P. Norris, "The Promise and Perils of Private Enforcement," *Virginia Law Review* 108 (2022): 1492.

106 Norris, "The Promise and Perils," 1493.

107 Norris, "The Promise and Perils," 1486. Jon D. Michaels and David L. Noll, "Vigilant Federalism," *Cornell Law Review* 108 (2023): 1191.

108 Michaels and Noll, *Vigilant Federalism*, 1191.

109 Samuel R. Bagenstos, *Law and the Contradictions of the Disability Rights Movement* (New Haven: Yale University Press 2009), 20; Dorfman, "Fear of the Disability Con," 1053.

110 Michael Waterstone, "A New Vision of Public Enforcement," *Minnesota Law Review* 92 (2007): 447–48; Ruth Colker, "The Power of Insults," *Boston University Law Review* 100 (2020): 43; Doron Dorfman and Mariela Yabo, "The Professionalization of Urban Accessibility," *Fordham Urban Law Journal* 47 (2020): 1240; Kristen L. Popham, Elizabeth F. Emens and Jasmine E. Harris, "Disabling Travel: Quantifying the Harm of Inaccessible Hotels to Disabled People," *Columbia Human Rights Law Review Forum* 55 (2023): 6.

111 Dorfman, "Suspicious Species," 1413–14.

112 Dorfman, "[Un]Usual Suspects," 600; Samuels, Fantasies of Identification, 139; Geoffrey P. Miller, "Norm Enforcement in the Public Sphere: The Case of Handicapped Parking," *George Washington Law Review* 29, no. 71 (2003): 895–908.

113 Dorfman, "[Un]Usual Suspects," 600.

114 Dorfman, "[Un]Usual Suspects," 600.

115 Dorfman, "[Un]Usual Suspects," 601.

116 Rabia Belt and Doron Dorfman, "Reweighing Medical Civil Rights," *Stanford Law Review Online* 72 (2020): 1.

117 Belt and Dorfman, "Reweighing Medical Civil Rights," 2. See also Jamelia Morgan, "On the Relationship Between Race and Disability," *Harvard Civil Rights–Civil Liberties Law Review* 58 (2023): 218.

118 Sharon N. Barnartt, "Disability as a Fluid State: Introduction," in *Disability as a Fluid State*, ed. Sharon Barnartt (Cambridge, MA: Emerald Insight, 2010), 2; Mark Priestley, *Disability: A Life Course Approach* (New York: Polity, 2003), 4.
119 Dorfman, "[Un]Usual Suspects," 609–11.
120 Wendy E. Parmet, *Populations, Public Health and the Law* (Washington, D.C.: Georgetown University Press, 2009), 20.
121 Wendy E. Parmet, "Vaccines and Abortion: Congruence, Divergence, and the Elusive Meaning of Medical Freedom," *Regulating the Body*, ed. Susanna Lee and Austin Sarat (New York: New York University Press, 2024), 30.
122 See, e.g., Marissa Ditkowsky, Ok, #DisabilityTwitter. . . . X (July 28, 2023), https://twitter.com/mditkowsky/status/1685018209294983168?s=46&t=pWmp4SJ_8tQEtCZorH69jA; Matthew Corland, Disabled, immunocompromised, public health expert . . . X (July 28, 2023), https://twitter.com/mattbc/status/1685037013299240960?s=46&t=pWmp4SJ_8tQEtCZorH69jA.

4

Vaccines and Abortion

Congruence, Divergence, and the Elusive Meaning of Medical Freedom

WENDY E. PARMET

"*My body, my choice!*" The cry for the "freedom" to decide which medical procedures to have or forego, sometimes conveyed by the phrases "medical freedom" and "health freedom," has a long history in the United States.[1] Since the start of the COVID-19 epidemic, the cry has been raised with heightened fervor against numerous public health regulations, including mask mandates, which Doren Dorfman discusses in chapter 3 of this volume. Here I explore the legal and political debates that have swirled around two other types of state regulations of the body: vaccine mandates and abortion bans.[2] Although opponents of both types of regulation frequently employ the rhetoric of medical or health freedom,[3] those who resist one often support the other, and vice versa. In addition, following the United States Supreme Court's dismantling of the constitutional right to an abortion in *Dobbs v. Jackson Women's Health Organization* (2022),[4] and the Court's embrace of new doctrines unsettling the constitutionality of vaccine mandates, vaccine mandates and abortion bans now appear to be on separate legal trajectories.

How can we understand the seemingly inconsistent resistance to the two types of regulation and their divergent fate in the courts? How can activists, politicians, and judges who see vaccine mandates as violative of freedom perceive no such problem with laws that compel pregnancy and childbirth? Likewise, how can those who demand reproductive choice support laws that require vaccination? Is there anything more to the apparent inconsistencies than hypocrisy or partisanship? Do the demands for medical or health freedom and rejection of the state's regulation of the body have any principled content?

This chapter considers these questions by exploring the congruent, divergent, and frequently intersecting histories of state-imposed vaccine mandates and abortion bans.[5] The first section begins by reviewing the current landscape of vaccine and abortion laws and discussing how both types of regulation relate to individual autonomy and public health. The second section offers a brief review of the law and politics of vaccine mandates and abortion in three different periods roughly delineated by regulatory and jurisprudential changes: the era of convergence, dating from the early nineteenth century until the middle of the twentieth century; the era of the first divergence, beginning in the middle of the twentieth century and continuing until the COVID-19 pandemic; and the era of the second divergence, which started during the COVID-19 pandemic and continues today. This review is not meant to provide a comprehensive history or analysis of vaccine mandates or abortion restrictions in any of the three periods. Nor does it attempt to provide a legal argument as to why or how the two different claims for bodily autonomy are distinct or similar. Rather, the discussion seeks to explore the ways in which debates about state regulation of vaccination and abortion have converged, intersected, and diverged while also highlighting some recurring themes—including the role of medical authority, partisanship, and gender norms. Finally, in the third section, I consider what the paradoxical relationship between vaccine mandates and abortion bans says about the state's role in regulating the body and the meaning of health or medical freedom.

The Current Landscape and the Relationship of Mandates and Bans to Autonomy and Health

That opponents of vaccine mandates and abortion bans employ a common rhetoric of medical freedom and individual choice should not be surprising. Both types of regulation interfere with an individual's ability to decide what happens to their body, albeit to different degrees and for different reasons.[6] After briefly reviewing the current status of state vaccine mandates and abortion bans, this section looks more closely at how such regulations impact individual autonomy as well as justifications offered in their support.

The Current Legal Landscape

Every state in the United States mandates that children entering daycare or school be vaccinated against several different vaccine-preventable diseases.[7] A few states also require health care workers to be vaccinated against influenza.[8] During the COVID-19 pandemic, at least 20 states required some workers or students to be vaccinated against COVID-19.[9] In contrast, twenty states passed laws prohibiting at least some COVID-19 mandates or "passports," which required proof of vaccination to enjoy a service or participate in an activity.[10]

Post-*Dobbs*, the states have also taken diverse paths regarding abortion restrictions. As of June 13, 2024, at least fourteen states banned almost all abortions at any stage of pregnancy; three did so after six weeks, which is before many women know they are pregnant.[11] Several other states have attempted to institute bans that are currently tied up in litigation.[12] In contrast, at least 27 states and the District of Columbia have relatively liberal abortion laws, and 22 states plus the District of Columbia have laws that aim to shield providers who perform abortions from prosecution by other states.[13]

Importantly, there is a significant overlap between the states that restrict abortion and those that banned COVID-19 vaccine mandates. Not surprisingly, these states have Republican legislatures and generally vote Republican.[14] In contemporary political parlance, these are "red" states. A different overlap exists between the states that try to secure abortion access and those that limit vaccine mandates. These are "blue" states in which the legislatures and voters veer Democratic.[15] To oversimply, the states that protect medical freedom from vaccine mandates are often willing to restrict medical freedom when it comes to abortion, and the states that restrict it with respect to vaccination usually seek to secure it with respect to abortion.

The Regulations' Impact on the Individual

As Martha Fineman's vulnerability theory insists, the experience of the human body is significantly one of vulnerability and dependency.[16] In our infancy and childhood, with our reproduction, disability, disease, and aging, we are not as invulnerable or independent as we would like to believe.

Despite the ubiquity of the body's vulnerability and dependency, contemporary American politics, culture, and law treat invulnerability as the norm and prioritize individual rights of autonomy, as if the individual can be independent of the state and others.[17] The cry for health freedom can be viewed as stemming, at least in part, from this denial of vulnerability and interdependence. It insists that individuals alone should be able to choose what happens to their bodies and that the state, at least in most cases, has no interest in the medical choices they make.

In different ways, both vaccines and abortions recognize and attempt to mitigate the body's vulnerability, in the former case with respect to the dangers of disease, in the latter case to the precarities of reproduction. Likewise, vaccine mandates and abortion bans assert the state's interest in what happens to the body and conflict with contemporary conceptions of individual autonomy. It should not be surprising that both types of regulations are challenged as violating health freedom.

Yet it is important to note that neither vaccine mandates nor abortion bans impose a total limit on individual autonomy. For example, contemporary vaccine mandates do not actually compel vaccination; rather, they require individuals to be immunized against specified diseases as a condition for engaging in certain activities, such as going to school or holding down a particular job. To be sure, such "choices" can be highly coercive and raise significant equity concerns. Not everyone can homeschool their child or afford to lose a job. Still, some semblance of choice or bodily autonomy remains.[18]

State vaccine mandates also offer the possibility of exemptions. In 1905, the Supreme Court in *Jacobson v. Massachusetts* (1905) implied that states had to provide exemptions to people with medical contraindications.[19] Recently, some lower courts have suggested that the Free Exercise Clause of the First Amendment requires states to grant religious exemptions.[20] And even if religious exemptions are not constitutionally compelled, almost every state includes such exemptions in their childhood vaccine laws.[21] At least 15 states go further and offer so-called personal belief exemptions, which allow parents to opt out of vaccinating their child based on a deeply held personal belief.[22] In such states, mandates are not all that mandatory.

Unlike vaccine mandates, abortion bans mostly (but not in all cases) operate as indirect regulations of the body in that they apply primarily to health care workers and others who might assist an individual in getting an abortion, rather than the individual who would have the abortion.[23] Nevertheless, because abortion bans and restrictions aim to and do restrict a pregnant individual's ability to have an abortion, they affect their bodily autonomy.

As with vaccine mandates, abortion bans often include some exemptions. For example, some states that restrict most abortions permit it very early in the pregnancy—sometimes before an individual knows they are pregnant—or when the life of the pregnant person is in serious or imminent jeopardy.[24] Some states also allow for abortion in the case of rape or incest. However, the actual availability of all of these "exceptions" is quite limited. For example, in 2023 the Texas Supreme Court held that a woman who carried a fetus with trisomy 18, a fatal genetic condition, and who faced a significant risk of loss of her future fertility if she went into labor and delivered a child, did not qualify for a medical necessity exemption under Texas law.[25] In a later case, that same court rejected plaintiffs' request to interpret the state's abortion law as permitting physicians to apply a good-faith standard when determining whether an abortion qualified for a medical exemption. Instead, the court ruled abortions are permissible only when "reasonable medical judgment" would find that the patient had a "life-threatening physical condition" that places them "at risk of death or poses a serious risk of substantial impairment of a major bodily function" unless they have an abortion.[26]

Because abortion bans like vaccine mandates occur (for now) primarily at the state level, abortion remains available (at least for now) to individuals who are able to travel from states that ban abortion to states that do not.[27] As with the choices that vaccine mandates offer, such choices raise significant equity implications, as many people lack the resources (time and money) to obtain an out-of-state abortion.[28] More accessible are abortion medications, which can be shipped to states that ban abortion from both legal and extralegal sources.[29] Whether abortion medications will remain legally available, however, is uncertain: although the Supreme Court recently rejected on standing grounds a challenge to decisions by the federal Food and Drug Administration to liberalize access to mifepristone, one of two widely used "abortion pills,"[30] other challenges are pending. It also remains to be seen whether the second

Trump administration will defend the Food and Drug Administration's position or try to limit access to abortion medication.

The impact of vaccine mandates and abortion bans on an individual's body is not confined to the moment of medical decision-making. Both types of regulation can have long-term effects on autonomy and health. This is most apparent with respect to abortion bans; they do not simply limit an individual's one-time medical choice but attempt to compel the individual to carry a pregnancy to term, which is far more dangerous from a medical perspective than abortion.[31] Bearing a child can also have significant long-term physical and mental health consequences and can constrict numerous choices for the rest of an individual's life.[32] Thus, bodily autonomy is not the only type of autonomy that is negated by abortion bans. Indeed, it is likely not the most important type of autonomy that is affected.

Nor is medical freedom the only type of autonomy at stake in the case of vaccine mandates. Although the vaccines that are mandated are very safe and the overwhelming weight of scientific evidence does not support many of the risks that critics have ascribed to them,[33] there are nonetheless risks. Some are serious. For example, studies have shown that mRNA COVID-19 vaccines increase the risk of myocarditis and pericarditis compared with unvaccinated individuals in the absence of infection with COVID-19.[34] The Centers for Disease Control and Prevention also notes a wide range of other—mostly quite mild—side effects from other common vaccines, including localized pain, soreness, and, more seriously, Guillain-Barré syndrome.[35] In addition, as discussed below, many people believe that vaccine mandates burden their religious liberty and that being vaccinated forces them to violate their faith every day for the rest of their lives. In that way, vaccine mandates, like abortion bans, can be viewed as imposing lifelong restrictions on autonomy.

The Impact on the Health of Others

Liberal theory generally accepts that the state may restrict an individual's bodily autonomy to prevent harm to others.[36] Vaccine mandates and abortion bans can be and have been defended on such grounds.

States mandate vaccination not only to protect the health of the individual subject to the mandate but also to protect the health of third parties and the greater community. Vaccine mandates can do this by increasing the rate of vaccination within a community.[37] This can lower a disease's prevalence, making it less likely that others will transmit infection or become ill. This lowered risk is especially important to individuals who cannot be vaccinated, due to medical contraindications, or who are less likely to benefit from vaccination, due to immune impairments.[38]

Polio offers a striking example of how vaccines (and vaccine mandates) can protect public health. As a result of high vaccination rates, the number of polio cases in the United States dropped from 58,000 to just 161 in the six years that followed the introduction of the polio vaccine.[39] Such public health benefits are most evident for diseases such as polio, smallpox, and measles in which high vaccine rates can create so-called herd immunity, in which there are so few individuals susceptible to a disease within a population that it can no longer spread. But even if the mandated vaccine—such as the influenza or COVID-19 vaccine—provides less robust immunity, thereby foreclosing the possibility of herd immunity, it can still lower the risk of transmission and the resulting danger to third parties.[40] Importantly, by so doing vaccine mandates can enhance the liberty of third parties who face a reduced risk of illness or death.

In addition to conferring public health benefits, traditional childhood vaccine mandates protect the health of children whose parents or guardians would, without a mandate, fail to have them vaccinated. Such failure may arise from religious or ideological grounds, lack of easy access to vaccination, or simply because the parent or guardian would not bother to get their child vaccinated in the absence of a mandate. Thus, childhood vaccine laws, like the proposed limits on genetic testing discussed by Allison Whelan in chapter 2 of this volume, impair the decisional autonomy of adults to protect the bodies of children.[41]

Supporters of abortion bans (or other regulations that restrict access to abortion) also justify these regulations as benefiting the health of pregnant persons as well as the fetus. First, supporters argue that restrictions on abortion are needed to protect pregnant persons from the health risks associated with abortion. This claim is contradicted by the weight of scientific evidence showing that abortion is far safer than pregnancy and childbirth.[42] This is especially true when abortion bans limit access to medically necessary abortions or other medical treatments that are necessary due to pregnancy complications or other serious medical conditions (such as cancer).[43]

Another justification given for abortion bans is the protection of what the Supreme Court in *Dobbs* termed an "unborn human being."[44] According to the Court, this makes abortion a "unique act,"[45] theoretically more worthy of the state's protection than the creation of gametes discussed in chapter 1 by Kim Mutcherson. Yet as the *Dobbs* Court seemed to accept, whether abortion is indeed "unique" depends upon "belief[s]" about the nature and moral status of an embryo or fetus, rather than empirical evidence. Thus, in sharp contrast to vaccine mandates, the claim for "health" benefits of abortion bans relies on moral or theological reasoning, rather than science. This is a point to which I will return.

The Changing Jurisprudence of Vaccine Mandates and Abortion Restrictions

For more than a century the law and politics relating to vaccine mandates and abortion restrictions have intersected, converged, and diverged. To understand these movements and consider what they may say about the meaning of medical freedom, it is useful to consider three separate periods. The first period began in the early nineteenth century and continued until the middle of the twentieth century. This was a time of congruence, in which the regulation of vaccines and abortion aligned. The second era started in the middle of the twentieth century and continued until the COVID-19 pandemic. This was a period of divergence, when courts recognized a constitutional right to abortion even as vaccine mandates proliferated. The third period, in which we are living today, is marked by new divergences in which once-settled understandings of the legality of vaccine mandates are being challenged even as once-prohibited abortion bans have taken hold. Yet it is too simple to say that the regulation of abortion and vaccines have diverged from each other. In this current period, the regulation of abortions and vaccines have diverged geographically and politically, as the law and politics of each type of regulation have become destabilized. This fracturing raises important questions about the scope of medical freedom and the appropriate role for state regulations of the body.

The Era of Congruence

Abortion bans and vaccine mandates emerged in the first half of the nineteenth century and became commonplace after the Civil War, even as jurists and legal scholars began to hold that the Due Process Clause of the newly ratified Fourteenth Amendment limited states' power to restrict certain unenumerated individual rights under a doctrine termed "substantive due process."[46] Despite the ascendence of this "substantive due process" doctrine, courts during this period ruled that reasonable health laws were constitutional, even if they restricted bodily autonomy.[47]

In 1827, Boston became the first jurisdiction in the United States to require children to be vaccinated against smallpox to attend schools.[48] In 1855, Massachusetts required all residents to be vaccinated against smallpox.[49] In the years that followed, as public health became professionalized and the medical profession attained greater status and credibility, smallpox vaccine mandates, especially when tied to attending public schools, became more common.

The mandates were often met with fierce opposition.[50] One reason was fear of the health risks associated with vaccination. In the nineteenth and early twentieth centuries, vaccines were more dangerous than they are today. Even though they lowered the risk of deadly diseases, especially smallpox, vaccines could be unsterile or tainted and spread diseases or be blamed for spreading diseases.[51] Describing the fear that took hold in the early twentieth century after an apparent rise in tetanus cases thought to be linked to vaccination, the historian Karen L. Wallach noted "the fact that few children developed tetanus in the course of thousands of vaccination did little to quell public outcry for some positive assurance of vaccine purity."[52]

Another reason for opposition to vaccination is that, as vaccination rates climbed and cases of smallpox fell, people began to fear smallpox less than the vaccine that prevented it.[53] This spurred a type of freeriding,[54] in which individuals could avoid both the disease and the risks posed by the vaccine as long as a sufficiently high number of others in their community were vaccinated. Of course, such freeriding could and did lead to declining vaccination rates and a concomitant increase in the risk of an outbreak. Mandates were one way that the state responded to that problem.

Opponents of mandates had other motivations as well. Some, such as the Reverend Henning Jacobson, the defendant in *Jacobson v. Massachusetts*, believed that vaccination was ungodly because it prevented illness.[55] But at the time, courts had not yet held that the First Amendment's Free Exercise Clause, which protects religious liberty, applied to the states. Accordingly, Jacobson and other vaccine opponents argued in court that mandates violated the liberty protected by the Fourteenth Amendment.[56]

With few exceptions, courts disagreed.[57] In 1905, the Supreme Court appeared to settle the question by rejecting Jacobson's Fourteenth Amendment challenge to a Cambridge, Massachusetts, ordinance that required all residents to show proof of vaccination or pay a $5 fine.[58] In so doing, the Court, in an opinion by Justice John Marshall Harlan, emphasized that states could use their police power to impose reasonable health measures.[59] Indeed, Harlan stressed that "real liberty" could "not exist under the operation of a principle which recognizes the right of each individual person to use his own, whether in respect of his person or his property, regardless of the injury that may be done to others."[60] Yet Harlan also suggested that there might be some constitutional protections for what we might today call "medical freedom," stating "there is, of course, a sphere within which the individual may assert the supremacy of his own will, and rightfully dispute the authority of any human government—especially of any free government existing under a written constitution to interfere with the exercise of that will."[61] Harlan added that courts might strike down vaccine laws that were "unreasonable, arbitrary, and oppressive, and, therefore, hostile to the inherent right of every freeman to care for his own body and health in such a way as to him seems best."[62] Thus, even as the Court upheld the state's power to mandate vaccines, it suggested for the first time that the United States Constitution offered some protection for an individual's ability to protect their health and make their own medical decisions.

Despite that important nod to individual autonomy, until the COVID-19 pandemic lower courts and the Supreme Court read *Jacobson* as settling the constitutionality of vaccine mandates. For example, in 1922 the Supreme Court relied on *Jacobson* to uphold a law that required schoolchildren to be vaccinated even in the absence of an outbreak.[63] And after the Court held that the Free Exercise Clause applied to the states, it cited *Jacobson* in rejecting a parent's religious liberty challenge to child labor laws, stating that a parent "cannot claim freedom from compulsory vaccination for the child more than for himself on religious grounds."[64]

Abortion laws developed during this same period. Under common law at that time (and earlier), life was recognized as beginning (at least for legal purposes) only at quickening, which could occur as late as 25 weeks of pregnancy.[65] Prior to quickening, in most states the termination of pregnancy was not legally actionable.[66]

That began to change in the 1820s, the same decade that saw the first vaccine mandates. The earliest abortion bans appeared as efforts to prevent poisoning.[67] As the century progressed, restrictions on abortion became more common, thanks largely to the efforts of the gynecologist Horatio Storer and the American Medical Association.[68] Their antiabortion advocacy was motivated by the desire to discredit midwives and other nonphysician healers and by eugenicist concerns that the white Protestant population in the United States was being overtaken by immigrants with different racial, religious, and ethnic identities.[69] Proponents of abortion bans also sought to enforce patriarchal gender roles that relegated women to marriage and reproduction.[70]

To be sure, the legal prohibitions of abortion did not stop all or most abortions, just as vaccine mandates did not achieve universal vaccination. Before the Supreme Court in 1973 recognized a constitutional right to abortion in *Roe v. Wade*,[71] large numbers of women had illegal abortions;[72] many others, usually those with financial resources, traveled abroad or convinced hospitals to approve so-called therapeutic abortions. However, during this period the jurisprudence of abortion was settled. Courts saw no greater problem with abortion bans than they saw with vaccine mandates. Both restrictions on bodily autonomy were accepted as squarely within the states' police power. For example, in 1898 in *Hawker v. People of New York*, the Supreme Court considered whether the state could convict a physician for continuing to practice medicine after he had been convicted of performing an abortion even though the law prohibiting the practice of medicine following a felony conviction was not in effect when he performed the abortion.[73] In an opinion by Justice David J. Brewer, the Court emphasized the state's authority to protect the public's health by ensuring that only people of good moral character practice medicine.[74] In dissent, Justice Harlan argued that the conviction violated the Constitution's ban on ex post facto laws.[75] Neither justice considered that the abortion ban might violate the autonomy of either the patient or the physician.[76]

The Court eventually took up the issue of autonomy in relation to reproduction (but not abortion) in the infamous case of *Buck v. Bell* (1927).[77] *Buck* was a test case designed to garner the Supreme Court's imprimatur for involuntary sterilization in service of eugenics.[78] It achieved that goal, with Justice Oliver Wendell Holmes stating: "The principle that sustains compulsory vaccination is broad enough to cover cutting the Fallopian tubes."[79] Although *Jacobson* was the only precedent the Court cited, it never noted that case's recognition of a "sphere within which the individual may assert the supremacy of [their] own will."[80]

The First Divergence

The regulation of vaccines and abortion began to diverge in the mid-twentieth century as vaccine mandates proliferated and abortion bans fell. In 1963, only 20 states plus the District of Columbia and Puerto Rico mandated that schoolchildren be vaccinated against one or more diseases.[81] But following the development of vaccines for polio (in 1955) and then measles (1963),[82] states added more vaccines to their mandates. By 1970, 20 states required that schoolchildren be vaccinated against measles; by 1983, all 50 states did so.[83] Importantly, almost all of these mandates allowed for religious exemptions.[84]

For several decades, public support for vaccines (and mandates) remained strong and bipartisan. As the public health historian James Colgrove has noted, the middle of the twentieth century was a "high-water mark for trust and respect in medical services."[85] This trust extended to vaccines, especially the polio vaccine, which was widely welcomed by parents terrified of what polio could do to their children.

And yet as the number and types of vaccines mandated grew and problems appeared with some vaccines,[86] resistance rose. In 1982, a group of parents who believed that their children were harmed by the diphtheria–pertussis–tetanus vaccine founded the National Vaccine Information Center, whose mission was "protecting health and informed consent rights,"[87] more specifically the rights of parents to reject vaccination for their children. Opposition to vaccines further intensified after a British physician, Dr. Andrew Wakefield, published a paper in the prestigious medical journal *The Lancet*, claiming to link the measles–mumps–rubella vaccine to autism.[88] Wakefield's findings have since been repudiated by numerous studies, and he has been stripped of his license to practice medicine in England for ethical violations.[89] Nevertheless, an increasingly zealous group of parents came to believe that vaccines caused autism and were dangerous to their children.[90] In that sense, their demands for informed consent and the liberty to reject vaccination are related to worries that vaccines were dangerous to children's health, as well as their distrust of the public health and medical establishments.[91]

Initially, many of the parents protesting vaccines were otherwise politically progressive.[92] Indeed, in the years between 9/11 and the Iraq War, it was the conservative Republican George W. Bush's administration that required that members of the military and some other government personnel be vaccinated against smallpox, which the administration believed could be used as a biological weapon.[93] The Bush administration also rolled out a campaign to offer smallpox vaccines to health care workers[94] and prioritized vaccine development in efforts to prepare the country for a possible avian influenza pandemic.[95]

The politics of vaccine mandates began to change in 2015 after California eliminated the personal belief exemption to its childhood vaccine mandate in the wake of a measles outbreak associated with Disneyland.[96] Responding to the repeal, "anti-vaccine activists mobilized their following beyond [their] traditional natural-living, left-leaning base through deliberate activation of, and outreach to, potential Tea Party and libertarian allies."[97] This alliance between antivaccination activists and conservative groups grew during the COVID-19 pandemic.

Until then, however, states continued to impose vaccine mandates on schoolchildren, and courts continued to uphold those mandates, even when states eliminated religious or personal belief exemptions.[98] Courts did this by relying on *Jacobson v. Massachusetts* and Justice Antonin Scalia's 1990 opinion for the Supreme Court in *Employment Division v. Smith*, which held that neutral laws of general applicability are subject only to the rational relationship test, the least strict form of judicial review, when challenged under the Free Exercise Clause.[99] That led lower courts to conclude that the Constitution does not require that state mandates include religious exemptions.[100]

Yet even as they rejected liberty challenges to vaccine mandates, courts began to accept such challenges to abortion bans. Although there had always been advocates for "family planning" and the legalization of abortion, the push for the liberalization or outright repeal of regulations restricting access to abortion accelerated in the middle of the twentieth century. In the 1950s, organized medicine, which had so successfully pushed for abortion bans in the prior century, began to question that position,[101] even as the profession supported expanded use of vaccine mandates.

The debate about abortion within the medical profession coincided with a reassessment within the legal establishment. In 1957, the American Law Institute proposed a Model Penal Code that would have permitted abortion by a licensed physician when the continuation of the pregnancy would create a substantial risk of harm to the physical or mental health of the woman, the child would be born with serious physical or mental defects, or in the case of rape or incest.[102] The push for reform, however, did not come only from elites. As Rosemary Nossiff explains, feminists began to claim that "access to abortion was a central component of women's liberty, and that the decision to have an abortion should be made by the woman involved, not by her doctor, the Church, or the State."[103]

Courts likewise began to view the restrictions on liberty imposed by the regulation of reproduction as constitutionally suspect. As far back as 1942, in *Skinner v. Oklahoma*, the Supreme Court appeared to reverse (although it did not overrule) its position in *Buck v. Bell* by holding that an Oklahoma law authorizing the involuntary sterilization of some felons violated the Equal Protection Clause.[104] Then in 1965, in *Griswold v. Connecticut* the Supreme Court held that a state law prohibiting prescribing or using birth control was unconstitutional, at least as it applied to married individuals.[105] In reaching that conclusion, the Court in an opinion by Justice William O. Douglas argued that the Constitution protects a "zone of privacy created by several fundamental constitutional guarantees."[106]

Justice Douglas's opinion did not mention *Jacobson*. Nor did he try to square his recognition of a zone of privacy with cases affirming vaccine mandates. But in a concurring opinion, Justice Byron White cited to *Jacobson* in a footnote attached to the statement that "such statutes, if reasonably necessary for the effectuation of a legitimate and substantial state interest, and not arbitrary or capricious in application, are not invalid under the Due Process Clause."[107] By so doing, Justice White marked the beginning of the divergence between how courts viewed state limitations on the body relating to vaccines and abortion. The latter would be viewed as an impermissible infringement on "privacy" or individual autonomy, even as the former continued to be accepted as effectuating a legitimate state interest.[108]

Following *Griswold*, the march toward liberalizing abortion laws intensified in statehouses and courthouses. By 1971, 12 states had passed laws that were similar to the American Law Institute's model law; one state, Oregon, "expanded the American Law Institute grounds to include a sociomedical ground," and four states "repealed all criminal penalties for abortion" performed early in pregnancy by a licensed physician.[109]

During this period, courts also changed their stance toward abortion. For example, in *People v. Belous* (1969) the Supreme Court of California relied heavily on *Griswold* to proclaim that individuals have a "'right of privacy' or 'liberty' in matters related to marriage, family, and sex."[110] The *Belous* court went on to hold that the state's new therapeutic abortion ban was unconstitutionally vague because its health and safety exception could result in a physician denying a woman the right to terminate her pregnancy.[111] In the years that followed, several other state and lower federal courts agreed that "the right of privacy, however based, is broad enough to cover the abortion decision."[112]

The major change in abortion law, of course, came with the Supreme Court's 1973 decision in *Roe v. Wade*.[113] Without restating much of what has been written elsewhere about *Roe*, two points are especially salient here. First, although Justice Harry Blackmun's opinion for the Court grounded the right to abortion in a right to "privacy," the term the Court employed in *Griswold*, much of his opinion emphasized the role of physicians as decision makers.[114] He also stressed that both the American Medical Association and the American Public Health Association had changed their views and had come to support abortion access.[115] Accordingly, just as vaccine mandates rested to some degree in this period on trust in the health professions, the constitutional right to an abortion was also tied to trust in medical authority. Second, the Supreme Court continued to see *Jacobson* as relevant to the constitutionality of the state's regulation of the body, although the justices appeared to differ as to how. The majority followed Justice White's opinion in *Griswold* by citing *Jacobson* (and *Buck*) for the proposition that rights of privacy are not unlimited.[116] Yet in his concurring opinion, in a companion case, Justice Douglas quoted *Jacobson* for a very different point: "There is, of course, a sphere within which the individual may assert the supremacy of his own will and rightfully dispute the authority of any human government."[117]

Despite these varied readings of *Jacobson*, *Roe* and its progeny solidified the divergence between abortion and vaccine law. Post-*Roe*, states continued to impose vaccine mandates, and courts continued to uphold them even after the Supreme Court in *Planned Parenthood of Southeastern Pennsylvania v. Casey* (1992) reaffirmed *Roe*'s "essential holding" and grounded it in respect for "personal liberty."[118] Interestingly, like Justice Douglas's concurring opinion to the companion case to *Roe*, the decisive joint opinion in *Planned Parenthood of Southeastern Pennsylvania v. Casey* cited *Jacobson* for the recognition of individual liberty.[119]

To be sure, during this post-*Roe*, pre-*Dobbs* period support for abortion rights was continuously contested. Although attitudes toward abortion were not closely aligned with partisanship before *Roe*,[120] in the years and decades that followed abortion became politically polarized and partisan[121] even as vaccine law continued to be largely nonpartisan. In this new climate, *Roe* eventually became a rallying point for a broader conservative attack on the courts.[122] At the same time, Republican-led states began to enact laws (including so-called Targeted Restrictions on Abortion [TRAP] laws) that sought to chip away at abortion rights, often under the guise of protecting the health of pregnant persons. Even before *Dobbs*, these regulations resulted in significant restrictions on abortion access in many Republican-led states.[123]

Other divergences between abortion and vaccine law also began to appear during this period. For example, in expanding vaccine mandates and rejecting constitutional challenges to them, lawmakers and courts accepted scientific expertise (usually in the form of recommendations from the Centers for Disease Control and Prevention's Advisory Committee on Immunization Practices). Likewise, the Supreme Court in *Roe* granted considerable weight to the views of physicians and the medical establishment.[124] But as the contestation over abortion intensified, some courts began to give credence to so-called scientific claims that existed well outside the medical consensus. For example, in *Planned Parenthood of Minnesota v. Rounds* (2012), the federal Eighth Circuit Court of Appeals upheld a South Dakota law that required doctors to tell patients that suicide was a "statistically significant risk[ ] factor to abortion,"[125] even though the weight of medical evidence showed that abortion very rarely causes psychological harm.[126] And in *Gonzales v. Carhart* (2007), the Supreme Court upheld a federal ban on what Congress termed "partial-birth" abortions, stating: "While we find no reliable data to measure the phenomenon, it seems unexceptionable to conclude some women come to regret their choice to abort the infant life they once created and sustained."[127] Although the Court in *Whole Woman's Health v. Hellerstedt* (2016)[128] returned to an approach that was heavily reliant on scientific evidence to determine whether a TRAP law at issue actually protected health, *Gonzales*'s disregard for scientific evidence would reappear during the COVID-19 pandemic in both abortion and vaccine law.

The Second Divergence and the Era of Chaos

During the COVID-19 pandemic, the law and politics of vaccination and abortion began to shift, creating new divergences. These were evident not only between the law and politics of abortion and vaccines but also within each domain, as political instability and regulatory chaos engulfed both types of regulation. Nevertheless, the regulation of abortion and vaccines continue to be propelled by common themes and intertwined in multiple ways.

One important distinction between the first and second eras of divergence relates to partisanship. As noted above, during the first divergence vaccine mandates remained relatively nonpartisan, even as abortion law became politically divisive. During the second divergence, that partisan divide spilled over to vaccine law as many Democratic political leaders, including President Joseph Biden, supported vaccine mandates while Republicans began to decry them as violations of medical freedom.[129] This led to a geographic and partisan divide.[130] It also helps to explain why Republicans had higher death rates from COVID-19 than Democrats following the introduction of vaccines.[131]

Another key distinction between the first and second eras of divergence relates to how courts treated challenges to abortion bans and vaccine mandates. As noted above, during the period of the first divergence, courts consistently upheld vaccine mandates even as they subjected restrictions on abortion to heightened judicial review. During the pandemic, the tables began to turn, as some courts began to block vaccine mandates and the Supreme Court overruled the right to abortion.

The roots of the doctrinal upheaval began early in the pandemic when many states imposed restrictions on in-person religious worship.[132] These social distancing measures became a partisan flashpoint when President Donald Trump called for reopening the country for in-person worship on Easter Sunday 2020 and US Attorney General William Barr warned that restrictions on worship could violate the Free Exercise Clause of the First Amendment.[133]

Initially most, but not all, lower courts rejected free exercise challenges to COVID-related restrictions.[134] In May and July 2020, the Supreme Court refused to block state restrictions on worship.[135] Although the majority did not write an opinion in either case, Chief Justice John Roberts wrote a concurring opinion in the first case, *South Bay United Pentecostal Church v. Newsom*, citing *Jacobson* for the proposition that the Constitution "principally entrusts" health policies to politically accountable officials.[136] Foreshadowing where the Court would later go, Justice Samuel Alito dissented in the second case, *Calvary Chapel Dayton Valley v. Sisolak*, arguing that *Jacobson* had no relevance in free exercise cases.[137]

After Justice Amy Coney Barrett replaced Justice Ruth Bader Ginsburg on the Supreme Court, the majority adopted Alito's views.[138] Although a full discussion of the Supreme Court's COVID-era free exercise cases is beyond the scope of this chapter,[139] several points are critical to understanding how those precedents affected vaccine law. First, after Barrett joined the Court, the majority ceased relying upon or even citing *Jacobson* in free exercise challenges to public health laws. Second, although the Court did not overrule *Smith*, it limited that case's impact. Notably, in April 2021, in *Tandon v. Newsom* the Court held that California could not apply a law limiting the number of people meeting in a private home to a bible study group because it did not limit the number of people in some retail establishments or places of public transportation.[140] In so doing, the

Court explained that strict scrutiny (the most stringent form of judicial review, which generally leads to the invalidation of the contested law) is required whenever a state places a greater burden on an individual's sincerely held religious beliefs than on *any* comparable secular activity.[141] The Court also failed to give any deference to the state's public health evidence in determining whether a secular activity was comparable to the exercise of religion that the plaintiffs claimed to be burdened. Then in *Fulton v. City of Philadelphia* (2021), the Court insisted that strict scrutiny was required whenever a state granted officials discretion to grant or deny an exemption.[142] Together, these cases granted religious claimants a type of "most favored nation status," which enables them to opt out of broadly applicable regulations.[143]

None of these cases concerned vaccine mandates, but their relevance to vaccine cases quickly became apparent. Using the Court's new approach to free exercise claims, litigants who objected to vaccine mandates, often relying on the false claim that the vaccines contained fetal tissue,[144] could and did claim that strict scrutiny was required because the state offered a medical but not a religious exemption. Although some lower courts have rejected that argument,[145] a federal district court in Mississippi relied on it in holding that that state's childhood vaccine law was unconstitutional because it failed to include a religious exemption.[146] Other courts have refused to dismiss free exercise challenges to vaccine mandates.[147] In addition, Justices Clarence Thomas, Samuel Alito, and Neil Gorsuch have indicated they believe that such challenges merit strict scrutiny.[148] In so doing, they noted that plaintiffs' religious objections related to their belief that the COVID-19 vaccines were developed with "fetal cell lines" or used "abortion-related materials" in their production.[149] Thus, the contestation over abortion helped destabilize the once-settled law pertaining to vaccine mandates.

Doctrinally, most cases challenging vaccine mandates seek to vindicate religious liberty rather than medical freedom, privacy, or substantive due process. But the distinction among types of liberty claims can be tenuous. First, as noted above, before the onset of COVID courts treated *Jacobson* (which did not rely on the Free Exercise Clause) as relevant in religious liberty claims. Second, individuals can reject vaccination for a mix of reasons—worries about vaccine safety, the desire to freeride on others' vaccination, the belief that the state is interfering in freedom of choice or the rights of parents, partisan affiliation, and religious concerns. Untangling those motives and distinguishing claims for religious liberty from those for secular liberty can be challenging, especially because individuals can have religious beliefs that clash with those professed by the leaders of their faith. As a result, courts generally give broad, albeit not unlimited, deference to claims that vaccination violates individuals' sincerely held religious beliefs.[150] This deference makes it relatively easy for individuals to couch objections that are primarily secular as religious.[151] Therefore, as a practical matter the legal movement in support of religious objections facilitates individuals' autonomy to opt out of vaccination regardless of their motivation.

In addition, the judiciary's newfound support for the autonomy to reject vaccines has not been limited to religious liberty cases. It has also appeared in cases challenging the Biden administration's authority to impose vaccine mandates. Technically these cases raised questions of statutory interpretation and separation of powers: Did the statute that the president or federal agency relied upon grant the authority to impose a vaccine mandate? In answering that question in the negative, the Supreme Court and lower courts relied upon the newly minted major questions doctrine, which holds that federal officials cannot regulate "major questions" without explicit congressional authorization.[152] Applying that doctrine, the Supreme Court held that the Occupational Safety and Health Administration (OSHA) lacked the authority to require large employers to have either a vaccine mandate or a testing and masking policy[153] but that the Centers for Medicare and Medicaid Services had the authority to require health care workers to be vaccinated.[154] Lower courts also blocked the president's ability to mandate vaccination (with religious exemptions) for federal workers or contractors.[155]

As some scholars have noted, there is no clear answer as to what questions are "major" so as to trigger the major questions doctrine.[156] In applying the doctrine, the justices have offered a variety of factors, including whether the regulation is novel, imposes substantial costs on the economy, is controversial, intrudes upon matters that were traditionally reserved to the states, or undermines individual autonomy.[157] The latter rationale was evident in *National Federation of Independent Business v. Department of Labor* (2022), in which the Supreme Court emphasized that OSHA's vaccine regulation constituted "a significant encroachment into the lives—and health—of a vast number of employees"[158] and explained that vaccination "'cannot be undone at the end of the workday.'"[159] Thus the Court's sense that individuals should have the power to decide what happens to their bodies with respect to vaccines seemed to underlie its decision to read OSHA's power narrowly.[160]

Yet even as courts seemed to grant greater protection for bodily autonomy with respect to vaccination, the Supreme Court overturned its past protection for reproductive autonomy, opening the door to abortion bans.[161] In *Dobbs v. Jackson Women's Health Organization*, the Supreme Court, in an opinion by Justice Alito, held that the Constitution does not protect an individual's liberty to terminate a pregnancy.[162] In reaching that decision, Alito offered an explanation that he did not seem to consider in the vaccination cases, arguing that the Court "must guard against the natural human tendency to confuse what that [the Fourteenth] Amendment protects with our own ardent views about the liberty that Americans should enjoy."[163] Instead, Alito explained, the determination of what types of liberty the Constitution recognizes must be "guided by the history and tradition that map the essential components of our Nation's concept of ordered liberty."[164] Alito then devoted much of his opinion to a recitation of the treatment of abortion at common law (as far back as the thirteenth century) and in the early days of the American republic. From this reading of "history and tradition," he concluded that the right recognized by *Roe* was not "deeply rooted" and therefore not constitutionally protected.

Many scholars have analyzed and critiqued *Dobbs*.[165] For this discussion, a few points stand out. First, the type of historical analysis that Alito employed in *Dobbs* was remarkably absent in the Supreme Court's recent free exercise and vaccine cases. Thus, the Court looked to the legal practices from the period of convergence (and even earlier) in denying a right to an abortion but failed to consider practices from that same period in upholding free exercise challenges to public health laws. Second, the *Dobbs* court never cited *Jacobson*, even though during oral argument Justice Barrett noted that "there is, without question, an infringement on bodily autonomy, you know, which we have in other contexts, like vaccines."[166] Third, as in the COVID cases, the *Dobbs* majority displayed little interest in either medical expertise or the health consequences (to already-born individuals) of its decision. Instead, and in sharp contrast to both *Roe* and *Jacobson*, the Court failed to suggest that state regulations of the body might have to provide exemptions to protect the health of the individual whose body is being regulated.

Dobbs, of course, is not the end of the story. After it was issued, numerous states banned abortion, some outright from the moment of conception, others at later periods and with some exceptions. Predictably, abortion advocates challenged those laws as violative of state constitutions.[167] In so doing, they often echoed the type of "medical freedom" language that was used politically—sometimes with success in the same states—against vaccine mandates.[168] At the same time, some abortion rights advocates relied on the Supreme Court's COVID-era free exercise jurisprudence to challenge abortion bans that lack religious exemptions.[169] Although at least one state appeals court has found for plaintiffs raising such claims,[170] the Free Exercise Clause scholars Micah Schwartzman and Richard Schragger argue that they are unlikely to gain wide traction because courts implicitly favor some types of religious liberty claims—those brought by conservative Christians—over others— those brought by non-Christians and liberals.[171] Their conclusion seems persuasive, but the very existence of religious liberty challenges to abortion laws, as well as the state-law claims and political advocacy focused on medical freedom, shows the tenuousness of the divergence: despite the significant health and liberty distinctions between vaccine mandates and abortion bans, arguments and doctrines developed in one arena continue to influence those in the other. As they do so, and as courts continue to consider myriad challenges to abortion bans and vaccine mandates, the legal status of both forms of regulation remains uncertain and increasingly unstable, with different courts issuing divergent and often hard to reconcile decisions—even as different parts of the country go in different directions.

Despite these divergences, signs of a potential new convergence may be visible. Since *Dobbs* was decided, political (as opposed to judicial) opposition to abortion restrictions has become more apparent, as voters in several conservative states have voted for referenda supporting abortion rights.[172] At the same time, opposition to vaccine mandates and even vaccines appears to be gaining ground in some statehouses and in Washington, as evident by President Trump's nomination of longtime vaccine skeptic Robert Kennedy Jr. to head the Department of Health and Human Services.[173] Although the public's support for vaccine mandates remains relatively high, and the opposition continues to be concentrated among Republicans, it is possible to imagine a new convergence in which both vaccine mandates and abortion bans are condemned in the name of health freedom. For now, however, the story remains one of divergence and instability.

Explaining the Divergences and the Elusive Meaning of "Medical Freedom"

Given the long history of congruence, intersections, and divergences between the regulatory and jurisprudential treatment of vaccine mandates and abortion bans, how can we understand the current era? How can it be that one type of regulation of the body appears ascendent, though its fate remains uncertain, while another is eroding, even as it remains politically popular?[174] And what does the divergence tell us about the meaning of "health freedom" and the accepted role for the state's regulation of the body?

One possible answer, at least for the jurisprudential divergence, is that the claims for freedom from state regulation in the abortion and vaccine contexts rely on different parts of the Constitution, with their own distinct text and precedent. More specifically, the claims for "freedom" from vaccine mandates frequently rest on the textually enumerated Free Exercise Clause, while the claims for abortion rights rest on the unenumerated right of substantive due process.

Although that "answer" may be correct, at least in some cases, as a matter of doctrine, it should be quickly cast aside as having little explanatory heft. First, as noted above, for decades courts dismissed free exercise claims leveled at vaccine mandates.[175] Nothing in the Constitution's text can explain the shift. Second, as also noted above, the Supreme Court has expressed concern for autonomy against vaccine mandates in cases in which religious rights were not at issue.[176] Likewise, the Court has supported and then withdrew its support for abortion rights without any change in the Constitution's history or text. But even more important, although the Supreme Court's decisions can and do influence the political sphere, court rulings alone cannot explain how the social and political meaning of medical freedom from state regulation in the context of abortion and vaccines has changed over time and across geographic and political borders.

The last observation suggests another, not necessarily wrong, answer. It's all politics or, more precisely, partisanship. In our highly polarized era, individuals on both sides of the political spectrum gather their "facts" from echo chambers and assess policy and ethical questions through the lens of party affiliation.[177] To some degree, this process had been going on with respect to abortion for decades.[178] What changed recently and helped mark the second divergence is that, during the pandemic, partisanship began to drive perceptions of the COVID-19 policies and eventually vaccine mandates.[179] This likely occurred because COVID-19 vaccine mandates rolled out when a Democrat (Joe Biden) was president. Because partisans often disdain the policies of their political opponents, Republicans began to assail vaccine mandates, even likening them to Nazi experiments.[180] Some Republican policymakers went further, enacting legislation to prohibit mandates, even those imposed by private employers.[181]

The heated political rhetoric may have seeped into the courts, helping to create the jurisprudential flip that characterizes the second divergence, due to the rise of "movement judges." According to Robert L. Tsai and Mary Zeigler, movement judges are jurists who are "socially embedded in influential networks outside of the legal system and [are] willing to use a judge's tools of the trade in the service of a movement's goals."[182] These judges—and Tsai and Ziegler include several sitting Supreme Court justices among their number—may view issues of bodily autonomy in both abortion and reproductive rights cases through the lens of the political movements to which they belong.[183] Through this process, a political divergence may have been converted into a jurisprudential one, unsettling long-settled precedent and causing courts to flip in how they approached challenges to vaccine mandates and abortion bans.

Sherry F. Colb and Michael C. Dorf offer (but ultimately reject) another possible explanation for the current divergence: both abortions and vaccines can be seen as interfering with nature's course.[184] Abortion disrupts the "natural order" of pregnancy, while vaccines impede the "natural order" of infection. From this perspective, abortion bans can be said to respect nature, while vaccine mandates can be seen as undermining it. Yet as Colb and Dorf explain, this let-nature-take-its-course distinction ignores the humanmade hardships that follow from compelled pregnancy and other forms of medical care that the state may prohibit.[185] It also cannot explain why *some* regulations of the body that interfere with nature are viewed as more problematic than others. For example, proponents of abortion bans are unlikely to argue that obstetricians should not be allowed to perform a cesarean section when it is needed to save the life of an unborn child, even though C-sections "interfere with nature." This suggests that the naturalistic argument provides less of a role in explaining the differential treatment of abortion bans and vaccine mandates than those who favor the former but abhor the latter may think.

What else can explain the current divergences? One possible answer is the decline of judicial reliance on and public trust in scientific expertise, particularly medical authority. During the era of congruence, courts ordinarily granted considerable deference to medical and public health authorities, accepting for the most part their conclusions as to what limitations on autonomy were reasonable or necessary to protect the public's health.[186] In effect, the consensus of public health or medical professionals was relied upon to delineate the boundary between bodily autonomy and the police power. In the nineteenth and early twentieth centuries, medical experts supported abortion bans and vaccine mandates.

As discussed above, that congruence in the medical profession's views about abortion and vaccines broke down during the era of the first divergence. Medical authority continued to support vaccines; in fact, health experts pushed for mandates to cover an expanded list of vaccines. Yet during this same period the weight of medical opinion began to change regarding abortion, a fact that was important to the Court not only in *Roe* but also in other cases upholding abortion rights.[187] In that sense, medical authority continued to mark the legal boundaries between autonomy and public health protection in both abortion and vaccine cases; it just led to different conclusions in the two cases, creating the divergence.

By the late twentieth century, the public's trust in medical "authority" began to dissipate, both in the courts and among social movements, from the women's health movement to HIV/AIDS activists.[188] This skepticism of scientific consensus, long apparent among vaccine resisters, also took hold in the battle over abortion as all sides began to question the relevance of medical authority and put forth their own versions of what the science teaches.[189] Feminist supporters of abortion rejected the *Roe* Court's reliance on medical authority, insisting that the right to an abortion was about a woman's right to autonomy.[190] Concurrently, abortion opponents began to push forward nonmainstream views of the science. This alternative claim to medical authority was especially apparent in the Fifth Circuit's 2023 decision in *Alliance for Hippocratic Medicine v. Food & Drug Administration*,[191] which challenged the Food and Drug Administration's approval of mifepristone, a key abortion medication. The case was brought by groups of physicians who opposed abortion and disagreed with the consensus held by "mainstream" medical groups. In supporting the challengers' contention that mifepristone is dangerous and that the FDA acted arbitrarily and capriciously in liberalizing access to at several points over the previous seven years, the Fifth Circuit consistently addressed the challengers as "Doctors," granting the challengers the mantle of science[192] even as it overrode a decision by the FDA, ignored numerous studies showing that mifepristone is far safer than many common medications,[193] and disregarded the conclusions of most medical experts. Going even further, in his opinion concurring in part and dissenting in part, Judge James Ho offered a litany of cases in which the FDA was found to have erred.[194] To him, faith in expert bodies was misplaced.

Although the Supreme Court ultimately reversed the Fifth Circuit's ruling, it did so on technical grounds, holding that the plaintiffs lacked standing to challenge the FDA's decisions regarding mifepristone.[195] The Court's opinion thus did not reach the merits or reaffirm that courts should offer deference to the FDA's expertise. It also did not shut the door to other challenges to the FDA's decisions regarding mifepristone.

This contestation about the science and the erosion of trust evident in the Fifth Circuit's opinion aligns with a broader cultural questioning of expertise and authority,[196] one that has its roots in the social movements of the 1960s and 1970s including, importantly, the women's health movement,[197] as well as the revelations of ethical breaches and downright fraud exemplified by the Tuskegee syphilis study and fake science supported by the tobacco companies and the Wakefield study.[198] While a full discussion of the populist turn against science is beyond the scope of this chapter, the critical point is that, by the time

Justice Barrett joined the Supreme Court, enabling it to change course on both abortion and vaccine law, trust in science had diminished significantly, especially but not only among conservatives.[199] As a result, conservative lawmakers and jurists were increasingly unwilling to rely upon "science" to demarcate the boundary between bodily autonomy and the state's role in regulating the body.[200] To put it another way: in both vaccine and abortion cases, science was no longer an accepted arbiter of when the protection of health justified limits on autonomy. In this climate of distrust, physicians and other health care providers are understandably wary of the potential consequences they face for performing an abortion, even when medical exemptions as in Texas rely on "reasonable medical judgement."[201]

To be sure, disregard of science has not overtaken the entire regulatory landscape with respect to either abortion or vaccines. Some legislatures and many (if not most) courts continue to stress the need for evidence-based policies and look to medical authority for guidance as to the boundaries between freedom and restraint.[202] That may lead them to hold fast (to the extent that Supreme Court precedent permits) to the jurisprudence from the first divergence, which upheld the state's power to mandate vaccination. But for many other politicians, government appointees, activists, and jurists the scientific consensus no longer seems to matter.

What has replaced the role once granted to established scientific authority? One answer, in both abortion and vaccine law, is religion, more specifically a particular conservative Christian theology that disapproves of both abortion and vaccines, often seeing vaccines as problematic precisely because of their (alleged) ties to abortion. Thus, the freedom that many abortion and vaccine opponents prize most may be the freedom to follow their religion and live in a society that adheres to its theology. That leads to support for freedom from vaccines and the imposition of abortion bans. From a conservative Christian perspective, there simply is no inconsistency.

There is yet one more way in which there is consistency in the apparently discordant positions of the second divergence. The battles over abortion bans and vaccine mandates are deeply tied to the contestation of gender roles. With abortion, the connection to gender is readily apparent. Although abortion bans do not impact only women (and not all pregnant persons are women), women are disproportionately affected.[203] Most obviously, the right to have an abortion enables many women to (at least partially) escape traditional gender roles by controlling their own reproduction. That is one type of freedom that abortion proponents seek. But to abortion opponents, the choice to reject reproduction is deeply inimical to what they view as women's appropriate and natural role. Some further argue that access to legal abortion undermines women's freedom to *choose* motherhood, by diminishing respect for motherhood and relieving men of responsibility for supporting mothers and children.[204] They thus see abortion bans as supporting a different type of freedom.

The gender dimensions of vaccine mandates are less glaring but nevertheless important. Recall that individuals who reject vaccines (and therefore mandates) often point to the use of cell lines derived from aborted fetuses in vaccine development and testing.[205] To these opponents, vaccines are problematic precisely because of their perceived connection to abortion, which itself is viewed as impeding traditional gender roles. But even without the abortion connection, vaccines and vaccine mandates have often been viewed as dangerous to women's maternal role. During the COVID-19 pandemic, for example, misinformation about the vaccines' purportedly harmful impact on fertility was widespread,[206] with 24 percent of Americans erroneously believing the claim that COVID-19 vaccines "have been proven to cause infertility" is "definitely true."[207] At least one study found that fear of the vaccines' adverse impact on fertility was a "major cause for COVID-19 vaccine hesitancy in the United States."[208]

Mandates for childhood vaccines are also seen by many critics as corrosive of women's maternal role, a perspective that opponents of vaccination exploit in their advocacy by utilizing a variety of tropes related to motherhood and the maternal role.[209] As Jennifer A. Reich noted before the pandemic, "intense cultural expectations of mothering define many aspects of gender," especially for middle- and upper-class white women.[210] As part of this expectation, mothers are viewed as "responsible for the physical, emotional, and psychological health of their children" and are expected to research and make healthy choices for their children, even when that challenges expert advice.[211] In addition, the work of intensive mothering, including breastfeeding, can be viewed as the key to boosting a child's immunity and health.[212] Vaccine mandates implicitly devalue that work, substituting the intervention of medicine and the conclusions of experts, as imposed by state law, for the choices and efforts of individual mothers.

Vaccine mandates also challenge gendered expectations of mothering in another way. Contemporary norms of intensive mothering are decidedly selfish. The "good" mother is expected to care for the well-being of her own children, rather than the good of other children or the broader community.[213] Thus "good" mothers need not and perhaps should not consider the third-party benefits of vaccines. Yet it is precisely those public health benefits of vaccination that leads states to impose mandates.

Importantly, this deference to maternal decision-making stands in stark contrast to the distrust of women's judgment evident in abortion restrictions. To those who support abortion bans and reject vaccine mandates, the state's regulatory role ends once a child is born. To those who support vaccine mandates and reject abortion bans, that is precisely when state regulation should commence.

Conclusion

We are in a moment of political and doctrinal instability. Many of the activists, lawmakers, and judges who champion "freedom" in the case of vaccines see no problem with the state limiting it in the case of abortion. And many who support vaccine mandates demand reproductive freedom and see no role for the state's restriction of abortion. In both domains, long-settled understandings of when the state can regulate the body and when individuals should have the freedom to make their own medical decisions have been upended.

In this era of uncertainty, divergences, and fractures, it is easy to believe that the claim for health freedom has no meaning: that people see and reject vulnerability and independence where they want to. For many, especially partisans, that may be true. Partisanship may trump all other factors. But the history and current politics and regulation of abortion and vaccines offer a more nuanced perspective. Our legal system has always accepted that the body is not wholly independent and that states may regulate the body to protect the health of others. What has changed, and what remains highly contested, is the authority that is accepted for determining when states may regulate the body to protect the health (and bodies) of others, as well as the identity of the other parties for whose such regulations may be imposed. Do we look to science? To theology? To mothers? Should the state regulate only to protect family members or also to protect strangers?

In a time of deep epistemic, cultural, and partisan divisions, the answers to those questions will remain contested and elusive, whether the issue is gender-affirming care, end-of-life treatment, vaccine mandates, or abortion. In each case, the cry for health freedom will be waged and contested; but without a shared understanding about the boundaries between our vulnerabilities and independence, the responsibilities we owe to one another, and the authorities to guide us as to when and how our actions affect others, the debates will remain unsettled. Although an emerging libertarian consensus is imaginable, the era of chaos is likely to continue.

NOTES

Many thanks to the editors and authors of this volume as well as Jeremy Paul and Katherine Kraschel for their helpful comments on a prior draft. Erica Brangwynne, Luke Colomey, Camden Connor, Catherine Kuchel, Danika Marzluff, Jennifer Morris, Anjika Pail, and Ruchi Ramamurthy provided excellent research assistance. All errors are my own.

1. Lewis A. Grossman, *Choose Your Medicine: Freedom of Therapeutic Choice in America* (New York: Oxford University Press, 2021), 10–23. Although the phrase "health freedom" has somewhat broader connotation than "medical freedom," in the discussion that follows I use the two phrases interchangeably.
2. Tina Rulli and Stephen Campbell, "Can 'My Body, My Choice' Anti-Vaxxers be Pro-Life?," *Bioethics* 36, no. 6 (April 2022): 708, https://doi.org/10.1111/bioe.13033. The issue of medical freedom has also risen recently in the context of trans health care.
3. Opponents of abortion bans also criticize them as violative of reproductive justice and equality. Aziza Ahmed et al., "*Dobbs v. Jackson Women's Health*: Undermining Public Health, Facilitating Reproductive Coercion," *Journal of Law, Medicine & Ethics* 51, no. 3 (Fall 2023): 488, doi:10.1017/jme.2023.137.
4. Dobbs v. Jackson Women's Health Org., 142 S. Ct. 2228 (2022).
5. For another discussion of this divergence, see Alyssa Curcio, "Immunizing *Roe*: How Court Treatment of COVID-19 Vaccine Mandates Supports Reproductive Freedom," *Columbia Journal of Gender and Law* 43, no. 1 (February 2023): 3, https://doi.org/10.52214/cjgl.v43i1.10714.

6 Rulli and Campbell, "'My Body, My Choice,'" 709. See also Jesse Hill, "The Constitutional Right to Make Medical Treatment Decisions: A Tale of Two Doctrines," *Texas Law Review* 86 (2007): 277; Deanna Pollard Sacks, "Judicial Protection of Medical Liberty," *Florida State University Law Review* 49 (2022): 515, http://doi.org/10.2139/ssrn.3801253.
7 National Conference of State Legislatures, "States with Religious and Philosophical Exemptions from School Immunization Requirements," National Conference of State Legislatures, www.ncsl.org, last modified August 3, 2023; Immunize.org, "State Requirements by Vaccine," Immunize.org, www.immunize.org, accessed August 21, 2023.
8 Centers for Disease Control and Prevention, "State Immunization Laws for Healthcare Workers and Patients," Centers for Disease Control and Prevention, November 19, 2014. www2a.cdc.gov.
9 Curcio, "Immunizing *Roe*," 1.
10 Ballotpedia, "State Government Policies About Vaccine Requirements (Vaccine Passports), 2021–2022," Ballotpedia, https://ballotpedia.org, accessed May 3, 2023.
11 "Tracking Abortion Bans Across the Country," *New York Times*, www.nytimes.com, last modified June 13, 2024.
12 Ibid; Adam Liptak, "Supreme Court to Hear Challenge to Idaho's Strict Abortion Ban," *New York Times*, January 5, 2024, www.nytimes.com.
13 "Tracking Abortion Bans," *New York Times*; Guttmacher Institute, "Interactive Map: US Abortion Policies and Access after Roe," Guttmacher Institute, www.guttmacher.org, last modified June 20, 2024.
14 Sabrina Tavernise, "'The Time is Now': States Are Rushing to Restrict Abortion, or to Protect It," *New York Times*, May 15, 2019, www.nytimes.com; Sophia Cai, "Red States Fight School Vaccine Mandates," *Axios*, January 9, 2022, www.axios.com.
15 Tavernise, "'The Time is Now'"; Cai, "Red States Fight."
16 Martha Albertson Fineman, "Reasoning from the Body: Universal Vulnerability and Social Justice," *Emory University School of Law Legal Studies Research Paper Series 22–18* (May 4, 2022): 6, http://dx.doi.org/10.2139/ssrn.4100709.
17 Martha Albertson Fineman, "Rights, Resistance, and Responsibility," *Emory Law Journal* 71, no. 7 (2022): 1435, 1444, http://dx.doi.org/10.2139/ssrn.4104731.
18 There was a time when officials forcefully vaccinated individuals, usually immigrants and people of color. Michael Willrich, "How the 'Pox' Epidemic Changed Vaccination Rules," interview by Terry Gross, *Fresh Air*, NPR, April 5, 2011, audio, 38:48, www.npr.org. See generally Michael Willrich, *Pox: An American History* (New York: Penguin Press, 2012).
19 Jacobson v. Massachusetts, 197 U.S. 11, 38 (1905).
20 E.g., Lowe v. Mills, 68 F.4 th 706 (1st Cir. 2023); Bosarge v. Edney, 669 F. Supp. 598 (S.D. Miss. 2023).
21 National Conference of State Legislatures, "States with Religious and Philosophical Exemptions from School Immunization Requirements," National Conference

of State Legislatures, www.ncsl.org, last modified May 25, 2022. Since the source was published, Mississippi began to offer religious exemptions. Mississippi State Department of Health, "Religious Exemptions for Immunizations Available," Mississippi State Department of Health, July 14, 2023, https://msdh.ms.gov.

22 National Conference of State Legislatures, "States with Religious and Philosophical Exemptions."

23 Farah Diaz-Tello and Sara Ainsworth, "The End of *Roe* and the Criminalization of Abortion: More of the Same," American Bar Association, April 12, 2023, www.americanbar.org.

24 Mabel Felix, Laurie Sobel, and Alina Salganicoff, "A Review of Exceptions in State Abortion Bans: Implication for the Provision of Abortion Services," Women's Health Policy, Kaiser Family Foundation, May 18, 2023, www.kff.org.

25 In re State, No. 23–0994, 2023 WL 8540008 (Tex. 2023).

26 State v. Zurawski, 690 S.W. 3d 644, 653 1 (Tex. 2024).

27 Some states have tried to prevent people from aiding minors who travel for out-of-state abortions. Sarah Varney, "Idaho AG Sued Over State's Teen Abortion Travel Ban," KFF Health News, *CNN*, July 12, 2023, www.cnn.com; Associated Press, "Alabama's Attorney General Says the State Can Prosecute Those Who Help Women Travel for Abortions," *ABC*, August 31, 2023, https://abcnews.go.com.

28 Liza Fuentes, "Inequity in US Abortion Rights and Access: The End of Roe is Deepening Existing Divides," Guttmacher Institute, January 17, 2023, www.guttmacher.org.

29 David S. Cohen, Greer Donley, and Rachel Rebouché, "Abortion Pills," *Stanford Law Review* 76 (2024): 329.

30 All. for Hippocratic Med. v. Food & Drug Admin., 78 F.4th 210 (5th Cir. 2023), rev'd 602 S. Ct. ___, 2024 WL 2964140 (June 13, 2024).

31 Elizabeth G. Raymond and David A. Grimes, "The Comparative Safety of Legal Induced Abortion and Child Birth in the United States," *Obstetrics and Gynecology* 119 (February 2012): 217, https://doi.org/10.1097/AOG.0b013e31823fe923; see M. Antonia Biggs et al., "Women's Mental Health and Well-Being 5 Years After Receiving or Being Denied an Abortion," *JAMA Psychiatry* 74, no. 2 (February 2017): 169, https://doi.org/10.1001/jamapsychiatry.2016.3478.

32 See Diana Greene Foster, *The Turnaway Study: Ten Years, a Thousand Women, and the Consequences of Having-or Being Denied-an Abortion* (New York: Scribner, 2020), 99–187.

33 Lindzi Wessel, "Vaccine Myths," *Science* 326, no. 6336 (April 28, 2017): 368–69, https://doi.org/10.1126/science.356.6336.368.

34 Abdallah Alami et al., "Risk of Myocarditis and Pericarditis in mRNA COVID-19-Vaccinated and Unvaccinated Populations: A Systemic Review and Meta-Analysis," *BMJ Open* 13 (June 20, 2023): 11, https://doi.org/10.1136/bmjopen-2022-065687.

35 Centers for Disease Control and Prevention, "Possible Side Effects from Vaccines," Centers for Disease Control and Prevention, www.cdc.gov, last modified July 31, 2024.

36 See John Stuart Mill, *On Liberty* (Walter Scott Publishing Co., Ltd., 2011), 17–18, www.gutenberg.org.
37 Michelle M. Mello et al., "Effectiveness of Vaccination Mandates in Improving Uptake of COVID-19 Vaccines in the USA," *The Lancet* 400, no. 10351 (August 2022): 535, https://doi.org/10.1016/S0140-6736(22)00875-3.
38 U.S. Department of Health and Human Services, "Vaccines Protect Your Community," U.S. Department of Health and Human Services, www.hhs.gov, last modified, April 29, 2021.
39 World Health Organization, "History of the Polio Vaccine," World Health Organization., www.who.int, last accessed July 26, 2024.
40 Mello et al., "Effectiveness of Vaccination Mandates," 535.
41 Emily R. Jones, "Who Calls the Shots? Parents Versus the Parens Patriae Power of the States to Mandate Vaccines for Children in New York," *Georgia State University Law Review* 37, no. 2 (March 2021): 653.
42 Raymond and Grimes, "The Comparative Safety," 217; Biggs et al., "Women's Mental Health," 169.
43 See, e.g., Zurawski v. Texas, No. D-1-GN-23-000968 (Travis Cty. Tex. 2023).
44 *Dobbs*, 141 S. Ct. at 2258.
45 Ibid. In his concurring opinion, Justice Thomas rejected the majority's distinction and argued that other decisions affirming rights to autonomy should also fall. See *Dobbs*, 141 S. Ct. at 3201 (Thomas, J., concurring).
46 Wendy E. Parmet, *Constitutional Contagion: COVID, the Courts, and Public Health* (Cambridge: Cambridge University Press, 2023), 37–49.
47 *Jacobson*, 197 U.S. at 11.
48 James Hodge and Lawrence O. Gostin, "School Vaccination Requirements: Historical, Social and Legal Perspectives," *Kentucky Law Journal* 90, no. 4 (2002): 851.
49 Ibid.
50 Anna North, "The Long, Strange History of Anti-vaccination Movements," *VOX*, March 4, 2022, www.vox.com.
51 Willrich, *Pox*, 167–71.
52 Karen L. Walloch, *The Antivaccine Heresy:* Jacobson v. Massachusetts *and the Troubled History of Compulsory Vaccination in the United States* (Rochester, NY: University of Rochester Press, 2015): 91.
53 Willrich, *Pox*, 192–210.
54 Yoko Ibuka et al., "Free-Riding Behavior in Vaccination Decisions: An Experimental Study," *PLoS ONE* 9, no. 1 (2014): 6–8, https://doi.org/10.1371/journal.pone.0087164.
55 Wendy E. Parmet, "Rediscovering Jacobson in the Era of COVID-19," *Boston University Law Review Online* 100 (2020): 121.
56 Parmet, *Constitutional Contagion*, 33–36.
57 Ibid., 33–49.
58 *Jacobson*, 197 U.S. at 11.
59 Ibid., 25–26.

60 Ibid., 26.
61 Ibid.
62 Ibid.
63 Zucht v. King, 260 U.S. 174, 176–77 (1922).
64 Prince v. Massachusetts, 321 U.S. 158, 166 n.12 (1944).
65 Brief for Respondents at 5–7, Dobbs v. Jackson Women's Health Org., 141 S. Ct. 2228 (2022) (No. 19-1392), 2021 WL 4341742, at *5–7.
66 Ibid.
67 Ibid., 14–15.
68 Ibid., 18.
69 Reva Siegel, "Reasoning from the Body: A Historical Perspective on Abortion Regulation and Questions of Equal Protection," *Stanford Law Review* 44, no. 2 (1992): 279–80, https://doi.org/10.2307/1228947.
70 Ibid., 279.
71 Roe v. Wade, 410 U.S. 113 (1973).
72 Willard Cates Jr., David A. Grimes, and Kenneth F. Schulz, "The Public Health Impact of Legal Abortion: 30 Years Later," *Guttmacher Institute* 35, no. 1 (January 2003): 25, doi: 10.1363/3502503.
73 Hawker v. People of New York, 170 U.S. 189 (1898).
74 Ibid., 192.
75 Ibid., 201 (Harlan, J., dissenting).
76 See also State of Miss. ex rel. Hurwitz v. North, 271 U.S. 40 (1926) (ruling that conviction of a physician for performing an abortion did not violate due process).
77 Buck v. Bell, 274 U.S. 200, 207–08 (1927).
78 Paul A. Lombardo, *Three Generations, No Imbeciles: Eugenics, The Supreme Court, and* Buck v. Bell (Baltimore: Johns Hopkins University Press, 2008): 101–02.
79 Ibid., 207.
80 *Jacobson*, 197 U.S. at 29.
81 Kevin M. Malone and Alan R. Hinman, "Vaccine Mandates: The Public Health Imperative and Individual Rights," in *Law in Public Health Practice*, 269, ed. Richard A. Goodman et al. (New York: Oxford University Press, 2003).
82 Ibid.
83 Ibid., 271.
84 Ibid., 273.
85 North, "The Long, Strange History."
86 The "Cutter Incident," in which a defectively manufactured polio vaccine infected thousands of children with polio and killed 10, helped to erode trust in vaccines and led to greater regulatory oversight. Paul A. Offit, *The Cutter Incident: How America's First Polio Vaccine Led to a Growing Vaccine Crisis* (New Haven: Yale University Press, 2005), 3, 51–52, 178–79.
87 National Vaccine Information Center, www.nvic.org, accessed July 26, 2023.
88 North, "The Long, Strange History."

89 Dorit Rubenstein Reiss and Lois A. Weithorn, "Responding to the Childhood Vaccination Crisis: Legal Frameworks and Tools in the Context of Parental Vaccine Refusals," *Buffalo Law Review* 63, no. 4 (2015): 889–90.
90 Gardiner Harris, "Journal Retracts 1998 Paper Linking Autism to Vaccines," *New York Times*, February 2, 2010, www.nytimes.com.
91 Many scholars have sought to understand the motivations of pre-COVID vaccine rejectors. Maya J. Goldenberg, *Vaccine Hesitancy: Public Trust, Expertise, and the War on Science* (Pittsburgh: University of Pittsburgh Press, 2021), 33; Heidi J. Larson, *Stuck: How Vaccine Rumors Start—and Why They Don't Go Away* (New York: Oxford University Press, 2020), 22–47.
92 Kolbeck v. Kramer, 202 A.2d 889, 890 (N.J. 1964), *modified by* 214 A. 2d 408 (N.J. 1965). See also Dalli v. Bd. of Educ., 267 N.E.2d 219, 222–23 (Mass. 1971) (finding vaccine exemption limited to members of recognized religions to violate First Amendment).
93 Robert Roos, "Bush Announces Smallpox Vaccination Plan for Military, Healthcare Workers," Center for Infectious Disease Research and Policy, December 13, 2002, www.cidrap.umn.edu.
94 Rebecca Onion, "George W. Bush Set Out to Vaccinate Health Care Workers in Case of Smallpox Bioattack. It Was a Disaster," *Slate*, February 9, 2021, https://slate.com.
95 Homeland Security Council, "The National Strategy for Pandemic Influenza," Homeland Security Council, November 2005, 5, www.cdc.gov.
96 Another precursor of the changing politics was conservative opposition to the HPV vaccine, which some believed supported adolescent sexual activity. Gillian Haber, Robert M. Malow, and Gregory D. Zimet, "The HPV Vaccine Mandate Controversy," *Journal of Pediatric and Adolescent Gynecology* 20, no. 6 (2007): 328, https://doi.org/10.1016/j.jpag.2007.03.101.
97 Richard M. Carpiano et al., "Confronting the Evolution and Expansion of Anti-Vaccine Activism in the USA in the COVID-19 Era," *The Lancet* 401, no. 10380 (March 2023): 967, https://doi.org/10.1016/S0140-6736(23)00136-8.
98 E.g., Brown v. Smith, 235 Cal. Rptr. 3d 218, 225 (Ct. App. 2018). See also Love v. State Dep't of Educ., 240 Cal. Rptr. 3d 861, 873 (Ct. App. 2018).
99 Emp. Div., Dep't of Hum. Res. of Oregon v. Smith, 494 U.S. 872, 879 (1990).
100 E.g., Workman v. Mingo County Bd. Of Educ., 419 Fed. Appx. 348, 351, 357 (4th Cir. 2011); Phillips v. City of New York, 775 F.3d 538, 542, 544 (2d Cir. 2015). See also Caviezel v. Great Neck Pub. Schs., 500 Fed. Appx. 16, 17, 20 (2d Cir. 2012).
101 Linda Greenhouse and Reva B. Siegel, "Before (and After) *Roe v. Wade*: New Questions About Backlash," *Yale Law Journal* 120 (March 2011): 2035.
102 Ruth Roemer, "Abortion Law Reform and Repeal: Legislative and Judicial Developments," *American Journal of Public Health* 61, no. 3 (March 1971): 500, https://doi.org/10.2105/ajph.61.3.500.
103 Rosemary Nossiff, *Before Roe: Abortion Policy in the States* (Philadelphia: Temple University Press, 2000), 30.

104 Skinner v. Oklahoma ex rel. Williamson, 316 U.S. 535 (1942).
105 Griswold v. Connecticut, 381 U.S. 479, 497–98 (1965).
106 Ibid., 485.
107 Ibid., 504 (White, J., concurring).
108 Doctrinally, this meant that liberty-based challenges to vaccine mandates were subject to "rational basis" review, whereas liberty-based challenges to abortion bans were subject to some level of heighted scrutiny.
109 Roemer, "Abortion Law Reform," 500.
110 People v. Belous, 458 P.2d 194, 199 (Cal. 1969).
111 Ibid., 205–06.
112 *Roe*, 410 U.S. at 155–56.
113 *Dobbs*, 142 S. Ct. at 2240 ("For the first 185 years after the adoption of the Constitution, each State was permitted to address [abortion] in accordance with the views of its citizens. Then, in 1973, this Court decided *Roe*.").
114 Siegel, "Reasoning from the Body," 275.
115 *Roe*, 410 U.S. at 141–47.
116 Ibid., 154.
117 Doe v. Bolton, 410 U.S. 179, 213–14 (1973) (Douglas, J., concurring) (quoting Jacobson, 197 U.S. at 29).
118 Planned Parenthood of Southeastern Pennsylvania v. Casey, 505 U.S. 833, 852–53 (1992).
119 Ibid., 857.
120 Greenhouse and Siegel, "Before (and After)," 2067–72.
121 Ibid., 2070–72, 2084–86. See also Mary Ziegler, *After Roe: The Lost History of the Abortion Debate* (Cambridge, MA: Harvard University Press, 2015), 22, 186–87.
122 Ziegler, *After Roe*, 27–31.
123 Marshall H. Medoff and Christopher Dennis, "TRAP Abortion Laws and Partisan Political Party Control of State Government," *American Journal of Economics and Sociology* 70, no. 4, (2011): 951, https://doi.org/10.1111/j.1536-7150.2011.00794.x.
124 *Roe*, 410 U.S. at 142–43.
125 Planned Parenthood of Minnesota, N. Dakota, S. Dakota v. Rounds, 686 F.3d 889, 904–95 (8th Cir. 2012) (en banc).
126 Nada Logan Stotland, Angela D. Shrestha, and Naomi E. Stoland, "Reproductive Rights and Women's Mental Health: Essential Information for the Obstetrician-Gynecologist," *Obstetrics and Gynecology Clinics of North America* 48, no. 1 (2021): 11, https://doi.org/10.1016/j.ogc.2020.11.002; National Collaborating Centre for Mental Health, "Induced Abortion and Mental Health: A Systematic Review of the Mental Health Impact of Induced Abortion" (London: Academy of Royal Colleges, 2011), 123–26.
127 Gonzales v. Carhart, 550 U.S. 124, 159 (2007).
128 Whole Woman's Health v. Hellerstedt, 579 U.S. 582 (2016).
129 Don Albrecht, "Vaccination, Politics and COVID-19 Impacts," *BMC Public Health* 22 (2022): 4–5, https://doi.org/10.1186/s12889-021-12432-x.

130 National Academy for State Health Policy, "State Efforts to Limit or Enforce Covid-19 Vaccine Mandates," National Academy for State Health Policy, https://nashp.org, last modified June 30, 2023. Republican congressional leaders pushed for and succeeded in passing a law terminating vaccine mandates for members of the military. Catie Edmonson and John Ismay, "Congress Poised to Repeal Covid Vaccine Mandate for Troops in Military Bill," *New York Times*, December 6, 2022, www.nytimes.com.

131 Jacob Wallace, Paul Goldsmith-Pinkham, and Jason L. Schwartz, "Excess Death Rates for Republicans and Democratic Registered Voters in Florida and Ohio During the COVID-19 Pandemic," *JAMA Internal Medicine* 183, no. 9, (July 24, 2023): 916, https://doi.org/10.1001/jamainternmed.2023.1154; Bradley Jones, "The Changing Political Geography of COVID-19 Over the Last Two Years," *Pew Research Center*, March 3, 2022, www.pewresearch.org.

132 Wendy E. Parmet, "From the Shadows: The Public Health Implications of the Supreme Court's COVID-Free Exercise Cases," *Journal of Law Medicine & Ethics* 49 (2021): 566, https://doi.org/10.1017/jme.2021.80.

133 Ibid., 564.

134 Ibid., 567.

135 S. Bay United Pentecostal Church v. Newsom, 140 S. Ct. 1613, 1613 (202); Calvary Chapel Dayton Valley v. Sisolak, 140 S. Ct. 2603, 2603 (2020).

136 S. Bay United Pentecostal Church, 140 S. Ct. at 1613 (Roberts, C.J., concurring).

137 Calvary Chapel Dayton Valley, 140 S. Ct. at 2608, 2614–15 (Alito, J. dissenting).

138 Parmet, *Constitutional Contagion*, 25–26.

139 Parmet, "From the Shadows," 568–75.

140 Tandon v. Newsom, 593 U.S. 61 (2021).

141 Ibid., 62.

142 Fulton v. City of Philadelphia, 141 S. Ct. 1868, 1888 (2021).

143 Zalman Rothschild, "Individualized Exemptions, Vaccine Mandates, and the New Free Exercise Clause," *Yale Law Journal Forum* 131 (2022): 1106.

144 Jessica McDonald, "COVID-19 Vaccines Don't Contain Fetal Tissue," *Fact Check*, July 1, 2022, www.factcheck.org.

145 E.g., We the Patriots USA, Inc. v. Conn. Off. Early Childhood Dev., 76 F. 4th 130 (2nd Cir. 2023); Doe v. San Diego Unified Sch. Dist., 19 F.4th 1173 (9th Cir. 2021).

146 Bosarge, v. Edney, 669 F. Supp. 598 (S.D. Miss. 2023).

147 Lowe, 68 F.4th 706, 724 (1st Cir. 2023); M.A. on behalf of H.R. v. Rockland Cnty. Dept't of Health, 53 F.4th at 39–40; Dahl v. Bd. of Trs. of Western Mich. Univ., 15 F.4th 728, 732 (6th Cir. 2021); Fox v. Makin, No. 2:22-cv-00251-GZS, 2023 WL 5279518 (D. Me. 2023).

148 Does 1–3, 142 S. Ct. 18, 21–29 (2021)(Gorsuch, J., dissenting); Dr. A. v. Hochul, 142 S. Ct. 552 (2021) (Gorsuch, J., dissenting).

149 Does 1–3, 142 S. Ct. at 18 (Gorsuch, J. dissenting). The concern about the use of fetal tissue from abortions in vaccine research and development predates COVID. Kyle Christopher McKenna, "Use of Aborted Fetal Tissues in Vaccines and Medi-

cal Research Obscures the Value of All Human Life," *Linacre Quarterly* 85, no. 1 (2018): 13, https://doi.org/10.1177/0024363918761715.
150 For an example of a court ruling that an individual's objection to vaccination "was insufficient to establish a plausible basis from which to infer that the beliefs or practices of her religion prevent her being vaccinated," see Griffin v. Massachusetts Dep't Rev., No. 22-cv-11991-FDS, 2023 WL 4685942 (D. Ma. 2023).
151 Mark E. Wojcik, "Sincerely Held or Suddenly Held Religious Exemptions to Vaccination?," *Human Rights Magazine* 47, no. 3/4, (July 2022); Dorit Reiss, "People Lie About Their 'Religious' Objections to Vaccines. Proving It Is Hard.," *Washington Post*, October 15, 2021, www.washingtonpost.com.
152 Congressional Research Service, "The Major Questions Doctrine," Congressional Research Service, https://crsreports.congress.gov, updated November 2, 2022.
153 Nat'l Fed'n of Indep. Bus. v. Dep't of Lab., OSHA, 142 S. Ct. 661, 665-67 (2022).
154 Biden v. Missouri, 142 S. Ct. 647, 650 (2022) (per curiam).
155 Lawrence O. Gostin et al., "Vaccination Mandates—An Old Public Health Tool Faces New Challenges," *Journal of American Medicine Association* 330, no. 7 (July 2023): 589, https://doi.org/10.1001/jama.2023.11059.
156 See Jonas J. Monast, "Major Questions About the Major Questions Doctrine," *Administrative Law Review* 68 (2016): 462–70; Kevin O. Leske, "Major Questions About the 'Major Questions' Doctrine," *Michigan Journal of Environmental and Administrative Law* 5, no. 2 (2016): 488–89.
157 Ala. Ass'n of Realtors v. HHS, 141 S. Ct. 2485, 2488–90 (2021); West Virginia v. EPA, 142 S. Ct. 2587, 2612 (2022).
158 *Nat'l Fed'n of Indep. Bus.*, 142 S. Ct. at 665.
159 Ibid. (quoting *In re MCP No. 165*, 20 F.4th 264, 274 (2021) (Sutton, C. J., dissenting)).
160 Although Justice Gorsuch's concurrence in *West Virginia v. Environmental Protection Agency* did not list the protection of liberty as a factor for deciding whether to apply the major questions doctrine, he invoked the concept repeatedly, explaining that the separation of powers, which the doctrine protects, is designed to protect liberty. 142 S. Ct. at 2618–24 (Gorsuch, J., dissenting).
161 *Dobbs*, 142 S. Ct. at 2243, 2248.
162 Ibid., 2228.
163 Ibid., 2247.
164 Ibid.
165 David S. Cohen, Greer Donley, and Rachel Rebouché, "The New Abortion Battleground," *Columbia Law Review* 123, no. 1 (2023): 41, http://doi.org/10.2139/ssrn.4032931; Siegel, "Reasoning from the Body," 278–90; Nina Varsava, "Precedent, Reliance and Dobbs," *Harvard Law Review* 136, no. 7 (May 2023): 1846–47, http://doi.org/10.2139/ssrn.4152020.
166 Transcript of Oral Argument at 56, Dobbs v. Jackson Women's Health Org., 142 S. Ct. 2228 (2022) (No. 19–1392).

167 Mabel Felix, Laurie Sobel, and Alina Salganicoff, "Legal Challenges to State Abortion Bans Since the Dobbs Decision," Women's Health Policy, KFF, January 20, 2023, www.kff.org.
168 For example, compare Complaint at 25, Oklahoma Call for Reprod. Just. v. O'Connor, No. 120543 (2022) (basing challenge in part on right to "personal autonomy and bodily integrity"); Complaint at 18, Planned Parenthood Ass'n of Utah v. Utah, No. 220903886 (2022) (basing challenge in part on "right to bodily integrity"); and Complaint at 19, Johnson v. Wyoming, No. 18732 (2022) (basing challenge in party on right to "privacy and bodily integrity") with Medical Freedom in Immunizations, N.H. Rev. Stat. §141-C:1-a (2022) ("Every person has the natural, essential, and inherent right to bodily integrity, free from any threat or compulsion by government to accept an immunization."); and An Act Prohibiting the Mandatory COVID-19 Vaccination of Pennsylvania Residents by the Commonwealth, Political Subdivisions or as a Condition of Employment, P.A. S.B. 471 (2021) ("Every resident in this Commonwealth has the inalienable right to bodily integrity and should be free from any threat or compulsion that the individual must receive a COVID-19 vaccination.").
169 Complaint at 1–2, Sobel v. Cameron, No. 22-CI-005189 (2022); Complaint at 20–21, Generation to Generation v. State of Florida, No. 2022-CA-000980 (2022).
170 E.g., Individual Members of Medical Licensing Bd. Ind. v. Anonymous Plaintiff 1, 233 N.E. 3d 416 (Ind. Ct. App 2024).
171 Micah Schwartzman and Richard Schragger, "Religious Freedom and Abortion," *Iowa Law Review* 108 (2023): 2323–28.
172 Alice Miranda Ollstein, Megan Messerly, and Jessica Pipier, "The Supreme Court Dismantled Roe. States are Restoring It One by One," *Politico*, November 9, 2023, www.politico.com.
173 Sheryl Gay Stolberg, "Trump Picks R.F.K. Jr. to Be Head of Health and Human Services Dept.," *New York Times*, November 14, 2024, www.nytimes.com; Lauren Weber, "How the Anti-Vaccine Movement is Gaining Power in Statehouses," *Washington Post*, December 22, 2023, www.washingtonpost.com; "American's Largely Positive Views of Childhood Vaccines Hold Steady," *Pew Research Center*, May 16, 2023, pewresearch.org.
174 Lydia Saad, "Broader Support for Abortion Rights Continues Post-Dobbs," *Gallup*, June 14, 2023, https://news.gallup.com.
175 Zucht, 260 U.S. at 176–77; Prince, 321 U.S. at 166 n.12; Brown, 235 Cal. Rptr. 3d at 225; Love, 240 Cal. Rptr. 3d at 873 (agreeing with *Brown*, 235 Cal. Rptr. at 218); Emp. Div., 494 U.S. at 879; Workman, 419 Fed. Appx. at 351, 357; Phillips, 775 F.3d at 542, 544; Caviezel, 500 Fed. Appx. at 17, 20.
176 Ala. Ass'n of Realtors, 141 S. Ct. at 2488–90; West Virginia, 142 S. Ct. at 2612.
177 Morgan Kelly, "Political Polarization and its Echo Chambers: Surprising New, Cross-Disciplinary Perspectives from Princeton," Princeton University, December 9, 2021, www.princeton.edu; Pew Research Center, "Section 3: Political Polarization and Personal Life," *Pew Research Center*, June 12, 2014, www.pewresearch.org.

178 Greenhouse and Siegel, "Before (and After)," 2067–86; Ziegler, *After Roe*, 186–87; Medoff and Dennis, "TRAP Abortion Laws," 951.
179 Xinyuan Ye, "Exploring the Relationship Between Political Partisanship and COVID-19 Vaccination Rate," *Journal of Public Health* 45, no. 1 (March 2023): 91, https://doi.org/10.1093/pubmed/fdab364.
180 E.g., Martin Pengelly, "Fox News Host Tucker Carlson Compares Vaccine Mandates to 'Nazi Experiments,'" *The Guardian*, January 22, 2022, www.theguardian.com.
181 Ron DeSantis, "Governor Ron DeSantis Signs Legislation to Protect Florida Jobs," November 18, 2021, www.flgov.com.
182 Robert L. Tsai and Mary Zeigler, "Abortion Politics and the Rise of Movement Jurists," *UC Davis Law Review* 57 (2024): 2149, https://ssrn.com/abstract=4492053.
183 Andrew Koppelman, "The Anti-Vax Tribalism of Republican Judges," *The Hill*, April 8, 2023, https://thehill.com.
184 Sherry F. Colb and Michael C. Dorf, "Mandating Nature's Course," *Cornell Legal Studies Research Paper 23-20* (September 14, 2023): 9.
185 Ibid., 42.
186 Edward P. Richards, "A Historical Review of the State Police Powers and their Relevance to the COVID-19 Pandemic of 2020," *National Security Law & Policy* 11, no. 1 (2020): 95.
187 *Whole Women's Health*, 579 U.S. at 624–27.
188 Wendy E. Parmet and Jeremy Paul, "Post-Truth Won't Set Us Free: Health Law, Patient Autonomy, and the Rise of the Infodemic," in *COVID-19 and the Law: Disruption, Impact and Legacy*, ed. I. Glenn Cohen et al., (Cambridge: Cambridge Univ. Press, 2023), 63–69.
189 Greenhouse and Siegel, "Before (and After)," 2070–72, 2084–86; Ziegler, *After Roe*, 186–87; Medoff and Dennis, "TRAP Abortion Laws," 951; Aziza Ahmed, "Abortion Experts," *University of Chicago Legal Forum* 2022, no. 1 (2023): 12.
190 Grossman, *Choose Your Medicine*, 145.
191 All. for Hippocratic Med., 78 F.4th 210, 245 (5th Cir. 2023), rev'd 602 S. Ct. ___, 2024 WL 2964140 (June 13, 2024).
192 Ibid.
193 Amy Schoenfeld Walker et al., "Are Abortion Pills Safe? Here's the Evidence," *New York Times*, April 7, 2023, www.nytimes.com.
194 All. for Hippocratic Med., 2023 WL 5266026 at *46–47 (Ho, J., concurring).
195 Food and Drug Admin. v. Alliance for Hippocratic Medicine, nos. 23–235, 23–236, 602 U.S. 367 (June 13, 2024).
196 Tom Nichols, *The Death of Expertise: The Campaign Against Established Knowledge and Why It Matters* (New York: Oxford University Press, 2017), 5–7, 27, 217–18.
197 The women's health movement has also questioned the role of medical authority. See Grossman, *Choose Your Medicine*, 145.
198 Parmet and Paul, "Post-Truth Won't Set Us Free," 61.
199 Oreskes and Conway, "From Anti-Government to Anti-Science," 111–13. For a critique of the claim that there has been a populist turn against science and an

argument that "science" itself is more divided than many claim, see Jacob Hale Russell and Dennis Patterson, "Post-Truth and the Rhetoric of 'Following the Science,'" *Critical Review* 35, no. 1–2 (August 10, 2023), https://doi.org/10.1080/089138 11.2023.2231782.

200 Jeff Tollefson, "Inside the US Supreme Court's War on Science," *Nature*, September 14, 2022, www.nature.com.
201 State v. Zurawski, no. 23–0623, 2024 WL 278913* 1 (Tex. May 31, 2024).
202 E.g., *We the Patriots USA, Inc.*, 76 F.4th at 153–55.
203 In *Dobbs*, the Supreme Court rejected the argument that abortion bans violate the Equal Protection Clause by discriminating against women. 142 S. Ct. at 2235 (citing *Geduldig*, 417 U.S. 284 496 n.20 (1974)).
204 Yvonne Lindgren, "Trump's Angry White Women: Motherhood, Nationalism and Abortion," *Hofstra Law Review* 48, no. 1 (2019): 27–31; Erika Bachiochi, "Embodied Equality: Debunking Equal Protection Arguments for Abortion Rights," *Harvard Journal of Law & Public Policy* 34, no. 3 (2011): 898.
205 McDonald, "COVID-19 Vaccines." E.g., *We the Patriots, Inc.*, at 142; *Lowe*, 68 F.4th at 724; M.A., 53 F.4th at 39–40.
206 Raj Mathur, "COVID-19 Vaccination and Fertility: Fighting Misinformation," *Obstetrics, Gynaecology and Reproductive Medicine* 33, no. 7 (2023): 203, https://doi.org/10.1016/j.ogrm.2023.04.004.
207 Lunna Lopes et al., "KFF Health Misinformation Tracking Poll," *KFF*, August 22, 2023, www.kff.org.
208 Parris Diaz et al., "Fear About Adverse Effect on Fertility is a Major Cause of COVID-19 Vaccine Hesitancy in the United States," *Andrologia* 54, no. 4 (May 2022): 1, https://doi.org/10.1111/and.14361.
209 Stephanie Alice Baker and Michael James Walsh, "'A Mother's Intuition: It's Read and We Have to Believe in It': How the Maternal is Used to Promote Vaccine Refusal on Instagram," *Information, Community & Society* 26, no. 8 (2023), 1675–79, https://doi.org/10.1080/1369118X.2021.2021269.
210 Jennifer A. Reich, "Neoliberal Mothering and Vaccine Refusal: Imagined Gated Communities and the Privilege of Choice," *Gender and Society* 28, no. 5 (October 2014): 679–704, https://doi.org/10.1177/0891243214532711.
211 Ibid.; Darryn Wellstead, "Narratives of Mothers' Medical Experiences on the Internet: A Challenge to Medical Dominance," in *From Band-Aids to Scalpels: Motherhood Experiences in/of Medicine*, ed. Rohini Bannerjee and Karim Mukhida (Demeter Press, 2021), 137–46, https://doi.org/10.2307/j.ctv1nj3505.
212 Reich, "Neoliberal Mothering."
213 Ibid.

5

Trans Disabled Inclusion

Disability Rights Include Trans Disabled People

CLAUDIA CENTER AND VICTORIA RODRÍGUEZ-ROLDÁN

Across the United States, and at dramatically escalating rates, legislators are proposing and passing punitive laws that discriminate against transgender people, particularly trans children and youth.[1] A large proportion of these proposals seek to limit or ban access to gender-affirming care for trans minors and to limit such care for trans adults. Increasingly, these bills seek to single out and deny care to trans people who may have other disabilities such as depression, anxiety, ADHD, and autism. The reasoning underlying these proposals intertwines anti-trans animus and ableism. First, the proposals posit that individuals who identify as trans or as having gender dysphoria are mistaken and are actually experiencing obsessions or delusions caused by other mental conditions (the Ohio legislature used the term "psychopathology"). Thus, trans people with disabilities should be directed, if anywhere at all, toward services to control or cure their purportedly distorted thinking and not to gender-affirming care. Second, these proposals presume that trans people with mental disabilities do not have the legal or mental capacity to make decisions about their own health care, including gender-affirming care.

Even when laws do not explicitly target trans people with disabilities, state officials assert the same ableist reasoning in litigation defending anti-trans laws. According to the testimony of expert witnesses hired by the states, the existence of other disabilities means that disabled trans people should not access gender care because trans people with disabilities are not truly trans and/or do not have the mental or legal capacity to decide to access gender care. These experts further argue that the continuance of mental disabilities after transition means that gender care was not appropriate.[2]

The impact of these anti-trans and ableist laws and statements is great. Many trans people, including trans youth, also have other disabilities. This congruence occurs in part due to the experience of living as a trans person in our society. These experiences can cause trans people to acquire disabilities such as PTSD, depression, and anxiety. Further, for reasons that are not fully understood, there is a correlation between being trans and having disabilities such as ADHD and/or autism. Ableist anti-trans regulations further marginalize, penalize, and erase the lived experiences of trans disabled people. Unsurprisingly, trans disabled people frequently report encountering ableist bias and discrimination when seeking gender-affirming care.

For trans disabled people, the onslaught of anti-trans and ableist laws compound existing barriers to care. Many trans disabled people live in areas of the country with little to no access to gender-affirming care. These areas include states like Indiana, Kentucky, and Tennessee, which share borders and now have regulations in effect that limit or bar such care.[3] Traveling to access care requires trans disabled people—people who disproportionately live below the poverty line—to spend scarce time and money. Those who rely on Medicaid to cover medical expenses cannot use this coverage across state lines.

Health care facilities and equipment are often inaccessible to wheelchair users.[4] Many fail to make the legally required adjustments needed by some disabled people, such as providing a sign language interpreter, providing information in plain language, or working effectively with a disabled person's supporter. Further, studies show that a large majority of health care providers hold ableist attitudes toward people with disabilities, believing that people with significant disabilities have a "worse" quality of life.[5] Many providers are not confident about their ability to serve disabled patients appropriately.[6] Some providers demonstrate bias in their treatment of autistic patients.[7]

These multifaceted access barriers function as a form of de facto regulation, limiting further the ability of trans disabled people to access gender care. Living without gender-affirming care can disrupt education and employment, exacerbate trauma and poverty, worsen existing disabilities, and cause new disabilities.

The new laws and many of the long-standing access barriers violate the Americans with Disabilities Act (ADA) and Section 1557 of the Affordable Care Act, laws that prohibit discrimination in health care based on actual or perceived disabilities and, in the case of Section 1557, gender. These laws cover trans people with physical or mental disabilities, protecting trans people not only with gender dysphoria[8] but also those with I/DD (intellectual/developmental disability), including autistic trans people and trans people with ADHD, trans people with mental health disabilities, trans people who use wheelchairs, trans people who are blind, trans people who are deaf, and trans people who have other or multiple disabilities. These trans disabled people include youth, immigrants, indigent people, rural people, and people under guardianship or conservatorship.

The disability rights movement can and must do more to include and support the rights and needs of trans disabled people as we encounter, navigate, and battle the latest waves of anti-trans rhetoric, laws, and policies. Disability rights organizations must come out publicly against ableist and anti-trans laws and policies and educate their members on the virulent ableism that infuses anti-trans measures. A statement recently issued by members of the Consortium for Constituents with Disabilities is a helpful example.[9] Disability rights advocates must commit to greater and more intentional collaboration with the trans rights movement to advance our shared values, interests, and experiences.

What Is Gender Dysphoria and What Is Gender-Affirming Care?

The National Center for Transgender Equality defines the term "transgender" (of which "trans" is a shorthand version) as someone whose gender identity is different from that with which they were assigned at birth.[10] "Cisgender" is the term for someone who identifies with the gender they were assigned at birth, which describes the large majority of the population.

"Gender dysphoria" is a clinical term and a diagnosis listed in the American Psychiatric Association's Diagnostic and Statistical Manual DSM-5-TR, which is the major compilation of mental health diagnoses utilized by health care professionals in the United States. In the words of the DSM-5-TR, gender dysphoria is "[a] marked incongruence between one's experienced/expressed gender and natal gender of at least 6 months in duration."[11]

Many transgender people, though not all, experience gender dysphoria. An integral reason why gender dysphoria may be defined as a disability by advocates and trans patients is that it can be fundamentally disabling due to the emotional distress it causes. As the DSM states, the condition is associated with clinically significant distress or impairment in social, school, or other important areas of functioning.[12] This distress worsens when authorities regulate bodies through laws banning gender-affirming care.

"Gender-affirming care" is the catch-all phrase encompassing the medical treatment that is accepted as the gold standard by the medical community for gender dysphoria. It means the use of medical treatment to help the person's physical secondary and primary sex characteristics come into congruence with their gender identity. For trans minors, gender-affirming care typically begins at or before puberty with medications referred to as "hormone blockers" or "puberty blockers," which delay puberty and the appearance of secondary sex characteristics that typically appear at puberty.[13] Puberty blockers play an important role for trans children and youth because they allow the child to delay or avoid acquiring secondary sex characteristics associated with the sex with which the child patient is discordant. These characteristics often heighten gender dysphoria and can be difficult or infeasible to change once they exist.[14] Hormone blockers are reversible in that they can be discontinued and the patient will enter the puberty associated with their original assigned sex.

Gender-affirming hormone therapy induces masculine or feminine secondary sex characteristics to help better align the body with an individual's gender identity. For some trans people, gender-affirming care includes certain surgeries, such as mastectomy for breast removal, breast augmentation, or, in the case of adults, genital surgeries to make one's primary sex characteristics match their gender identity.

Although the appropriateness and efficacy of gender-affirming care for minors with gender dysphoria is hotly contested by anti-trans lawmakers and their expert witnesses, such care is part of evidence-based standards of care accepted by all major medical organizations in the United States and recognized as medically appropriate and necessary for some transgender children.[15]

The siege of proposed and enacted anti-trans laws banning gender-affirming care to trans minors, and limiting or banning such care to trans people of all ages, seeks to regulate and control trans bodies and minds through the omission and criminalization of care.

The Correlation Between Being Trans and Having Other Disabilities

Among people who are transgender, there is a higher likelihood of having a disability. In the 2015 U.S. Trans Survey performed by the National Center for Transgender Equality,[16] respondents reported identifying as disabled at a rate of 39 percent.[17] For comparison, the U.S. Census Bureau reported that 15 percent of people in the United States have a disability.[18] More than 20 percent of respondents to the Trans Survey reported having difficulty doing errands alone due to reasons of disability, versus 6 percent of the general population. Thirty percent of respondents reported having difficulty making major decisions due to a disability. About one in ten reported receiving disability income from the Social Security Administration, a status requiring a significant impairment in the ability to work. Academic and medical studies find similar results, particularly for autism, ADHD, and mental health disabilities such as PTSD and major depressive disorder.[19] This correlation or overlap of statuses and identities is well known in the trans and disability communities.[20]

One obvious source or cause of the correlation is that being trans can itself be disabling, simply by virtue of how society treats and has treated trans people, both historically and in the present. Trans people have historically faced very high amounts of discrimination, harassment, and mistreatment at all levels and facets of society throughout recent history, up to and including the anti-trans onslaught of legislation and political rhetoric we have seen in many states across the country. For example, the 2021 National School Climate Survey performed by GLSEN reported that transgender students experienced the most hostile school climates compared to their cis LGBQ peers.[21] More than 45 percent of trans students reported missing school due to safety concerns compared to 23.5 percent of cis LGBQ+ students.[22] Similarly, the Williams Institute at UCLA School of Law found that almost half of transgender respondents experienced discrimination in the workplace based on their transgender status, and more than 40 percent reported experiencing verbal harassment in workplaces due to their transgender status.[23]

It is therefore logical and to be expected that a population that undergoes such extreme levels of stigmatized mistreatment by society will experience higher levels of emotional distress, manifested in grim figures such as the fact that 41 percent of transgender respondents in the Trans Survey reported having attempted suicide at one point or other in their lives. This manifests by extension in the acquiring of mental health disabilities. The experience of being trans in American society can be described as inherently disabling. There is a distinct correlation where transgender people are much more likely to experience disability, in large part because of the mistreatment of the world around them against them.

But the effects of discrimination and harassment are likely not a complete explanation for the overlap between trans people and people with disabilities. People with I/DD, including autistic people and people with ADHD, disproportionately identify as transgender or nonbinary. Self-advocacy organizations, including the Autistic Self Advocacy Network and the Autistic Women and Nonbinary Network, identify the needs of their trans constituents as an increasing concern and priority.[24] Trans autistic authors have published resource guides for teens and adults and their supporters and providers.[25]

Some correlations with disabilities exist without complete explanations. For example, lawyers are much more likely than the general population to be diagnosed with mood and anxiety disorders found in the DSM.[26] One explanation may be the negative effects and experiences of law school and lawyering, but this is likely not a complete explanation. It may be that, for reasons we do not completely understand, the same type of person who gravitates toward law school and the legal profession is also more likely to have mental health diagnoses. This does not mean we should exclude people with disabilities from law school; instead we should make the profession inclusive and welcoming.

Similarly, while we may not have a complete explanation for why trans people are more likely to be autistic or to have ADHD or mental health conditions, disability and trans advocates should continue to fight for the rights of trans people with disabilities to access the gender care they need.[27] Disability organizations that focus on the targeted disabilities—intellectual and developmental disabilities, including or specifically autism and/or ADHD, and mental health conditions such as depression and anxiety—should advocate publicly for the rights of their trans constituents who may need to access care.

Discrimination Faced by Trans People with Disabilities

Trans people with disabilities—including mental health, intellectual, and developmental disabilities—face distinct forms of discrimination and challenges. One of the most common forms of discrimination is the denial of transition-related and gender-affirming health care to disabled trans people based on the presumptions that their disability is somehow causing their trans status and/or that their disability impairs their ability to consent to such health care.

People with disabilities should be presumed competent to make their own decisions about their health care (with supports where necessary). As discussed herein, supports may include plain language, visual aids, supported decision-making, patience, and trauma awareness. The denial of gender-affirming care to trans disabled people is a form of disability discrimination against the transgender patient. It is a particularly harmful form of discrimination, as mental health generally deteriorates with the lack of access to gender-affirming health care. There are many anecdotal instances of disabled trans people who have been refused access to gender-affirming care based on depression, other mental health disabilities, autism, or another type of I/DD.

Refusing gender-affirming care based on mental health or I/DD diagnosis status, without clear and convincing evidence that the person is incapable of making an informed decision, even with supports, violates the Americans with Disabilities Act and Section 1557 of the Affordable Care Act, as well as constitutional principles of autonomy and relevant applicable state disability discrimination laws such as the Maryland Human Rights Act.

This presumption of lack of competence is manifested also in the context of guardianship and conservatorship applications, where we have seen anecdotal cases in the community of unsupportive anti-trans parents who will weaponize their adult child's disability as a tool to seek a guardianship or conservatorship and prevent them from transitioning, leaving it up to a potentially biased court to decide the case. When this occurs, the unsupportive parent seeks to be legally deputized to regulate their adult child's mind, body, and gender identity. Disability and trans rights advocates should propose and support state laws that ban the use of LGBTQ status or the receipt of gender-affirming care as any sort of criterion for the granting of a guardianship or conservatorship for a disabled adult.

Virtually every ban on conversion therapy focuses solely on people under the age of 18, leaving some trans disabled adults vulnerable to this abusive practice. The scope of these laws responds to the fact that people under 18 can be legally coerced by parents or guardians to submit to therapy, whereas most adults can make such a legal decision on their own. However, these statutes leave out adults who are under guardianship or conservatorship because of their disabilities, creating a group of disabled adults who can be legally coerced into forms of anti-trans conversion therapy. The District of Columbia is the only jurisdiction in the United States that has addressed this gap by banning conversion therapy for adults under guardianship.[28]

These forms of disability discrimination specific to trans disabled people exacerbate existing barriers to health care faced by people with disabilities. Health care providers often do not understand their obligations under the ADA and are likely to be biased against people with disabilities.[29] They often fail to provide legally required effective communication for people with disabilities, including alternative formats for blind people and appropriate sign language interpreting for deaf people (including integrated captions and/or sign language interpreting in video telemedicine).[30] There are few providers, including mental health counselors, who are fluent in sign language.[31] Provider websites and appointment portals often have barriers for people who use screen readers. Medical offices and equipment are not accessible.[32] Transit and hotels are also difficult and inaccessible.[33]

Providers have little awareness about using plain language or implementing appropriate supports for patients with intellectual, developmental, and psychiatric disabilities. Such supports might include the use of plain language at accessible reading levels (e.g., a person might need text or spoken words at a fourth-grade reading level) and visual aids. They can include the use of supported decision-making, which is a method of allowing adults with disabilities to make their own decisions with the support of trusted advisers selected by the disabled adult.[34] Needed support may simply be patience and trauma awareness.

Lawmakers Single Out Trans People with Disabilities

State law bans on gender-affirming care regulate trans bodies by blocking access to medications and other treatments. Legislatures that enacted these bans have included pseudo-scientific legislative "findings" that emphasize the correlation between being trans and having other disabilities such as mental health diagnoses or autism. These findings weaponize this correlation to dispute the legitimacy of trans status and even the existence of trans people. For example, Ohio and Arkansas enacted laws including this finding:

> Scientific studies show that individuals struggling with distress at identifying with their biological sex often have already experienced psychopathology, which indicates these individuals should be encouraged to seek mental health care services before undertaking any hormonal or surgical intervention.[35]

Along the same lines, Georgia's legislature enacted a law finding that "[g]ender dysphoria is often comorbid with other mental health and developmental conditions, including autism spectrum disorder."[36]

Similarly, in Illinois, Representative Thomas Morrison introduced a bill that would ban gender-affirming care to people under 18. The bill includes 15 pages of "findings," including statements from anti-trans medical providers and academics averring that mental health problems are causing people to become trans:

> The idea that mental health problems, including suicidality, are caused by gender dysphoria rather than the other way around (i.e., mental health and personality issues cause a vulnerability to experience gender dysphoria) is currently popular and politically correct. It is, however, unproven and as likely to be false as true. [quoting J. Michael Bailey, Professor of Psychology at Northwestern University, and Dr. Raymond Blanchard, former psychologist in the Adult Gender Identity Clinic of Toronto's Centre for Addiction and Mental Health] . . .
>
> Mounting evidence over the last decade points to increased rates of autism spectrum disorders (ASD) and autism traits among children and adults with gender dysphoria, or incongruence between a person's experi-

enced or expressed gender and the gender assigned to them at birth. . . . It is possible that some of the psychological characteristics common in children with ASD—including cognitive deficits, tendencies toward obsessive preoccupations, or difficulties learning from other people—complicate the formation of gender identity. [quoting from the American College of Pediatricians[37]] . . .

[O]ur central contention is that transgender children don't exist. [quoting two UK academics].[38]

These types of statements seek to create a "scientific" counternarrative against the provision of gender-affirming care to trans bodies. In Arkansas, the law permits malpractice actions against a health care provider for any negative effects from gender-affirming care provided to a minor. Actions can be brought up to 15 years after the person turns 18. The provider may defend themselves, but only if they can demonstrate a number of elements, including certifications "that the minor suffered from no other mental health concerns, including without limitation depression, eating disorders, autism, attention deficit hyperactivity disorder, intellectual disability, or psychotic disorders."[39] A similar law was introduced in North Carolina permitting medical malpractice claims for gender-affirming care provided to a minor unless the provider can show "that the minor suffered from no other mental health concerns or conditions, including depression, eating disorders, autism, attention deficit hyperactivity disorder, intellectual disability, or psychotic disorders."[40]

Missouri's Attorney General issued rules—later rescinded—that prohibited the provision of or referral to gender-affirming care unless the patient "received a full psychological or psychiatric assessment" of at least 15 sessions over 18 months to determine "whether the person has any mental health comorbidities," which must then be "treated and resolved" before lawful care can be provided.[41] Under the rules, "informed consent" required a disclosure that a study found that "[y]ouths with a history of mental health issues were especially likely to have taken steps to socially and medically transition."[42] The rules also required that the patient have received "a comprehensive screening to determine whether the patient has autism."[43]

In Ohio, the law bars physicians from providing minors with gender-affirming medical care but also prohibits mental health providers from treating minors for gender dysphoria and other issues related to transgender status "without screening [for] . . . [o]ther comorbidities that may be influencing the minor individual's gender-related condition, including depression, anxiety, attention deficit hyperactivity disorder, autism spectrum disorder, and other mental health conditions; [and] [p]hysical, sexual, mental, and emotional abuse and other traumas."[44]

At the time of this writing, the case challenging a Tennessee law is at the U.S. Supreme Court. The sponsors of that law published an op-ed stating:

> [C]hildren who say they're transgender are at least 300% more likely to have mental health issues, ranging from anxiety to depression to ADHD. There are also much higher rates of autism among children seeking to change genders. These underlying conditions should be treated before children are subjected to body-altering sex-change drugs, much less surgeries.[45]

These statements from anti-trans lawmakers communicate that disabled people—including minors with disabilities who identify as trans and who seek gender-affirming care—are not truly transgender but are actually experiencing the effects of their disabilities. They further suggest that people with disabilities lack the mental capacity to assert their gender identity. These presumptions then create a purported basis for regulations that delay or deny care to people who are both disabled and trans.

Given that the mental disabilities cited in these laws are long-lasting and often lifelong, these laws essentially prevent any gender-affirming care—and even supportive mental health care—to disabled trans people.

States defending anti–trans care bans in court similarly focus on the correlation between trans status and other disabilities and the stereotype that disabled people lack the mental or legal capacity to make their own decisions. Through their expert witnesses, these defendants argue that the existence of disabilities among trans people—including disabilities that are typically long-lasting or lifelong whatever medical or mental health care is or is not provided—is a basis for blocking access to gender-affirming care.

For example, the defense expert James Cantor, Ph.D., avers that the research is "strongly consistent with the hypothesis that mental health issues, such as Borderline Personality Disorder (BPD),[46] cause both suicidality and unstable identity formation (including gender identity confusion)."[47] He also describes a purported profile of "rapid onset gender dysphoria" in which cases "commonly appear . . . among people with autism or other mental health issues."[48] Thus, Cantor argues, "diverting distressed youth toward transition necessarily diverts youth away from receiving the psychotherapies designed for treating the issues actually causing their distress."[49]

Other defense experts similarly emphasize correlation. Paul W. Hruz, M.D., Ph.D., states that gender dysphoria "may be linked to trauma, developmental issues, or psychological comorbidities" and that the majority of trans adolescent boys "have significant mental health problems and neurocognitive comorbidities such as autism-spectrum disorder or ADHD."[50] The defense psychiatrist Sven Román likewise emphasizes the higher prevalence of autism, ADHD, depression, and other mental disabilities among trans people.[51] These experts argue that these *other* (nontrans) conditions are the "primary" or true conditions. Thus, these experts opine, mental health treatment for the "primary" condition may be appropriate but gender-affirming care is not.

These defense experts further argue that the existence of these disabilities means such trans people lack the mental or legal capacity to consent to gender-affirming care. States Hruz: "[I]ndividuals with transgender identity who also have clinical depression or other serious psychiatric comorbidity may have limited capacity to objectively weigh proposed clinical interventions with potentially irreversible consequences."[52] He also describes people seeking gender-affirming care as having an "underlying belief" that prevents informed consent, as unknown number of patients "reporting gender dysphoria suffer from mental illness(es) that complicate and may distort their judgments and perceptions of gender identity."[53]

Judges hearing challenges to the bans on gender-affirming care have criticized and discounted the testimony of Cantor, Hruz, and other state experts—but have not yet identified the ableism embedded within. In the Tennessee litigation (now at the U.S. Supreme Court), the federal trial court held that "the testimony of Dr. Cantor and Dr. Hruz is minimally persuasive given that neither of them state that they have ever diagnosed or treated a minor with gender dysphoria."[54] A federal court in North Carolina found that Dr. Hruz was not qualified to testify about gender dysphoria: "Hruz is not a psychiatrist, psychologist, or mental healthcare professional. He has never diagnosed a patient with gender dysphoria, treated gender dysphoria, treated a transgender patient, conducted any original research about gender dysphoria diagnosis or its causes, or published any scientific, peer-reviewed literature on gender dysphoria."[55] Similarly, a federal court in the Middle District of Alabama gave Cantor's testimony "very little weight" given that he had never provided care to a transgender minor under the age of 16.[56]

A federal court in the Northern District of Georgia discounted the testimony of Cantor and Hruz, noting the "inconsistency between, on the one hand, Defendants' experts' insistence on a very high threshold of evidence in the context of claims about hormone therapy's safety and benefits, and on the other hand their tolerance of a much lower threshold of evidence for [their] claims about its risks[.]"[57] In the Middle District of Florida, the court wrote:

> [A]n unspoken suggestion running just below the surface in some of the proceedings that led to adoption of the statute and rules at issue—and just below the surface in the testimony of some of the defense experts—is that transgender identity is not real, that it is made up. And so, for example, one of the defendants' experts, Dr. Paul Hruz, joined an amicus brief in another proceeding asserting transgender individuals have only a "false belief" in their gender identity—that they are maintaining a "charade" or "delusion."
>
> Dr. Hruz fended and parried questions and generally testified as a deeply biased advocate, not as an expert sharing relevant evidence-based information and opinions. I do not credit his testimony.[58]

The Florida court's reference to "delusion" comes close to naming the ableism this article seeks to surface and highlight.

These ableist assaults by anti-trans lawmakers and their experts build on and exacerbate the existing disability discrimination faced by trans people with disabilities. The disability rights community must do more to expose the ableism, intertwined with anti-trans bias, that underlies these regulations banning gender-affirming care for trans people. Disability and trans advocates should work together to raise public awareness of the ableism that is fueling attacks on trans people. Too often, media reports on anti-trans legislation and related litigation fail to report on underlying ableism.

Application of the ADA and Section 1557 to Disability Barriers to Gender-Affirming Care

The Americans with Disabilities Act and Section 1557 of the Affordable Care Act prohibit discrimination in health care on the basis of actual or perceived disabilities.[59] Federal disability nondiscrimination laws define "disability" as a "physical or mental impairment" that limits or substantially limits a major life activity. A person with a disability so defined is legally entitled to nondiscrimination and reasonable accommodation necessary to ensure equal access to important social institutions including education, employment, health care, and the government. People who are transgender may have trans-related diagnoses under the Diagnostic and Statistical Manual such as gender dysphoria; they may also have other disabilities.

Diagnoses contained in the DSM are typically considered impairments that may, depending on the facts, limit major life activities. Prior to the enactment of the ADA in 1990, several district courts had found that trans plaintiffs could plead claims of discrimination under the Rehabilitation Act, ADA's precursor statute.[60] This modest line of federal case law was disrupted by the enactment of the ADA and, two years later, the Rehabilitation Act Amendments of 1992.[61] After a hate-filled hearing dominated by then-Senator Jesse Helms,[62] featuring attacks on gay people, trans people, and people with HIV/AIDS, Congress explicitly excluded from the term "disability" a number of statuses including "gender identity disorders not resulting from physical impairments."

Since then, however, some federal courts—including the federal Fourth Circuit Court of Appeals—have construed federal disability laws to cover trans people who assert a disability based on gender dysphoria.[63] Several of these rulings reason that the language in the ADA and the Rehabilitation Act does not exclude "gender dysphoria," which did not appear in the DSM in 1990 or 1992 and has important differences from the prior "gender identity disorder" diagnosis.[64] These rulings find support in the concept of "constitutional avoidance"—that is, if trans people with disabling DSM diagnoses were excluded from the ADA and the Rehabilitation based on discriminatory animus, then it is proper to construe the statutory language in such a way as to avoid the equal protection issue raised by such a "bare desire to harm" an unpopular minority.[65]

While the question of whether gender dysphoria is a disability under the ADA and the Rehabilitation Act will continue to be reviewed by courts, trans people who have other disabilities—including ADHD, autism, depression, anxiety, and other intellectual, developmental, and mental health conditions—are plainly covered by the federal disability laws for those conditions.[66] Trans disabled people are entitled to nondiscrimination and reasonable accommodations. In other words, trans and disability rights advocates can use disability rights protections to fight back against anti-trans ableist laws and actions. Disability rights lawyers should offer their advocacy skills to support trans organizations that are fighting discriminatory laws and policies and to trans disabled constituents who are experiencing discrimination.

NOTES

1 Trans Legislation Tracker, "Tracking the Rise of Anti-Trans bills in the U.S.: The United States Has Experienced a Long Rise in Anti-Trans Legislation, Now It's Surging," https://translegislation.com; Lindsey Dawson and Jennifer Kates, "Policy Tracker: Youth Access to Gender Affirming Care and State Policy Restrictions," KFF, www.kff.org, last updated March 13, 2024.

2 While many studies show improvements in mental health status following medical transition, defense experts theorize that any improvement was due to concurrent psychotherapy and further note that people with more significant psychiatric illnesses were purportedly screened out from medical transition. See defense expert reports filed in L.W. v. Skrmetti, 3:23-cv-00376 (M.D. Tenn.): James Cantor, Ph.D. at ¶¶ 22–23, 60, 62, 69, 153; Paul W. Hruz, M.D., Ph.D. at ¶ 128 (hypothesizing that patients with significant disabilities were screened out in Turban 2020 and Tordoff 2022 studies). This argument is in tension with their emphasis on the correlation between trans and disability status and its related suggestion that other mental conditions are causing trans status.

3 See K.C. v. Individual Members of the Med. Licensing Bd. of Ind., No. 23–2366, 2024 U.S. App. LEXIS 4705, at *4 (7th Cir. Feb. 27, 2024) (staying preliminary injunction and permitting Indiana law banning gender care to minors to go into effect); Doe v. Thornbury, 75 F.4th 655, 657 (6th Cir. 2023) (refusing to lift stay and permitting Kentucky law banning gender care to minors to go into effect); L.W. v.

Skrmetti, 83 F.4th 460, 491 (6th Cir. 2023) (reverse preliminary injunctions issued in Kentucky and Tennessee and permitting Tennessee law banning gender care to minors to go into effect), *cert. granted*, United States v. Skrmetti, No. 23-477, 2024 U.S. LEXIS 2780 (June 24, 2024).

4   Nancy R. Mudrick, M.S.W., Ph.D., et al., "Presence of Accessible Equipment and Interior Elements in Primary Care Offices" (2019), https://dredf.org.
5   H Lisa I. Iezzoni et al., "Physicians' Perceptions of People with Disability and Their Health Care," 40:2 *Health Affairs* (February 2021), www.ncbi.nlm.nih.gov. Gina Kolata, "These Doctors Admit They Don't Want Patients With Disabilities," *New York Times* (October 19, 2022), www.nytimes.com (reviewing Iezzoni study and describing account of disability discrimination experienced by August Rocha, a trans disabled person who uses a wheelchair and a walker).
6   Iezzoni, "Physicians' Perceptions."
7   Dominique H. Como et al., "Examining Unconscious Bias Embedded in Provider Language Regarding Children with Autism," 22:2 *Nurs. Health Sci.* 197 (2020); Deanna Pistono, "'Above All Else, Believe Us': Advocates Say Doctors Can Show Biased Behavior Toward Autistic Adults," *Cronkite News* (March 6, 2023).
8   In 1989, Senator Jesse Helms and others successfully added an amendment to the Americans with Disabilities Act of 1990 excluding from the act's coverage a laundry list of conditions including compulsive gambling, kleptomania, pyromania, pedophilia, exhibitionism, voyeurism, sexual behavior disorders, transvestism, transsexualism, and gender identity disorders not resulting from physical impairments. See 42 U.S.C § 12211. However, a recent body of case finds that the ADA nevertheless applies to people with gender dysphoria, a subsequently developed diagnosis within the Diagnostic and Statistical Manual of Mental Disorders (DSM).
9   "Consortium for Constituents with Disabilities Members Denounce Attacks on LGBTQI+ Rights, Call for Comprehensive Nondiscrimination, Care and Accessibility Measures" (July 19, 2023), https://dredf.org, www.c-c-d.org.
10 National Center for Transgender Equality, "Understanding Transgender People: The Basics" (January 27, 2023), https://transequality.org.
11 American Psychiatric Association, DSM-5-TR (2022) at 511.
12 Ibid.
13 Secondary sex characteristics include characteristics such as breasts and softer skin for women and teenage girls and facial hair and a more muscular body for men and teenage boys.
14 See Doe v. Ladapo, No. 4:23cv114-RH-MAF, 2024 U.S. Dist. LEXIS 105334, at *89–90 (N.D. Fla. June 11, 2024) ("The choice these plaintiffs face is binary: to use GnRH agonists and cross-sex hormones, or not. It is no answer to say the evidence on the yes side is weak when the evidence on the no side is weaker or nonexistent. There is substantial and persuasive, though not conclusive, research showing favorable results from these treatments. A decision for the plaintiffs and many class members cannot wait for further or better research; the treatment decision must be made now.").

15 See, e.g., Doe v. Thornbury, No. 3:23-cv-230-DJH, 2023 U.S. Dist. LEXIS 111390, at *8–9 (W.D. Ky. June 28, 2023) (citing amicus brief of more than twenty organizations including the American Academy of Pediatrics, the American Academy of Child & Adolescent Psychiatry, the American Medical Association, the Endocrine Society, the Pediatric Endocrine Society, the Society for Adolescent Health and Medicine, and the World Professional Association for Transgender Health); Doe v. Ladapo, 29 Fla. L. Weekly Fed. D 177 (U.S. N.D. Fla. 2023) ("The overwhelming weight of medical authority supports treatment of transgender patients with GnRH agonists and cross-sex hormones in appropriate circumstances. Organizations who have formally recognized this include the American Academy of Pediatrics, American Academy of Child and Adolescent Psychiatry, American Academy of Family Physicians, American College of Obstetricians and Gynecologists, American College of Physicians, American Medical Association, American Psychiatric Association, and at least a dozen more. The record also includes statements from hundreds of professionals supporting this care. At least as shown by this record, not a single reputable medical association has taken a contrary position."); Eknes-Tucker v. Marshall, 603 F. Supp. 3d 1131, 1141 (M.D. Ala. 2022) (citing testimony that "at least twenty-two major medical associations in the United States endorse transitioning medications as well-established, evidence-based methods for treating gender dysphoria in minors"); Poe v. Labrador, No. 1:23-cv-00269-BLW, 2023 U.S. Dist. LEXIS 229332, at *16, *45 (D. Idaho Dec. 26, 2023) ("After carefully considering the voluminous evidence on this point, the Court finds that the treatment for gender dysphoria—when provided in accordance with the guidelines published by WPATH and the Endocrine Society, and which may include medical interventions such as puberty blockers, hormone therapy, and surgeries—is safe, effective, and medically necessary for some adolescents. . . . As plaintiffs' experts have explained, allowing gender dysphoric youth to go untreated can increase the risk of anxiety, depression, self-harm, and suicidality."); Koe v. Noggle, No. 1:23-CV-2904-SEG, 2023 U.S. Dist. LEXIS 147770, at *56–57 (N.D. Ga. Aug. 20, 2023) ("Defendants' characterization of hormone therapy significantly understates the benefits with which it is associated. These principally include improved mental health outcomes caused by the relief of distress including but not limited to reduced suicidality and self-harm, reduced anxiety and depression, and improved social and psychological functioning. Such benefits are supported by research as well as the extensive clinical experience of Plaintiffs' experts.").

16 The NCTE performed a new iteration of the survey in 2022 but has yet to publish the final report of this survey.

17 S. E. James et al., "The Report of the 2015 U.S. Transgender Survey, National Center for Transgender Equality" (2016), 57.

18 Ibid.

19 Jennifer R. Pharr and Kavita Batra, "Physical and Mental Disabilities Among the Gender-Diverse Population Using the Behavioral Risk Factor Surveillance System,

BRFSS (2017–2019): A Propensity-Matched Analysis," 9:10 *Healthcare (Basel)* 1285 (Sept. 2021).
20 Gabriel Arkles, "Right-Wing Attacks on Trans Health Care Rely on Ableist Logic: To Resist State-level Attacks on Trans Health Care, We Also Need to Tackle Ableism," *Truthout*, https://truthout.org.
21 Joseph C. Kosciw et al., "The 2021 National School Climate Survey: The Experiences of Lesbian, Gay, Bisexual, Transgender, and Queer Youth in Our Nation's Schools," GLSEN (2002), 84–86, 93 and figs. 3.10, 3.11, 3.12.
22 Ibid., 90 and fig. 3.14.
23 Brad Sears et al., "LGBTQ People's Experiences of Workplace Discrimination and Harassment," Williams Institute (September 2021), https://williamsinstitute.law.ucla.edu.
24 See, e.g., Autistic Self Advocacy Network, "A Self-Advocate's Guide to Gender Affirming Health Care" (June 2024), https://autisticadvocacy.org. Author Victoria Rodriguez-Roldan was a board member of both of these organizations until recently.
25 Yenn Purkis and Wenn B. Lawson, *The Autistic Trans Guide to Life* (2021); Yenn Purkis and Sam Rose, *The Awesome Autistic Guide for Trans Teens* (2022); Finn V. Gratton, *Supporting Transgender Autistic Youth and Adults* (2019).
26 See, e.g., Matthew S. Thiese, PhD, MSPH, et al., "Depressive Symptoms and Suicidal Ideation Among Lawyers and Other Law Professionals," 63:5 *Journal of Occupational and Environmental Medicine* 381 (May 2021); Patrick R. Krill, JD, LLM, et al., "The Prevalence of Substance Use and Other Mental Health Concerns Among American Attorneys," 10:1 *Journal of Addiction Medicine* 46 (Jan./February 2016), https://journals.lww.com; see also American Bar Association, "Depression" ("Some studies suggest that lawyers experience depression at higher rates than the general population. While there's no way to determine exactly why this occurs, demanding schedules and other stresses inherent in the practice of law may contribute to higher rates of depression."), www.americanbar.org.
27 See CCD; "ASAN Condemns Restrictions on Gender-Affirming Care" (March 22, 2023), https://autisticadvocacy.org; see also Katie Jo Glaves and Leah Kolman, "Gender Diversity in Autistic Clients: an Ethical Perspective," 14 *Front Psychiatry* 1244107 (September 2023) ("the onus is on us, as professionals, to make sure we are fostering autonomy in persons with developmental or intellectual disabilities"); Marianthi Kourti, ed., *Working with Autistic Transgender and Non-Binary People: Research, Practice, and Experience* (Jessica Kingsley Publishers, 2021).
28 See D.C. Law 22–247.
29 Lisa I. Iezzoni et al., "US Physicians' Knowledge About the Americans with Disabilities Act and Accommodation of Patients with Disability," 41:1 *Health Affairs* 96 (2022), www.healthaffairs.org (abstract); Iezzoni et al., "Physicians' Perceptions"; Kolata, "These Doctors."
30 28 C.F.R. § 35.160; 45 C.F.R. § 92.102; U.S. Department of Health and Human Services & U.S. Department of Justice, "Guidance on Nondiscrimination in Tele-

31 health" (July 2022), www.hhs.gov/civil-rights/for-individuals/disability/guidance-on-nondiscrimination-in-telehealth/index.html.
31 See Tugg v. Towey, 864 F. Supp. 1201, 1211 (S.D. Fla. 1994) (granting preliminary injunction requiring defendants to include mental health counselors "with sign language ability" and who possess "an understanding of the mental health needs of the deaf community").
32 Mudrick, "Presence."
33 Kristen L. Popham et al., "Disabling Travel: Quantifying the Harm of Inaccessible Hotels to Disabled People," 55 *Colum. Human Rts. L. Rev. F.* 1 (2023), https://blogs.law.columbia.edu; "DREDF and TLDEF File Claims Against TSA for Discrimination Against Transgender Couple with Disabilities" (March 21, 2023), https://dredf.org.
34 Support without Courts, https://supportwithoutcourts.org; ACLU, Supported Decision-Making Resource Library, www.aclu.org.
35 OH HB 68, sec. 2(D) (2023), https://legiscan.com/OH/text/HB68/id/2863440; AR 1570, sec. 2(4) (2021), www.arkleg.state.ar.us; see also GA SB141, sec. 1(4) (2023), https://legiscan.com/GA/text/SB141/id/2692266 (same "finding").
36 GA SB 140, sec. 1(2) (2023), https://legiscan.com/GA/text/SB140/id/2754936.
37 The American College of Pediatricians, founded in 2002, is a socially conservative advocacy group of pediatricians and other health care professionals in the United States. The group's primary focus is advocating against abortion rights and against rights for gay, queer, and transgender people.
38 IL HB 3515, sec. 1(15)(d), (20) (2019), www.ilga.gov/legislation/101/HB/PDF/10100HB3515lv.pdf.
39 AR SB 199, sec. 1 (2023) (adding Arkansas Code Title 16, Chapter 114, sec. 16-114-403), www.arkleg.state.ar.us.
40 NC SB 560 (2023), https://legiscan.com/NC/text/S560/id/2770823.
41 Emergency Rule, Tit. 15, Div. 60, Ch. 17, https://ago.mo.gov. These rules were blocked by the state court, www.aclu-mo.org/sites/default/files/order.pdf, and then subsequently rescinded via notation: "This emergency rule terminated effective May 16, 2023."
42 Emergency Rule.
43 Emergency Rule.
44 OH HB 68, sec. 1.
45 "Tennessee Senate and House Leaders: Why We Defend Gender-Affirming Care Ban," *Tennessean Online*, August 7, 2023 (Senator Jack Johnson is the Senate majority leader and Representative William Lamberth is the House majority leader in the Tennessee General Assembly), https://drupal-files-delivery.s3.amazonaws.com/public/2023-06/Boe-v-Marshall-2023-05-19-Cantor-Report.pdf.
46 The diagnosis of "borderline personality disorder" is controversial and has been often criticized for its unclear meaning and its inconsistent, uneven, stigmatizing, and punitive application. Critics contend that many people with this diagnosis should instead receive a trauma-based diagnosis.

47 Report of Cantor filed in L.W. v. Skrmetti, 3:23-cv-00376 (M.D. Tenn.) at ¶ 152.
48 Cantor at ¶ 136.
49 Cantor at ¶ 152; see also Cantor at ¶ 24 (citing with approval guideline that puberty blockers and hormones should not be provided unless needed "after [any] other psychiatric symptoms have ceased").
50 Report of Hruz filed in L.W. v. Skrmetti, 3:23-cv-00376 (M.D. Tenn.) at ¶¶ 61, 128 (2011 De Vries); see also Hruz at ¶¶ 128 (2019–2020 Turban) (reviewing critique of study relying on survey tool for failing to "control for comorbid psychiatric illness" and underplaying "confounding effects of co-existing mental health problems"); 2022 Tordoff (critiquing study where patients had depression and anxiety before and after gender-affirming care), 146 (noting children with a history of psychiatric illness, children with mental developmental disabilities, and children on the autistic spectrum are "disproportionately affected by gender discordance").
51 Report of Román filed in L.W. v. Skrmetti, 3:23-cv-00376 (M.D. Tenn.) at ¶¶ 2, 17, 30 and table 1.
52 Hruz at ¶ 109.
53 Hruz at ¶¶ 110, 139.
54 L.W. v. Skrmetti, No. 3:23-cv-00376, 2023 U.S. Dist. LEXIS 111424, at *45 (M.D. Tenn. June 28, 2023). The trial court blocked the law but a divided panel of the Sixth Circuit Court of Appeals later let the ban go into effect. L.W. v. Skrmetti, 83 F.4th 460 (6th Cir. 2023).
55 Kadel v. Folwell, 620 F. Supp. 3d 339, 364 (M.D.N.C. 2022).
56 Eknes-Tucker v. Marshall, 603 F. Supp. 3d 1131, 1142 (M.D. Ala. 2022).
57 Koe v. Noggle, No. 1:23-CV-2904-SEG, 2023 U.S. Dist. LEXIS 147770, at *63 (N.D. Ga. Aug. 20, 2023).
58 Doe v. Ladapo, 29 Fla. L. Weekly Fed. D 177 and n.8 (U.S. N.D. Fla. 2023).
59 Section 1557 also prohibits discrimination based on gender.
60 Blackwell v. United States Dep't of Treasury, 639 F. Supp. 289, 290 (1986) (finding that plaintiff stated a claim under the Rehabilitation Act, noting that the defendant "acknowledges that transvestitism is recognized by the American Psychiatric Association as a mental disorder."); see also Blackwell v. United States Dep't of Treasury, 656 F. Supp. 713, 715 (1986), *vacated on other grounds*, 830 F.2d 1183 (1987) ("[W]hile homosexuals are not handicapped it is clear that transvestites are, because many experience strong social rejection in the work place as a result of their mental ailment made blatantly apparent by their cross-dressing life-style."); Doe v. U.S. Postal Service, Doe v. USPS, No. 84-3296, 1985 U.S. Dist. LEXIS 18959 (June 12, 1985) (plaintiff's allegations stated a claim where she alleged that she was handicapped by reason of her "medically and psychologically established need for gender reassignment surgery" as "impairment" can be any mental or psychological disorder). Ultimately, the plaintiff in *Blackwell* did not prevail. Following discovery, the court concluded that the adverse action occurred because the interviewer found the plaintiff's "apparent homosexual aspect"—and not his transgender status—undesirable. *Blackwell*, 656 F. Supp. at 715.

61 42 U.S.C. § 12211(b)(1); 106 Stat. 4344, 102–569 (H.R. 5482) (amending statute now at 29 U.S. Code § 705).

62 135 Cong Rec S 10765 (Sept. 7, 1989).

63 Williams v. Kincaid, 45 F.4th 759 (4th Cir. 2022), *cert. denied*, 143 S. Ct. 2414 (2023) (holding that the plaintiff "has plausibly alleged that gender dysphoria does not fall within the ADA's exclusion for 'gender identity disorders not resulting from physical impairments.'"); Blatt v. Cabela's Retail, Inc., No. 5:14-cv-04822, 2017 U.S. Dist. LEXIS 75665, 2017 WL 2178123 (E.D. Pa. May 18, 2017) (interpreting the statutory exclusions narrowly such that they do not "exclude from ADA coverage disabling conditions that persons who identity with a different gender may have—such as Blatt's gender dysphoria, which substantially limits her major life activities of interacting with others, reproducing, and social and occupational functioning"); Doe v. Mass. Dep't of Corr., No. 17-12255-RGS, 2018 U.S. Dist. LEXIS 99925, at *17–18 (D. Mass. June 14, 2018); Doe v. Triangle Doughnuts, LLC, 472 F. Supp. 3d 115, 134–35 (E.D. Pa. 2020); cf. Parker v. Strawser Construction, Inc., 307 F. Supp. 3d 744 (S.D. Ohio 2018) (holding that plaintiff's "disability claims under the ADA . . . are foreclosed[,]" because the plaintiff failed to "allege that her gender dysphoria was caused by a physical impairment or that gender dysphoria always results from a physical impairment"); Doe v. Northrop Grumman Systems Corp., 418 F. Supp. 3d 921 (N.D. Ala. 2019) (holding the lack of "'clear allegations[ ]' that plaintiff's gender dysphoria results 'from a physical impairment[ ]' . . . is fatal to plaintiff's ADA claim").

64 Williams v. Kincaid, 45 F.4th at 767 ("[T]he definition of gender dysphoria differs dramatically from that of the now-rejected diagnosis of 'gender identity disorder.' Rather than focusing exclusively on a person's gender identity, the DSM-5 defines 'gender dysphoria' as the 'clinically significant distress' felt by some of those who experience 'an incongruence between their gender identity and their assigned sex.'"); *Doe v. Mass. Dep't of Corr.*, 2018 U.S. Dist. LEXIS 99925, at *17–18 ("In contrast to DSM-IV, which had defined 'gender identity disorder' as characterized by a 'strong and persistent cross gender-identification' and a 'persistent discomfort' with one's sex or 'sense of inappropriateness' in a given gender role, the diagnosis of GD in DSM-V requires attendant disabling physical symptoms, in addition to manifestations of clinically significant emotional distress.").

65 Williams v. Kincaid, 45 F.4th at 772; Blatt, 2017 U.S. Dist. LEXIS 75665, at *6; Doe v. Triangle Doughnuts, LLC, 472 F. Supp. 3d at 134.

66 28 CFR § 35.108(d)(2)(iii) ("[I]t should easily be concluded that . . . Intellectual disability substantially limits brain function; . . . Autism substantially limits brain function; . . . Major depressive disorder, bipolar disorder, post-traumatic stress disorder, traumatic brain injury, obsessive compulsive disorder, and schizophrenia each substantially limits brain function."); Glaser v. Gap Inc., 994 F. Supp. 2d 569, 575 (S.D.N.Y. 2014) (autistic employee); Adams v. Crestwood Med. Ctr., 504 F. Supp. 3d 1263, 1293 (N.D. Ala. 2020) (employee with intellectual disability); Hebert v. Ascension Par. Sch. Bd., 396 F. Supp. 3d 686, 698 (M.D. La. 2019) (employee with PTSD and depression).

6

Controlling Condemned Bodies

Regulation and Dehumanization of Death Row Inmates

JOHN H. BLUME AND ALLISON FRANZ

Body regulation is an essential tool for states that seek to kill their citizens. The regime of capital punishment depends on another, deeper regime of civil death—the ability to ensure that a condemned person is metaphorically dead before the time comes to literally kill him.[1] This dehumanization is necessary for the very existence of capital punishment itself. For correctional staff tasked with carrying out executions, it is difficult to kill a fellow human being, but it is easy to kill a nonhuman entity—an "inmate"—who has spent the previous 20 years with little human contact, made no meaningful decisions of his own, and has virtually no rights to speak of.

Death rows accomplish this systemic dehumanization through a regime of constant body regulation that culminates in a series of illusory "choices" in the final days of a condemned person's life. First, people on death row spend years experiencing physical and mental anguish before they are ultimately killed, their bodies regulated at every step. Condemned prisoners are told where to go, when to go there, when to sleep, when to wake up, what, when, and how much to eat or drink, whether they can go outside, when and how often they can shower, who can visit them and when, and even whether and how often they receive access to natural light.[2] They can be forcibly medicated at trial to allow the state to procure a death sentence,[3] and such forced medication can continue throughout their time on death row.[4] Physical contact with loved ones, or even with any person who is not applying handcuffs, is strictly regulated or forbidden outright,[5] and several death row inmates have engaged in legal battles for the right to have a spiritual adviser touch them in the execution chamber.[6] Access to medical services is severely limited, strictly controlled, and inadequate,[7] and inmates are exposed to violence at the hands of prison officials with little to no protection or recourse.

Finally, after spending years, often decades, in prison, the condemned person is presented with a series of illusory choices in the final days of his life, including his last words, his last meal, and in some states his method of execution. These choices retransform people on death row into individual, autonomous actors, who are endowed with free will and must now suffer the consequences of exercising it, in the eyes of both the public and the executioners.[8] To accomplish the "rehumanization" of the offender, the state frames these decisions as grants of the "privilege" of bodily autonomy, however temporary and however limited. However, even these moments are carefully controlled. Last meals and last words are frequently limited or censored, and the illusion of a decision between execution methods is the state's failed attempt to mask the underlying threat that if the prisoner refuses to accept the state's brief benevolent concession of body regulation—that is, if he refuses to choose an execution method—the state will take even that decision into its own hands. The state then exerts further dehumanizing control by forcing inmates to accept execution by especially brutal methods that inflict extreme pain and body mutilation.[9] In states that offer no choice of execution method, if a condemned person believes that the state's method will cause him extreme pain, he is forced to investigate and propose an alternative method by which the state may kill him.[10] All of this regulation reinforces the message that, for the entirety of the condemned prisoner's life, the state is in complete control.

The regulation and torture of death row inmates are necessary for capital punishment's existence. We do not consider it hyperbole to assert that correctional systems systematically dehumanize people on death row (and in prisons generally) to make it easier for their fellow human beings to punish and ultimately kill them.[11] Simultaneously, the temporary regranting of bodily autonomy before a person is executed bestows a paradoxical status on condemned persons on death row. The surface-level goal of the modern execution system is to dispose of those who commit the most heinous crimes in the most rational and unemotional manner possible—in essence, to function as a human toxic waste management system.[12] However, for capital punishment to maintain its cultural and retributive relevance, people on death row must simultaneously be viewed as human agents being punished for improperly exercising their free will. Thus, "[t]he offender is alternatively presented as both morally culpable and morally irrelevant, unpredictable and easily classified, endowed with free will and incapable of change."[13] For the death penalty to exist, states must successfully create and maintain both regulatory systems.

In this chapter, we will discuss the state-regulated life cycle of a person on death row. We begin by discussing the myriad ways in which the state systematically dehumanizes people on death row through body regulation, and then we discuss the ways the state exerts control to rehumanize them at the end of their lives to justify their executions. Throughout a condemned person's time on death row, the state exerts bodily regulation to present inmates with apparent moments of choice that only reinforce the state's complete control.

The Life Cycle of a Death Row Inmate

From the first courtroom appearance, every second of every day of death row inmates' lives is controlled by the state, which results in inflicting gratuitous punishment and dehumanizing them in the eyes of the corrections employees tasked with ultimately ending their lives.[14]

Pretrial and Trial

The state exerts control over the bodies of people charged with capital crimes before their trials even begin. Defendants who are incompetent to stand trial can be forcibly medicated to render them competent, and states may shackle defendants in the courtroom, in front of the judge and jury, despite the obvious prejudice to the defendant.

FORCIBLE COMPETENCE TO STAND TRIAL

A defendant who is otherwise incompetent to stand trial may be forcibly medicated if the defendant is a danger to himself or others[15] or to restore competency.[16] In *Sell v. United States* (2003), the United States Supreme Court established that, where a defendant is not a danger to himself or others, he may nonetheless be forcibly medicated to restore competency if (1) important governmental interests are at stake; (2) forced medication is "substantially likely to render the defendant competent to stand trial" and will not significantly interfere with the defendant's ability to assist in his defense; (3) "any alternative, less intrusive treatments are unlikely to achieve substantially the same results"; and (4) administration of medication is medically appropriate (i.e., in the defendant's best medical interests).[17] If a defendant is found incompetent, he is typically moved to a medical facility for treatment to be restored, if possible, to legal competency, most often through forcible administration of psychotropic medication.[18] The issue of competency typically presents a capital defendant with his first illusory choice: he can "choose" to medicate himself to become competent, but if he chooses not to, the state can medicate him anyway.

Forced medication interferes with a variety of a defendant's rights, including his right to counsel and right to testify on his own behalf.[19] It is particularly problematic in the capital context, where mitigation evidence is the difference between whether the defendant lives or dies. Forced medication prevents the jury from seeing the defendant in his unaltered, baseline state, and "[t]he side effects of antipsychotic drugs may alter demeanor in a way that will prejudice all facets of the defense."[20] Neuroleptics in particular can significantly reduce a person's affect and make them appear lethargic—and, to a jury, disinterested and remorseless.[21] As the American Psychiatric Association explained:

> By administering medication, the State may be creating a prejudicial negative demeanor in the defendant—making him look nervous and restless, for example, or so calm or sedated as to appear bored, cold, unfeeling, and unresponsive. . . . That such effects may be subtle does not make them any less real or potentially influential.[22]

"[S]erious prejudice could result" in the penalty phase "if medication inhibits the defendant's capacity to react and respond to the proceedings and to demonstrate remorse or compassion."[23] In a capital sentencing proceeding, the state's decision to force medication on a defendant and the jury's subsequent perception of the defendant's character and lack of remorse may be the difference between whether the defendant lives or dies.[24]

SHACKLING

The state can choose to remove what little bodily autonomy a defendant has in the courtroom by shackling or otherwise restraining him in view of the jury. Capital defendants may be shackled at both the guilt and penalty phases of their trial if the use of shackles is "justified by an essential state interest—such as the interest in courtroom security."[25] Shackling, in theory, is heavily disfavored because it (1) undermines the presumption of innocence; (2) can interfere with a defendant's ability to communicate with his lawyer and prepare his own defense; and (3) is an affront to the dignity and decorum of the judicial process.[26] Further, it inherently prejudices the jury against the defendant.[27] "During the guilt phase of a trial, the use of visible restraints seriously jeopardizes a defendant's right to a presumption of innocence."[28] At the penalty phase, the defendant no longer enjoys the presumption of innocence, but using visible shackles, which insinuates to the jury that the defendant would be dangerous if not restrained, places an extra thumb on the state's side of the "future dangerousness" scale.

The "essential state interest" identified in *Deck v. Missouri* (2005) has been interpreted broadly, diluting the protection that *Deck* was intended to provide. Perhaps most notoriously, in the case of James Holmes, the Aurora theater shooter, the trial judge initially justified shackling solely on the grounds that "the defendant has been accused of multiple violent crimes."[29] Further, even where a trial court fails to determine on the record that shackling is justified by an essential state interest, appellate courts have declined to find prejudice in the face of overwhelming evidence against a defendant. When a court orders shackling without providing sufficient justification, "[t]he State must prove 'beyond a reasonable doubt that the [shackling] error complained of did not contribute to the verdict obtained.'"[30] If, in the court's view, the evidence against the defendant is so overwhelming that visible shackles could not possibly have made a difference, the court will consider the standard satisfied.[31]

Further, the *Deck* standard applies only to visible shackling.[32] Courts have permitted the use of "invisible" wrist restraints, leg restraints, belly chains, and even stun belts on defendants.[33] In extreme situations, a particularly disruptive defendant may be bound and gagged in the courtroom.[34] Stun belts in particular are ripe for abuse by judges. James Calvert, who represented himself at his Texas capital trial, was forced to wear a stun cuff on his leg capable of delivering a jolt of 50,000 volts.[35] Calvert struggled to comply with the court's rigid rules regarding when he should sit down and stand up, which angered the judge to the extent that he tasked courtroom deputies with physically pushing Calvert back into his chair if he did not sit down quickly enough after addressing the judge.[36] After repeatedly threatening to activate the stun belt throughout the trial, the judge followed through on the threat when Calvert forgot to stand up before addressing him.[37] When Calvert screamed, the judge revoked Calvert's right to represent himself.[38] Another Texas judge was reprimanded for "barbarism" after he ordered a defendant to be shocked three times for making objections.[39] A third judge in Maryland was removed from office after shocking a defendant who did not stop talking when asked.[40] Courts have recognized that forcing a defendant to wear a stun belt, thus making him constantly wary that he could be shocked at any moment, has a "chilling effect" on a defendant's ability to participate in his trial.[41]

Shackling serves to further dehumanize the defendant and make it easier for the jury to imagine and rationalize sentencing him to death. As one juror observed in a shackling case, "the shackles seemed like a short lead on a vicious dog."[42] In addition, in cases with Black defendants, shackling exacerbates any racial stereotypes already at play in the minds of the jury; the federal Third Circuit Court of Appeals even noted that shackling "evokes the dehumanizing specter of slavery."[43] In an extreme example of the dehumanizing effect of shackling, in a Georgia capital trial, Frederick Whatley was compelled to stand, shackled, in front of the jury while the prosecutor gave him a toy gun and told him to reenact his crime, with the prosecutor playacting as the victim.[44] With the image of Whatley, a shackled Black man, shooting the prosecutor fresh in their minds, Whatley's jury sentenced him to death.

Daily Life on Death Row

After being sentenced to death and shipped off to death row, where many persons will remain for decades, they are reminded at every moment of their daily lives that their bodies are the property of the state. In many states, people on death row are locked in their cells for 22 hours a day or more. Their physical contact with visitors, if allowed at all, is strictly controlled, and they are arbitrarily punished for any "forbidden" human contact. Shower and recreation times are strictly controlled or arbitrarily denied, and they are deprived of all sexual stimulation and punished for seeking it. Access to what limited medical services are available is governed by strict rules that limit the type of care that inmates can receive and when they can receive it, a problem exacerbated by the fact that incarcerated individuals are fed nutritionally inadequate diets that create or aggravate health problems. Finally, inmates are routinely subjected to violence by prison guards from which the grievance and court systems offer little to no protection. Death row is an inherently dehumanizing place, and the practices of death rows throughout the country make it easier to inflict an ultimately inhumane punishment on people who are no longer seen as human.[45]

SOLITARY CONFINEMENT AND RESTRICTIONS ON STIMULATION

From the instant a condemned prisoner arrives on death row, he loses almost all control over where he can go, when and what he can eat, when and how much he can sleep, whether he can go outside, and whether he can shower. The control that prisons maintain over the physical movement of death row inmates is most potently illustrated by states' practices of solitary confinement on death row. Twelve states mandate automatic, indefinite solitary confinement for people on death row.[46] In those states, inmates are generally confined to cells of between 36 and 100 square feet for 23 hours per day.[47] Some states allow as little as one hour of solitary recreation, which often also takes place in a cell.[48] People on death row in solitary confinement can go months or years without experiencing sunlight or fresh air.

Courts across the country have recognized the deleterious physical and psychological effects of long-term solitary confinement.[49] Physically, people held in solitary confinement are more likely to experience heart palpitations, insomnia, joint pain, eyesight deterioration, and aggravation of preexisting medical problems.[50] The psychological consequences of solitary confinement are plentiful and varied and can include anxiety, depression, anger or hostility, panic attacks, psychotic hallucinations, long-term social withdrawal and gradually diminished ability to engage with the outside world, heightened sensitivity to sounds, light, or smells, shortened attention span and memory, increased paranoia, dissociation, and, at worst, self-harm or suicidal behavior.[51] As with physical effects, prolonged segregation exacerbates any preexisting mental health problems. Anthony Graves, who spent eighteen years in solitary confinement on Texas's death row before his exoneration, described the effects of solitary on others on the row:

> I saw guys who dropped their appeals because of the intolerable conditions. Before his execution, one inmate told me he would rather die than continue existing under these inhumane conditions. I saw guys come to prison sane, and leave this world insane, talking nonsense on the execution gurney. One guy suffered some of his last days smearing feces, lying naked in the recreation yard, and urinating on himself.[52]

In states that mandate solitary confinement, time outside the cell is also strictly regulated, including whether inmates can interact with others. In Alabama, Arkansas, Georgia, Idaho, Kansas, Mississippi, Texas, and Wyoming death row inmates are not allowed group recreation, and in Florida, Nevada, and Oklahoma they are allowed group recreation only in small groups of three or four.[53] Physical contact with visitors, or even with any person who is not applying handcuffs, is limited or forbidden outright. Inmates have no right to contact visitation; however, most states allow limited contact visitation with family. Mississippi, Texas, Kansas, South Carolina, and South Dakota do not allow contact visitation.[54] Even when states allow contact visitation, visits are supervised by guards, and the type of contact in which inmates may engage (e.g., hugging) is carefully monitored and restricted. Rules are enforced arbitrarily, and depending on which guard is on duty, something as simple as hugging or kissing a family member too long for a guard's liking can get an inmate written up and punished.[55]

Physical movement and physical contact with others are kept to a minimum even on the least restrictive rows in the country, South Carolina and Tennessee. In both states, inmates assigned to the least restrictive security classification are allowed out of their cells for a majority of the day, but still they cannot hold jobs outside their unit.[56] They are allowed limited contact visitation and, in Tennessee, unlimited phone use during the day.[57] However, these conditions apply only to inmates with the least restrictive custody classification. Inmates classified in the most restrictive levels are kept in solitary confinement with conditions and privileges similar to those in states that automatically place death row inmates in solitary confinement.[58]

States impose restrictions on physical contact for people on death row up to the moment of execution by regulating the presence of spiritual advisers in the execution chamber and fighting to deny inmates the opportunity to have a spiritual adviser physically touch them as they are executed. These practices were previously common, but over the past five years states have attempted to control new and increasingly minute details of the execution process.[59] As a result, religious freedom issues, particularly the question of whether spiritual advisers may be present during executions, have been a large part of the Supreme Court's death penalty docket.

The Court has largely been receptive to such claims. In 2019, the Court stayed the Texas execution of Patrick Henry Murphy until Texas permitted "Murphy's Buddhist spiritual advisor or another Buddhist reverend of the State's choosing to accompany Murphy in the execution chamber during the execution."[60] In 2020, it stayed the execution of Ruben Gutierrez after Texas refused to allow his spiritual adviser to accompany him to the execution chamber by asserting its interest in "not allowing outsiders into such a highly-charged environment" as the execution chamber.[61] The Court remanded this case for a hearing on "whether serious security problems would result if a prisoner facing execution is permitted to choose the spiritual adviser the prisoner wishes to have in his immediate presence during the execution."[62] In 2021, the Court required Alabama to allow Willie Smith's pastor to be present in the execution chamber.[63]

The Court's jurisprudence on the issue came to a head in 2022, when John Ramirez appealed Texas's refusal to allow Ramirez's pastor to "lay hands" on him and pray audibly during his execution.[64] Texas had revised its execution protocol in 2021 in response to the Gutierrez case to allow advisers in the execution chamber but informed Ramirez that advisers in the chamber were not allowed to touch the inmate.[65] Ramirez filed suit in federal district court alleging that the prison's refusal to allow the pastor to physically touch Ramirez and audibly pray during his execution violated his rights under the Religious Land Use and Institutionalized Persons Act (RLUIPA) and the First Amendment.[66] The Supreme Court enjoined the execution until Texas could create procedures that allowed for physical touch and audible prayer, on the ground that failing to do so violated Ramirez's free exercise rights under RLUIPA.

Notably, all of these decisions have been rooted not in an inmate's right to bodily autonomy but in their right to the free exercise of religion.[67] The Supreme Court has made clear that people on death row have religious rights *in spite* of their confinement.[68] *Ramirez v. Collier*, the 2022 case allowing physical touch, in particular raised the question of whether Ramirez's religious rights would have been recognized at all if the remedy for their violation had been slightly more complicated—that is to say, if vindicating Ramirez's rights would have even remotely impaired the state's and the victims' "important interest in the timely enforcement of a sentence."[69] The Court granted relief only "[b]ecause it is possible to accommodate Ramirez's sincere religious beliefs without delaying or impeding his execution."[70]

Finally, death rows police inmates' bodies by forbidding inmates from seeking any kind of sexual stimulation. If people on death row are caught attempting to seek sexual gratification even through private means such as masturbation, they are punished, including with further isolation with the outside world, such as the loss of visitation or phone privileges. Further, states are trending toward stricter enforcement of sexual deprivation: in this century the number of states allowing conjugal visits has decreased from 20 to four—California, Connecticut, Washington, and New York.[71] It is worth noting that the evidence strongly suggests that sexual deprivation is associated with a higher incidence of rape in prison and increased violence.[72]

ACCESS TO MEDICAL SERVICES

Death rows and prisons exercise extensive control over inmates' bodies by heavily restricting medical care. Incarcerated people in general are sicker than the noninstitutionalized population and consequently require more frequent care.[73] Compared to noninstitutionalized Americans of the same age, incarcerated individuals are more likely to have diabetes, hypertension, persistent kidney problems, cirrhosis, hepatitis, and HIV/AIDS.[74] Nonetheless, access to medical services is severely limited and strictly controlled, and as a result prison care is far inferior to that of the outside world.[75] Inmates have virtually no control over their own care; they are not allowed to choose their doctor, facility, or treatment method.[76] It can take weeks or more to receive treatment after requesting it. As one South Carolina inmate put it: "Getting to medical is like getting a ticket to a sold-out concert."[77]

The state has an affirmative duty under the Eighth Amendment (which, among other things, prohibits cruel and unusual punishment) to provide incarcerated people with proper medical care.[78] However, prisons are largely not required to provide the same quality of health care that individuals would receive in the outside world, partly because, from a punitive perspective, denial of quality health care is viewed as part of an inmate's punishment.[79] A state actor does not violate the Eighth Amendment by denying a prisoner medical care unless the state actor is "deliberately indifferent" and unless the medical need is sufficiently serious.[80] A violation will not be found unless an official "knows of and disregards an excessive risk to inmate health or safety; the official must both be aware of the facts from which the inference could be drawn that a substantial risk of serious harm exists, and he must also draw that inference."[81]

The phrase "serious medical need" has been defined largely on a case-by-case basis, depending on whether a physician determines that a condition is serious enough to warrant treatment.[82] Courts have found that a serious medical need may exist if a layperson could recognize the need for medical attention[83] or if the individual is in serious pain.[84] A serious medical need may also exist if an inmate's condition affects his daily life[85] or could cause a lifelong handicap.[86] However, because medical problems are endlessly wide-ranging, courts have found it almost impossible to establish a bright-line rule for what constitutes a serious medical need. As a result, determinations of the severity of medical problems have become a balancing test between the cost of treatment and the incarcerated person's need for it,[87] and medical providers in prisons are forced to balance cost-saving measures against providing the full extent of care that an individual needs.[88] Health care thus presents another illusory choice between two evils: "choose" not to receive care at all, or risk receiving care that is subpar or even downright detrimental.

Persons on death row in particular bear the burden of the balancing act that prisons perform between caring for inmates and saving money.

Inmates in the general prison population receive medical care on the premise that they might one day return to society. For death row inmates, this is not a consideration, and their care suffers as a result.[89] Death rows around the country are rife with health care neglect. One of our clients, Herman Hughes, complained for years on death row of leg pain. Because of his low IQ, others on the row with him also advocated (to no avail) for Herman to be seen by a doctor. The South Carolina Department of Corrections did nothing until his leg shattered, and only then was it discovered that he had bone cancer and his leg needed to be amputated at slightly below the hip. He was ultimately removed from death row (he was a juvenile at the time of the offense) and now uses a wheelchair because the prison refuses to give him a functional prosthesis.

Individuals on North Carolina's death row reported that the state stopped giving cancer medication to patients when the COVID-19 pandemic hit.[90] Two more North Carolina death row inmates died of complications from hepatitis C, a curable illness, after the state refused to properly treat prisoners with hepatitis C unless they also had HIV or hepatitis B or there was "significant liver scarring and the risks of further significant injury are higher."[91] On federal death row, some inmates with dental problems chose to have all their teeth removed rather than endure pain during the long wait to receive dental care.[92] Further, the average age of people on death row is steadily increasing, thereby also increasing the likelihood that they will need more extensive medical attention. As of 2021, the average age of people on death row was 51, with more than 22 percent of death row inmates over age 60.[93] By comparison, in 2000 people on death row were on average 38 years old, and just 2.7 percent of them were over age 60.[94]

NUTRITION

Diet is yet another aspect of prison life that is strictly regulated to the inmates' detriment. Incarcerated people are served too-small portions of food of little nutritional value, and the food is often spoiled. Consequently, inmates must rely on commissary items to keep from starving[95]—yet another illusory choice between surviving on insufficient, unhealthy prison food or spending limited funds on (very) overpriced commissary food. Inmates who cannot afford to buy commissary food lose weight at an alarming rate.[96]

Underfeeding inmates is ubiquitous. In 2014, investigations into the Gordon County Jail in Georgia revealed that inmates were fed two insufficient meals a day, and some were forced to resort to eating toothpaste and toilet paper.[97] At the Montgomery County Jail in New York, one inmate lost 90 pounds in less than six months, and another could not fit into his prosthetic leg because he had lost so much weight.[98] One Montgomery inmate was also so malnourished that he resorted to eating toothpaste and lotion and suffered a variety of health problems as a result, including exhaustion, bleeding gums, and skin rashes.[99] The lack of food led to increased violence among the inmates.[100] A group of incarcerated persons at the Schuylkill County Prison in Pennsylvania filed a federal civil rights lawsuit claiming the portions they received are "not even enough to fill a 5-year-old child."[101] In Arizona, a federal circuit court granted relief to inmates who brought a class-action suit against the Arizona Department of Corrections, where inmates on the intake unit were given a sack at four or five o'clock in the morning containing their two meals for the day, which was "mostly bread and served cold."[102] Some prisons have used, and continue to use, COVID-19 as an excuse not to provide incarcerated people with adequate nutrition. In jails in Orange County, California, the Orange County Sheriff's Department stopped serving hot meals at the start of the pandemic and instead served inmates moldy bologna sandwiches three times a day.[103] Those who could not afford commissary became sick, and even those who could still could not get enough nutrition.[104]

Both the quantity and quality of food provided to incarcerated people are regulated using a cost-benefit analysis, and corrections employees typically decide that the cost of feeding inmates a healthy or even adequate diet is very rarely outweighed by the benefit. Corrections officers consistently try to outdo each other to serve the cheapest food, and in some states there are statutory incentives for corrections administrators to dream up ever more creative ways to provide inmates with the cheapest possible diet. In 2013, the former Arizona sheriff Joe Arpaio bragged about serving Maricopa County inmates a 56-cent Thanksgiving dinner.[105] In Alabama, until 2019, local sheriffs were legally allowed to pocket any funds they could save from the prison food budget ($1.75 per inmate per day) for their own personal use. However, this practice backfired on one former Morgan County sheriff, who was locked up in his own jail for misusing state funds after pocketing over $200,000 from the food budget by feeding incarcerated people approximately 1,500 calories a day.[106]

GUARD VIOLENCE

Inmates are exposed to violence at the hands of prison officials with little to no protection or recourse.[107] Corrections officers have almost unlimited power and control over incarcerated people,[108] which is exacerbated by the fact that it is difficult for inmates to protect themselves against violence by correctional officers who use this power as a constant (and often explicit) reminder to inmates that their bodies are not their own and that they are powerless to stop the state's violence against them.[109]

Further, it is extremely difficult for incarcerated people subjected to violence from guards to obtain any relief. Any individual with a complaint is required to jump through a number of administrative hoops within the prison,[110] a process that is intentionally cumbersome and can be (and often is) actively thwarted by prison employees.[111] Problems can also arise if an incarcerated person is taken directly to segregated housing—solitary confinement, or "lockup"—following an encounter with a guard, which delays access to the grievance process.[112] In other circumstances, guards block inmates from accessing the grievance process at all.[113] Even if an individual is able to successfully file a grievance, any claim they try to assert against a guard can be blocked if they do not properly appeal the denial of the grievance.[114] Repeated denials of appeals broadcast to guards and other incarcerated people the message that the inmates' bodies are the property of the state and that guards are free to inflict physical punishment with near impunity.

Rehumanization

Just as dehumanization throughout the life cycle of a death row inmate is necessary for the inmate to become a nonhuman entity who can be acceptably killed without a second thought, his rebirth as an autonomous being is necessary for the execution to retain its original meaning. Consequently, a portion of a death row inmate's humanity is abruptly restored to him in the last days or even hours of his life. The state accomplishes this "rehumanization" in the same way it accomplishes dehumanization—through bodily control and a series of illusory choices. A condemned person who attempts to commit suicide before his execution date will be rushed to the hospital to receive the best medical care he has ever received in prison. In addition, inmates who are not competent to be executed can be forcibly medicated so that they have a sufficient understanding of their punishment that their execution will serve a retributive goal. Finally, inmates are offered the opportunity to "choose" their last words, their last meal, and their execution method—all subject, of course, to the state's approval. The reintroduction of choice in the last days of the inmate's life enables the public and corrections employees who will kill him to view the condemned not as a "helpless pawn[] of the modern execution drill"[115] but as a free-acting, autonomous individual who made his own choices throughout his life. Such practices are as much or more for the executioners as for the condemned. The consequences, particularly at the method selection stage, are that an inmate is forced to become a willing participant in his own execution—"to consecrate his own punishment."[116]

Final-Hour Suicide Attempts

As discussed above, prisons deny medical care or provide only the barest minimum care to death row inmates throughout their lives. However, if a person on death row attempts to commit suicide, they are provided with prompt and extensive medical attention to keep them alive so that the state is not deprived of its opportunity to dispense final "justice." We provide a few examples below.

DAVID LONG

David Long, a paranoid schizophrenic, was sentenced to death in Texas in 1987.[117] The night before his scheduled execution, Long overdosed on prescribed antidepressants.[118] He was found unresponsive in his cell and rushed to the hospital.[119] Over two days in the hospital, Long's condition improved from critical to serious, but his intensive care physician warned state officials that Long would require continual medical care past his execution date and refused to authorize transportation back to death row.[120] Undeterred, Lieutenant Governor Rick Perry denied Long's request for a thirty-day stay of execution, and officials arranged a medically supervised airplane transport to the execution chamber, with Long flown back to the prison on a ventilator.[121] In the middle of his execution by lethal injection, Long vomited a blackish-brown substance that disturbed one witness enough to leave the witness chamber, which prison officials claimed was a charcoal solution that the hospital had administered less than two days earlier to neutralize the toxicity of the drugs Long had taken in his suicide attempt.[122]

PEE WEE GASKINS

Donald Henry "Pee Wee" Gaskins was initially sentenced to death in South Carolina in 1976. That sentence was commuted to life in prison,[123] but in 1982 a murder victim's son hired Gaskins to kill Rudolph Tyner, a fellow inmate who had murdered the son's parents. Gaskins rigged a homemade bomb, gave it to Tyner disguised as an intercom speaker, and detonated the bomb remotely when Tyner held to it his ear.[124] The bomb blew Tyner's head off, earning Gaskins the title "Meanest Man in America"[125] and another death sentence that would not be commuted.

Gaskins frequently said that he would not allow the state to kill him,[126] and true to his word, the night before his scheduled execution in 1991, Gaskins hid under a blanket[127] and slit his wrists and the crooks of his arms with a razor blade that he had swallowed and regurgitated while six armed guards stood watch outside his cell.[128] When Gaskins passed out due to blood loss, he rolled over and his body weight acted like a tourniquet on the most serious injury, preventing him from dying. When guards discovered the suicide attempt, he was rushed to the hospital, where his wounds were sutured and his blood replenished.[129] As a result of the suicide attempt, Gaskins was prohibited from seeing his family on his final day and was allowed to see only his attorneys, a chaplain, and the corrections commissioner.[130] He was electrocuted less than 24 hours later.[131]

Execution Competence

In *Ford v. Wainwright* (1986),[132] the United States Supreme Court established that the Eighth Amendment prohibits the execution "of one whose mental illness prevents him from comprehending the reasons for the penalty or its implications."[133] In reaching this decision, the

Court noted the lack of "retributive value of executing a person who has no comprehension of why he has been singled out and stripped of his fundamental right to life"[134]—in other words, for the execution to hold meaning, the condemned person must retain his humanity, his rational understanding, and his autonomy and must be viewed as such.[135] In a concurrence that has since become the operative standard for *Ford* competency, Justice Lewis Powell suggested that, under the Eighth Amendment, prisoners are not competent to be executed if they are "unaware of the punishment they are about to suffer and why they are to suffer it."[136] Powell further explained, in an ominous footnote, that "if petitioner [Ford] is cured of his disease the state is free to execute him."[137]

Subsequently, in *Panetti v. Quarterman* (2007), the Court clarified that a determination of whether an inmate is competent to be executed requires an analysis of whether the individual has a rational understanding of the reason why he is being executed. The Court elaborated on its reasoning in *Ford* to establish that courts may not discount the possibility that a condemned person's delusions may prevent him from actually understanding the meaning of his punishment despite being aware of the relevant facts.[138] In sum, courts have applied the *Ford* standard to mean that an inmate sentenced to death may be executed only if he understands that he will be executed (and that execution means that he will die) and he has a rational understanding that he is being executed by the state for the crimes he committed. When determining competency to be executed, courts look to the inmate's current mental state, not his mental state at the time he committed the crime.[139]

This standard for competency means that mentally ill inmates whose illness is moderated by medication may be competent to be executed only while medicated. In applying the *Ford* rule, states have relied on Justice Powell's suggestion that they are free to execute otherwise incompetent people as long as they have been "cured." In a twisted perversion of the typical purpose of medical treatment, the "cure" for a psychotic person whom the state wants to execute is forcible medication to create the illusion of competency. In every state except Louisiana[140] and South Carolina,[141] mentally ill inmates can be forcibly medicated for the purpose of rendering them competent to be executed. The United States Supreme Court has never explicitly ruled on the issue of whether an inmate may decline medication when medication would result in the inmate's execution.

FORCIBLE COMPETENCE: CHARLES SINGLETON

Charles Singleton was convicted of murder and sentenced to death in Arkansas in 1979.[142] Once on death row, the state placed him on psychotropic medications to alleviate anxiety and depression.[143] His mental health began to deteriorate further around 1987, at which time he came to believe that his cell was possessed by demons, that his thoughts were being stolen from him when he read the Bible, and that a prison doctor had placed an implement in his ear.[144] Singleton's psychiatrist subsequently diagnosed Singleton with schizophrenia and placed him on antipsychotic medication, after which his mental health improved.[145]

Over the next four years, Singleton endured a constant cycle of involuntary medication followed by improvement in his condition, which led his doctor to discontinue his medication, upon which Singleton rapidly decompensated into psychosis and would be again forcibly medicated.[146] Singleton was evaluated for *Ford* competency in 1995 and was determined to be competent. He was psychotic again within six months, and within roughly a year he believed that he was God, that he was on a mission to kill the president, and that he had already been executed.[147] In August 1997, Singleton shredded his mattress, stuffed it in his toilet, sink, and air vents, and flooded his cell.[148] He was again involuntarily medicated, and his condition slowly improved over the next 13 months, until his psychiatrist believed that his psychosis was in remission.[149] The state then scheduled his execution for March 1, 2000.[150]

Singleton's execution was subsequently rescheduled several times amid appeals on the competency issue. The Arkansas Supreme Court determined that involuntarily medicating Singleton was permissible under *Washington v. Harper* (1990)[151] on the ground that "the intent of the state was not to make [Singleton] competent to be executed" but rather to treat him.[152] Subsequently, a panel of the federal Eighth Circuit Court of Appeals permanently barred Singleton's execution and ordered that he be sentenced to life in prison.[153] On rehearing en banc, a starkly divided Eighth Circuit reversed that ruling, holding that it was permissible for the state to treat Singleton to make him sane enough to be executed.[154] Chief Judge Roger Wollman, writing for the majority, callously observed that "eligibility for execution is the only unwanted consequence of the medication."[155] The United States Supreme Court rejected arguments from Singleton's lawyers that taking medication was not in Singleton's best interest, as medication would directly result in execution.[156]

Thus, forcibly medicated and found to understand that he was being executed and why, Singleton was executed in 2004.[157] His last words were a rambling written statement, which read in part: "The blind think I'm playing a game. They deny me, refusing me existence. But everybody takes the place of another. You have taught me what you want done—and I will not let you down."[158]

CHOOSING INCOMPETENCE: SOUTH CAROLINA AND LOUISIANA

The supreme courts of Louisiana and South Carolina have established that people on death row may not be forcibly medicated to ensure their competency to be executed. In 1992, in *State v. Perry*, the Louisiana Supreme Court held that forcibly medicating death row inmates for execution violated their rights under Louisiana's constitution—specifically, that forced medication violated the "right to privacy or personhood," "would constitute cruel, excessive[,] and unusual punishment," and "fail[ed] to measurably contribute to the social goals of capital punishment."[159] The Louisiana court noted that *Washington v. Harper* implied that involuntary medication was only appropriate as medical treatment in the inmate's best interest, and "forcible administration of drugs to implement execution is not medically appropriate."[160]

Similarly, in South Carolina, the state's supreme court held that forcible medication for the purpose of restoring an individual to execution competency would violate the person's right to privacy and to be "free from unwanted medical intrusions," even as the court noted that "[a]n inmate in South Carolina has a very limited privacy interest when weighed against the State's penological interest."[161] The South Carolina Supreme Court further suggested that medicating a condemned person for execution likely violated medical ethics and the Hippocratic oath.[162] Ultimately, the court concluded, "justice can never be served by forcing medication on an incompetent inmate for the sole purpose of getting him well enough to execute."[163]

In these states, however, mentally ill inmates who are competent while on medication but incompetent off medication have a lethal decision to make: take care of their mental health and be executed, or preserve their lives but allow themselves to decompensate into psychosis. In a 1993 case, *Singleton v. State*, the South Carolina Supreme Court overturned the postconviction judge's commutation of Fred Singleton's death sentence on the ground that Singleton was currently incompetent, specifically noting that "the ebb and flow of medical science" might provide a method whereby Singleton could be restored to competence in the future.[164] Particularly for individuals with schizophrenia, choosing to save their own lives and voluntarily stop their medication can have profound consequences. In severe cases, decompensation can mean that a mentally ill inmate becomes disoriented to person, place, or time or loses his ability to communicate or care for himself.

The case of Jamie Wilson in South Carolina illustrates the consequences of the decision to risk execution or descending into psychosis.[165] Wilson was born into a family with a long history of mental illness—four generations' worth of schizophrenia.[166] He exhibited symptoms of mental illness by the time he was five.[167] Wilson had a number of voluntary (and involuntary) admissions to psychiatric hospitals when he was a teenager. But when his father lost his job, and thus his medical insurance, hospitals would no longer admit the youth. Without treatment or medication, he became increasingly disorganized and began experiencing auditory hallucinations. At age 19, five months after being refused admission to a psychiatric hospital, Wilson entered a Greenwood, South Carolina, elementary school with a revolver and opened fire, killing two eight-year-old students.[168] After the shooting, Wilson stated that a goat had told him to commit the crime.[169] He was found guilty but mentally ill at a bench trial, where the judge found that Wilson, due to his mental illness, was not able to conform his conduct to the requirements of the law.[170] Nevertheless, the judge sentenced him to death.[171]

On death row, Wilson's mental health continued to decline. When an execution date became imminent, Wilson's attorneys filed a petition challenging his competency to be executed. Despite his severe schizophrenia, which was acknowledged by numerous mental health care providers within the state's department of corrections, there was still a chance that Wilson, if he continued taking his antipsychotic medications, would be found competent to be executed given *Ford*'s low bar and the fact that he could articulate, although not rationally, that was on death row for "some murders" and that he didn't want to die.

Thus, Wilson's attorneys advised him to stop taking his medication in an attempt to induce clear incompetency to be executed. Due to issues with informed consent, a legal guardian was appointed, who concurred. As predicted by psychiatrists, Wilson decompensated. He lost the ability to rationally communicate—his speech became unintelligible ("word salad" is the psychiatric term), and he no longer recognized his attorneys. He defecated and urinated on himself and paced continuously, often screaming at nonexistent people. At the evidentiary hearing to determine Wilson's competency to be executed, the state could find no mental health professional who would opine that he was competent.

Wilson remains on death row in legal limbo because of the theoretical (but not realistic) possibility that he could be restored to competency. In the meantime, Wilson's schizophrenia has advanced to the point that he requires others to make sure he eats, bathes, changes clothes, and cleans his cell. Correctional officers are unable (and unwilling) to provide the level of basic human care that Wilson needs; consequently, the other condemned men on South Carolina's death row have assumed responsibility for his care, cleaning up after him as best they can, making sure he eats, and, to the extent possible, keeping him calm.[172] Wilson's decision may have cheated the executioner, but the price the state demanded for refusing body regulation was his sanity (and any semblance of human dignity).

Last Words and Last Meals

Even in the context of re-creating the death row inmate as a free-willed, morally culpable person, multiple states censor inmates' last words, or require them to be submitted to prison employees in advance subject to approval, or cut off inmates whose statements the warden finds too long or too offensive.[173] While last meal requests are generally published as received, multiple states impose restrictions on last meals in practice. In Oklahoma, the meal is limited to $25;[174] in Florida, "to avoid extravagance," the cost limit is $40 and the food must be available locally.[175] Texas abolished last meal requests altogether in 2011 after one inmate, Lawrence Henry Brewer, requested steak, fried okra, a triple bacon cheeseburger, three fajitas, an omelet, pizza, half a loaf of bread, Blue Bell ice cream, peanut butter fudge, and three root beers but was too terrified of his impending execution to eat any of it.[176] Even states that do not impose official restrictions will unilaterally modify an inmate's last meal request as it sees fit, usually in the interest of cost. An inmate who requests lobster might receive a filet of processed fish; sometimes the prison will reduce a request it thinks is too large.[177]

Execution Methods and Procedure

Once an execution date is set, the state exerts control in the form of forcing inmates not only to be complicit in their own deaths but also willing participants. In some states, inmates are asked to select the manner of their own death, and in states that do not offer a choice, an inmate who believes the state's chosen method will cause him unreasonable pain is required to propose his own alternative method and a procedure by which the state may carry it out. If an inmate attempts to assert autonomy by refusing to choose, or if he selects an alternative method that the state does not want to use, the state will reject the inmate's choice and execute him by its chosen method. After the choice is made, executions are carried out by often untrained correctional staff, which, particularly in executions by lethal injection, result in a painful, drawn-out execution process whereby inmates are subjected to incompetent corrections employees poking and prodding them with needles for hours. Finally, various problems with properly administering lethal injections have led some states to return to antiquated methods of execution that are more painful and torturous and also mutilate the inmate's body more than lethal injection.

Further, in most executing states, in a final bodily indignity, the execution team stuffs the death row inmate's rectum and puts a rubber band around their penis so they will not offend the sensibilities (and senses) of the witnesses and execution participants by defecating or urinating on themselves during the execution event.[178]

METHOD "CHOICE"

In some states, inmates are presented with an illusory "choice" of the method by which they will die, with the caveat that, if the inmate refuses to actively participate in his own execution by choosing a method, the state will simply choose for him. Some states, however, do not even bother with the pretense of offering a choice and execute all inmates by a default method.[179] Further, if an inmate has reason to believe that a state's compulsory execution method will cause him extreme pain, the Supreme Court has held that he must propose an alternative method by which the state may kill him.[180] In other words, the state is free to abdicate any responsibility for causing an inmate pain and instead place the burden on an inmate to search for and propose the method of his own death.

In the case of Russell Bucklew, the U.S. Supreme Court in 2019 allowed Missouri to execute Bucklew by lethal injection because it thought he failed to identify a feasible and readily available alternative method and because "the Eighth Amendment does not guarantee a prisoner a painless death."[181] Bucklew suffered from a rare condition, cavernous hemangioma, which caused blood-filled tumors to develop in his head, neck, and throat.[182] He argued, among other things, that a throat tumor could burst during an execution by lethal injection, causing him to die not by the drugs but by choking on his own blood.[183] Bucklew proposed execution by nitrogen hypoxia, which he claimed would significantly reduce the risk of severe pain.[184] Bizarrely, however, the Court denied this proposal on the ground that Bucklew failed to present the state with a prepackaged, ready-made, extensively detailed protocol for carrying out an execution by nitrogen hypoxia—the creation of which is supposed to be squarely the responsibility of the state:

> [Bucklew] has presented no evidence on essential questions like how nitrogen gas should be administered (using a gas chamber, a tent, a hood, a mask, or some other delivery device); in what concentration (pure nitrogen or some mixture of gases); how quickly and for how long it should be introduced; or how the State might ensure the safety of the execution team, including protecting them against the risk of gas leaks.[185]

Requiring an inmate to present evidence at this level of detail to avoid an excruciatingly painful execution places the inmate in the position of having not only to advocate for the method of his own death but also to teach the state how to carry it out. Justice Stephen Breyer, in dissent, agreed, noting that prior precedents did not refer to any of these requirements; today's majority invents them. And to insist upon them is to create what, in a case like this one, would amount to an insurmountable hurdle for prisoners like Bucklew. That hurdle, I fear, could permit States to execute even those who will endure the most serious pain and suffering, irrespective of how exceptional their case and irrespective of how thoroughly they prove it. I cannot reconcile the majority's decision with a constitutional Amendment that forbids all "cruel and unusual punishments."[186]

UNTRAINED WORKERS AND PROLONGED EXECUTIONS

Once the execution method has been selected, inmates may be forced to participate in their own deaths by helping often untrained and incompetent prison workers carry out the execution protocol. Professional groups like the American Medical Association consider participation in executions highly unethical for doctors and other medical professionals; consequently, well-trained medical staff is hard to come by in the execution chamber.[187] The details of execution teams and their members are often carefully guarded state secrets, but in general teams are composed of willing corrections officers who must meet very few requirements.[188] As Dr. Jay Chapman, the Oklahoma coroner who developed the modern lethal injection protocol, regretfully noted: "It never occurred to me when we set this up that we'd have complete idiots administering the drugs."[189]

The result is that inmates being executed by lethal injection frequently find themselves in the position of having not only to submit to their own execution but also to actively help incompetent execution teams place the needles that then deliver poison to their bodies. In Arizona's 2022 execution of Frank Atwood, after several failed attempts to insert an IV line in Atwood's left arm, the execution team, which was composed of nonprofessional prison employees because prison medical staff did not participate in executions, told Atwood that they were going to cut into his groin to set a line in his femoral vein.[190] "Why?" Atwood asked. "They draw blood from my right arm all the time."[191] The execution team was unable to set a line in his arm, so Atwood then suggested his hand.[192] By the time the executioners managed to set the IV line in Atwood's hand, they had been sticking him with needles for 40 minutes.[193]

Problems with carrying out lethal injections have prompted Alabama to expand its execution timeline to essentially allow the execution team to subject inmates to execution procedures for days on end. In 2022, following the three-and-a-half-hour execution of Joe Nathan James Jr. (during which James appeared to be unconscious on the gurney throughout the time he was visible to witnesses[194]), Alabama was forced to call off the executions of two inmates, Alan Miller and Kenneth Smith, after it was unable to find veins to execute them within the time frame of a 24-hour warrant.[195] In response, the Alabama Supreme Court issued an order amending a procedural rule[196] to give Governor Kay Ivey a 30-day window within which to choose her own time frame to carry out a death sentence.[197] Ivey set the window for the execution of James Barber, the first person executed under the revised statute, as a period of 30 hours ending at 6:00 a.m. on July 21. It took the execution team two hours after the start of the window to execute Barber, but if they have difficulties with future executions, they can simply leave the inmate to bleed through the night in his cell and pick up where they left off the next morning. The imprecise time frame is problematic to say the least: inmates will be suspended in an execution limbo knowing that they are about to be put to death but not knowing when.

A RETURN TO ANTIQUITY

Lethal injection is currently the most frequently used method of execution.[198] There is ample evidence suggesting that lethal injection, depending on the drugs used or if they are improperly administered, can be far from painless.[199] Nonetheless, multiple states have sought to turn back the clock and return to more antiquated methods that are widely considered to be even more painful and mutilate the body more severely than lethal injection.

In 2021, after 10 years without an execution because the state could not procure the drugs for lethal injection, South Carolina passed a bill making electrocution the default method of execution and also providing for execution by firing squad.[200] An inmate could be executed by lethal injection only if lethal injection was deemed "available," and the statute gave the director of the South Carolina Department of Corrections virtually unlimited discretion to determine what "available" meant and whether any given method was available. Any inmate whose chosen method was deemed "unavailable" would be electrocuted. The statute provided no way to confirm the director's assertion of a method's availability or otherwise hold him accountable for such assertions, providing no safeguard other than the director's assumed good faith.[201]

In September 2022, a South Carolina state trial judge struck down the statute and held that both the electric chair and the firing squad were unconstitutional.[202] The state responded by enacting a "shield law" to protect the identities of anyone who sold the state the drugs to perform lethal injections to make it easier to obtain the drugs,[203] and it announced that the corrections department had obtained lethal injection drugs on September 19, 2023.[204] The South Carolina Supreme Court reversed the trial judge's decision, finding by a 4–1 margin that judicial electrocution did not violate the South Carolina Constitution and, by a 3–2 margin, that the firing squad was also constitutional.[205] In doing so, the state's supreme court relied heavily on a condemned individual's ability to choose their method of execution.[206]

Similarly, in March 2023 Idaho passed a bill to revive the firing squad after it scheduled and then canceled two execution dates because it did not have the drugs to undertake lethal injection.[207] As in South Carolina, Idaho lawmakers contended in supporting the bill that as long as lethal injection drugs remained unavailable, and with no alternative method in place, death sentences could never be carried out.[208] The bill went into effect on July 1, 2023.[209] Other states provide for even more antiquated alternative methods if lethal injection is not possible. For example, Utah allows for execution by firing squad if the state cannot obtain lethal injection drugs 30 days before a scheduled execution, and New Hampshire allows for hanging "if for any reason the commissioner [of corrections] finds it to be impractical to carry out the punishment of death by administration of the required lethal substance or substances."[210] Finally, Alabama recently executed two inmates with nitrogen gas, a previously untested method that evoked comparisons to Nazi Germany[211] and that produced "violent" executions in which Alan Miller and Kenneth Smith "writhed" and "gasped for air" on the gurney for several minutes, "in thrashing spasms and seizure-like movements."[212]

In light of these policies, it is clear that "allowing" prisoners to select their method of execution is nothing more than the illusion of state control disguised as a "choice." This allowance, framed by states as a fleeting but generous grant of bodily autonomy, belies the underlying threat that if a prisoner attempts to exert some amount of actual control—for example by proposing an alternative method if a state's existing methods will cause him unreasonable pain or by refusing a selection to avoid active participation in his own execution—the state will simply exert its will and execute the inmate by whatever method it deems fit and regardless of the inmate's choice. This false choice feels particularly surreal in states that have reintroduced crueler, more corporal, antiquated methods of execution. A choice between two or more unreasonably painful (and potentially unconstitutional) options is no choice at all.

Conclusion

From pretrial to postmortem, every second of a death row inmate's life is strictly regulated by the state. Even moments of apparent "choice," which to the public establish the inmate's autonomy and thereby justify his punishment, are carefully choreographed to ensure that people on death row can never actually act outside the power of the state. This regulation is necessary to dehumanize people on death row so that they can be executed and to ensure that they maintain just enough humanity that their execution retains its retributive and deterrent significance. This necessity places people on death row (and their punishment) in a position of ambivalence: for their punishment to be carried out, people sentenced to death can be neither fully human nor fully inhuman. It is a contradiction that undermines the stated retributive and deterrent goals of capital punishment and suggests that there is truly no way for us to carry out the death penalty while retaining our own humanity.

NOTES

1 See Ruffin v. Commonwealth, 21 Gratt. 790, 796 (Va. Sup. Ct. App. 1871) (articulating the concept of civil death for criminal offenders as rendering the offender "the slave of the State" who has "forfeited . . . all his personal rights except those which the law in its humanity accords to him").
2 ACLU, "A Death Before Dying: Solitary Confinement on Death Row," July 2013, www.aclu.org.
3 Sell v. United States, 539 U.S. 166 (2003).
4 Washington v. Harper, 494 U.S. 210 (1990).
5 Merel Pontier, "Cruel but Not Unusual: The Automatic Use of Indefinite Solitary Confinement on Death Row: A Comparison of the Housing Policies

of Death-Sentenced Prisoners and Other Prisoners Throughout the United States," *Texas Journal of Civil Liberties and Civil Rights* 26, no. 1 (2020): 134, https://sites.utexas.edu.

6   Ramirez v. Collier, 142 S. Ct. 1264 (2022); Dunn v. Smith, 141 S. Ct. 725 (2021); Gutierrez v. Saenz, 141 S. Ct. 127, 127 (2020); Murphy v. Collier, 139 S. Ct. 1111 (2019).
7   Marc J. Posner, "The Estelle Medical Professional Judgment Standard: The Right of Those in State Custody to Receive High-Cost Medical Treatment," *American Journal of Law and Medicine* 28, no. 4 (1992): 347.
8   See generally Daniel LaChance, "Last Words, Last Meals, and Last Stands: Agency and Individuality in the Modern Execution Process," *Law and Social Inquiry* 32, no. 3 (2007).
9   E.g., S.C. Code Ann. § 24-3-530; Idaho Code § 19-2716.
10 Baze v. Rees, 553 U. S. 35, 52 (2008).
11 J. Clark Kelso, "Corrections and Sentencing Reform: The Obstacle Posed by Dehumanization," *McGeorge Law Review* 46 (2014): 899–900, https://scholarlycommons.pacific.edu. As a California corrections employee articulates, dehumanization provides the basis for draconian sentencing and prison policies and mistreatment of prison inmates. Dehumanization "makes it easier to impose extremely long and disproportionate sentences," "for legislators and governors to underfund and neglect corrections," "for corrections leaders to establish draconian punishment policies, such as indeterminate solitary confinement, and apply those policies broadly to inmates where solitary confinement really doesn't advance any legitimate goals," "for custody officers to employ excessive force," and "causes even healthcare professionals who work in the prisons to treat their patients at arm's length and with fear and distrust." Ibid.
12 LaChance, "Last Words," 703.
13 LaChance, "Last Words," 703.
14 We will use "he," "him," and similar words throughout this chapter because the overwhelming number of death row inmates are men. However, everything we describe applies equally to female death row inmates; in fact, their bodies may be subject to even more state control, including increased risk of sexual assault by correctional officers.
15 Washington v. Harper, 494 U.S. 210 (1990).
16 Sell v. United States, 539 U.S. 166 (2003) (citing Harper and Riggins v. Nevada, 504 U.S. 127 (1992)).
17 Sell v. United States, 539 U.S. 166, 180–81 (2003). In the competency context, these are generally considered to be the government's interest in timely bringing to trial a person accused of a serious crime. Id. 181.
18 American Bar Association (ABA), "Severe Mental Illness and the Death Penalty" (December 2016): 19, www.americanbar.org.
19 Riggins v. Nevada, 504 U.S. 127, 144–45 (1992).
20 Riggins v. Nevada, 504 U.S. 127, 142 (1992).
21 Riggins v. Nevada, 504 U.S. 127, 143 (1992).

22 Brief for American Psychiatric Association as Amicus Curiae, Riggins v. Nevada, 504 U.S. 127 (1992).
23 Riggins v. Nevada, 504 U.S. 127, 143–44 (1992).
24 Riggins v. Nevada, 504 U.S. 127, 143–44 (1992). See also William Geimer and Jonathan Amsterdam, "Why Jurors Vote Life or Death: Operative Factors in Ten Florida Death Penalty Cases," *American Journal of Criminal Law* 15, no. 1–2 (1987–1988): 51–53.
25 Deck v. Missouri, 544 U.S. 622 (2005); see also Holbrook v. Flynn, 475 U.S. 560, 568 (1986).
26 Deck v. Missouri, 544 U.S. 622, 630–32 (2005).
27 Illinois v. Allen, 397 U.S. 337, 344 (1970).
28 Whatley v. Warden, 927 F.3d 1150, 1189 (11th Cir. 2019).
29 Beth Schwartzapfel, "The Garb of Innocence," *The Marshall Project*, January 23, 2015, www.themarshallproject.org. Holmes's lawyers later successfully overturned the shackling order. See also, e.g., Andrade v. Martuscello, 2013 U.S. Dist. LEXIS 77670, *71 (S.D.N.Y. 2013) (upholding judge's decision to shackle defendant because he was a gang member, was accused of a violent crime, and had accrued multiple disciplinary infractions in prison); and Sekou v. Warden, 216 Conn. 678, 692–93, 583 A.2d 1277 (1990) (concluding that, notwithstanding trial court's failure to articulate its reasons for restraining petitioner at his criminal trial, record "amply demonstrate[d]" that restraints were reasonably necessary due to petitioner's history of violence while incarcerated).
30 Deck v. Missouri, 544 U.S. 622, 635 (2005) (quoting Chapman v. California, 386 U.S. 18, 24 (1967)).
31 United States v. Alexander, 732 Fed. Appx. 88, 89–90 (2d. Cir. 2018) (declining to find prejudice where trial court failed to make a finding that shackling was necessary because "[g]iven the overwhelming evidence presented against him, Alexander fails to demonstrate that the outcome of the proceedings was affected by the shackling without the requisite finding or by the jury's possible observation of the restraints"); United States v. Calhoun, 600 Fed. Appx. 842, 846–47 (3d Cir. 2015); Clyde v. Rock, 2015 U.S. Dist. LEXIS 171858 *52–53 (N.D.N.Y. 2015) (no prejudice from unjustified shackling in the face of overwhelming evidence of guilt); People v. Reese, 102 N.E.3d 126, 141 (Ill. 2017); People v. Best, 979 N.E.2d 1187, 1189 (N.Y. 2012).
32 Earhart v. Konteh, 589 F.3d 337, 349 (6th Cir. 2009); Alkebulanyahh v. Byars, 2015 U.S. Dist. LEXIS 65041 *43 (D.S.C. 2015); Andrade v. Martuscello, 2013 U.S. Dist. LEXIS 77670 *71 (S.D.N.Y. 2013); Slater v. Conway, No. 11-CV-0047, 2012 U.S. Dist. LEXIS 30291, 2012 WL 777481 *14 (W.D.N.Y. Mar. 7, 2012) ("In contrast to Deck, here there is no indication that the stun belt—assuming that [petitioner] was forced to wear it during his trial—was, in fact, visible to the jury," (citation omitted)); Pruitt v. Brown, No. 08-CV-1495, 2011 U.S. Dist. LEXIS 90543, 2011 WL 3555829 *15 (E.D.N.Y. Aug. 9, 2011); Rush v. Lempke, No. 09-CV-3464, 2011 U.S. Dist. LEXIS 10101, 2011 WL 477807 *11 (E.D.N.Y. Feb. 2, 2011) ("When a court jus-

tifiably orders that the defendant be shackled, the defendant suffers no prejudice if the court takes precautions to keep the restraints hidden from the jury."); State v. Dixon, 250 P.3d 1174 (Ariz. 2011); Hoang v. People, 323 P.3d 780 (Colo. 2014).

33 Courts have approved more extreme practices in certain situations. See, e.g., State v. Brewer, 301 So. 2d 630, 636 (La. 1974) (holding that it was not abuse of discretion for the trial judge to order that one of the defendant's hands be tied behind his back and his mouth be "taped"); State v. Forrest, 609 S.E.2d 241, 246 (N.C. Ct. App. 2005) ("[T]he trial court did not abuse its discretion in requiring that defendant be secured to his chair, handcuffed, and masked during his trial.").

34 Illinois v. Allen, 397 U.S. 337, 344 (1970).

35 Amended Petition for Writ of Habeas Corpus, Calvert v. Lumpkin, No. 6:21-cv-436-JCB-KNM, 82 (E.D. Tex. Jan. 19, 2023).

36 Petition, Calvert v. Lumpkin, 83.

37 Petition, Calvert v. Lumpkin, 83.

38 Petition, Calvert v. Lumpkin, 88. See also Jack Brook, "Shock Treatment in Court," *The Marshall Project*, July 29, 2019, www.themarshallproject.org.

39 Brook, "Shock Treatment."

40 Brook, "Shock Treatment."

41 Hawkins v. Comparet-Cassani, 251 F.3d 1230, 1239–40 (9th Cir. 2001).

42 Walker v. Martel, 709 F.3d 925, 948 (9th Cir. 2013) (Gould, J., concurring in part and dissenting in part).

43 See United States v. Brantley, 342 F. App'x 762, 770 (3d Cir. 2009).

44 Reply Br. of Petitioner, Whatley v. Warden, No. 20-363, 11 (U.S. Nov. 9, 2020), www.supremecourt.gov.

45 Robert Johnson, "Reflections on the Death Penalty: Human Rights, Human Dignity, and Dehumanization in the Death House," *Seattle Journal for Social Justice* 13, no. 2 (2014): 589–90, https://digitalcommons.law.seattleu.edu.

46 Those twelve states are Alabama, Arkansas, Florida, Georgia, Idaho, Kansas, Mississippi, Nevada, Oklahoma, South Dakota, Texas, and Wyoming. Pontier, "Cruel but Not Unusual," 134. The United States is an international outlier in its use of indefinite solitary confinement, which is internationally considered inhuman and degrading punishment. Pontier, "Cruel but Not Unusual," 126. The Inter-American Court of Human Rights, the European Court of Human Rights, and the African Court on Human and Peoples' Rights have all ruled that the use of extended solitary confinement violates their respective conventions on human rights. Further, the international consensus is that solitary confinement should not be imposed solely based on the prisoner's punishment or crime and should be used only as a last resort. Juan E. Méndez (Special Rapporteur), U.N. Off. On Drugs and Crime, Interim Rep. of the Special Rapporteur on Torture and Other Cruel, Inhuman or Degrading Treatment or Punishment, ¶ 61 UN Doc. A/68/295 (Aug. 9, 2013) ("no prisoner, including those serving life sentences and prisoners on death row, shall be held in solitary confinement merely because of the gravity of the crime"). The Mandela Rules, promulgating rules for the treatment of

prisoners, explicitly prohibit the use of solitary confinement when it is prolonged or indefinite, G.A. Res. 70/175, Nelson Mandela Rules, 16 (Dec. 17, 2015), and the United States has ratified the Convention Against Torture and the International Covenant on Civil and Political Rights (ICCPR), which require consideration of the Mandela Rules. United Nations Convention Against Torture and Other Cruel, Inhuman or Degrading Treatment or Punishment, December 10, 1984, 1465 U.N.T.S. 85; United Nations International Covenant on Civil and Political Rights, December 16, 1966, 999 U.N.T.S. 171.

47 American Civil Liberties Union, "A Death Before Dying: Solitary Confinement on Death Row" (July 2013), www.aclu.org. Cells typically contain only a steel bed or concrete slab, a steel toilet, and a small writing table. Inmates eat alone in their cells and receive their food and health care through slots in their cell doors.

48 See generally Pontier, "Cruel but Not Unusual."

49 Glossip v. Gross, 576 U.S. 863, 926 (2015) (Breyer, J., concurring) (observing that "it is well documented that [] prolonged solitary confinement produces numerous deleterious harms" and it is therefore unsurprising that many death row inmates volunteer for execution); Incumaa v. Stirling, 791 F.3d 517, 534 (4th Cir. 2015) ("prolonged solitary confinement exacts a heavy psychological toll that often continues to plague an inmate's mind even after he is resocialized"); Williams v. Sec'y, Penn. Dep't of Corr., 848 F.3d 549, 566–67 (3d Cir. 2017) (finding a "scientific consensus" that solitary confinement "is psychologically painful, can be traumatic and harmful, and puts many of those who have been subjected to it at risk of long-term damage").

50 Sharon Shalev, "A Sourcebook on Solitary Confinement," Mannheim Centre for Criminology (2008): 15, https://178e280b-c2be-42ec-b126-29a57b080d80.filesusr.com.

51 See generally Shalev, "Solitary Confinement." The effects of solitary confinement are exacerbated (and vice versa) by "death row phenomenon," the additional psychological torture that results from day-to-day life under the certainty of a death sentence. Glossip v. Gross, 576 U.S. 863, 926 (2015) (Breyer, J., concurring) (observing that "the dehumanizing effect of solitary confinement is aggravated by uncertainty as to whether a death sentence will in fact be carried out").

52 ACLU, "Death Before Dying," 3.

53 Pontier, "Cruel but Not Unusual," 134–35.

54 Pontier, "Cruel but Not Unusual," 135.

55 See, e.g., Diana Nguyen, "Tackling a Huge Taboo: Sexual Desire Behind Bars," *The Marshall Project* (November 18, 2021), www.themarshallproject.org.

56 Pontier, "Cruel but Not Unusual," 139–40.

57 Pontier, "Cruel but Not Unusual," 139–40.

58 Pontier, "Cruel but Not Unusual," 139–40.

59 Alabama had previously required the presence of a prison chaplain at executions and disallowed the practice only when the Court barred states from providing spiritual advisers of only one faith. *Dunn* 725. Similarly, Texas had long allowed

chaplains to pray audibly and touch inmates at executions. Ramirez v. Collier, 142 S. Ct. 1264, 1276 (2022).
60 Murphy v. Collier, 139 S. Ct. 1111, 1111 (2019).
61 Br. in Opposition, Gutierrez v. Collier, Nos. 19–8695, 19A1052, 30 (Jun. 15, 2020).
62 Gutierrez v. Saenz, 141 S. Ct. 127, 127 (2020).
63 Dunn v. Smith, 141 S. Ct. 725, 725 (2021). Alabama had previously required the presence of a prison chaplain at executions, and disallowed the practice only when the Court barred states from providing spiritual advisers of only one faith. Id.
64 Ramirez v. Collier, 142 S. Ct. 1264, 1273–74 (2022).
65 Ramirez v. Collier, 142 S. Ct. 1264, 1274 (2022).
66 Ramirez v. Collier, 142 S. Ct. 1264, 1274 (2022).
67 See, e.g., Dunn v. Smith, 141 S. Ct. 725, 725 (2021).
68 See, e.g., Ramirez v. Collier, 142 S. Ct. 1264, 1282 (2022) ("By passing RLUIPA, Congress determined that prisoners like Ramirez have a strong interest in avoiding substantial burdens on their religious exercise, even while confined").
69 Ramirez v. Collier, 142 S. Ct. 1264, 1282 (2022).
70 Ramirez v. Collier, 142 S. Ct. 1264, 1282 (2022).
71 Molly Hagan, "Controversy and Conjugal Visits," *JStor Daily* (February 13, 2023), https://daily.jstor.org; Dana Goldstein, "Conjugal Visits," *The Marshall Project* (February 11, 2015), www.themarshallproject.org.
72 James B. Jacobs and Eric H. Stelle, "Sexual Deprivation and Penal Policy," *Cornell Law Review* 62, no. 2 (1977): 292, https://scholarship.law.cornell.edu.
73 See Andrew P. Wilper et al., "The Health and Health Care of US Prisoners: Results of a Nationwide Survey," *American Journal of Public Health* 99, no. 4 (2009): 669.
74 Wilper, "The Health and Health Care of US Prisoners," 669.
75 See, e.g., Brown v. Plata, 563 U.S. 493 (2011). The Court in *Plata* described deficiencies in California's prison health care system:

Prisoners in California with serious mental illness do not receive minimal, adequate care. Because of a shortage of treatment beds, suicidal inmates may be held for prolonged periods in telephone-booth sized cages without toilets. A psychiatric expert reported observing an inmate who had been held in such a cage for nearly 24 hours, standing in a pool of his own urine, unresponsive and nearly catatonic. Prison officials explained they had "no place to put him." Other inmates awaiting care may be held for months in administrative segregation, where they endure harsh and isolated conditions and receive only limited mental health services. Wait times for mental health care range as high as 12 months. . . .

Prisoners suffering from physical illness also receive severely deficient care. . . . A correctional officer testified that, in one prison, up to 50 sick inmates may be held together in a 12- by 20-foot cage for up to five hours awaiting treatment. The number of staff is inadequate, and prisoners face significant delays in access to care. A prisoner with severe abdominal pain died after a 5-week delay in referral to a specialist; a prisoner with "constant and extreme" chest pain died after an 8-hour delay

in evaluation by a doctor; and a prisoner died of testicular cancer after a "failure of MDs to work up for cancer in a young man with 17 months of testicular pain."
  Brown v. Plata, 563 U.S. 493, 503–05 (2011) (internal citations and quotations omitted).

76 Marc J. Posner, "The Estelle Medical Professional Judgment Standard: The Right of Those in State Custody to Receive High-Cost Medical Treatment," *American Journal of Law and Medicine* 18, no. 4 (1992): 361 n. 101 ("In essence, Estelle holds that a prisoner is constitutionally entitled to the treatment prescribed by a medical professional. This right would not seem to encompass second opinions or choice of doctors or treatments.").

77 Emily Bohatch, "SC Inmate's Baby Died in Toilet: Lawsuits Allege Rampant Medical Neglect in Prisons," *Greenville News* (April 11, 2019), www.greenvilleonline.com.

78 Estelle v. Gamble, 429 U.S. 97, 102 (1976).

79 Christina Pazzanese, "Supreme Court May Halt Health Care Guarantees for Inmates," *The Harvard Gazette* (March 2, 2023), https://news.harvard.edu.

80 Estelle v. Gamble, 429 U.S. 97, 104 (1976).

81 Farmer v. Brennan, 511 U.S. 825, 837 (1994).

82 Monmouth Cnt.y Corr. Inst. Inmates v. Lanzaro, 834 F.2d 326, 347 (3d Cir. 1987) (quoting Pace v. Fauver, 479 F. Supp. 456, 458 (D. N.J. 1979). *aff'd* 649 F.2d 860 (3d Cir. 1981)).

83 Monmouth Cnt.y Corr. Inst. Inmates v. Lanzaro, 834 F.2d 326, 347 (3d Cir. 1987).

84 East v. Lemons, 768 F.2d 1000, 1001 (8th Cir. 1985) (holding that arm cramps during physical work were a serious medical need).

85 Scott v. Garcia, 370 F. Supp. 2d 1056, 1057 (S.D. Cal. 2005) (holding that severe gastrointestinal condition was a serious medical need because it interfered with ability to eat).

86 Layman ex rel. Layman v. Alexander, 343 F. Supp. 2d 493 (W.D.N.C. 2004) (holding serious medical need evident when arrestee hit his head, fell unconscious, and suffered brain damage as a result of lack of medical attention).

87 See, e.g., Ralston v. McGovern, 167 F.3d 1160, 1161 (7th Cir. 1999) (noting that defining a serious medical need "is a function both of objective need and of cost. The lower the cost, the less need has to be shown, but the need must still be shown to be substantial.").

88 See, e.g., Bowring v. Godwin 551 F.2d 44, 48 (4th Cir. 1977) (the right to a specific treatment is "limited to that which may be provided upon a reasonable cost and time basis and the essential test is one of medical necessity and not simply that which may be considered merely desirable").

89 See generally Michelle Masotto, "'Death is Different': Limiting Health Care for Death Row Inmates," *Health Matrix* 24, no. 1 (2015), https://scholarlycommons.law.case.edu/cgi/viewcontent.cgi?article=1011&context=healthmatrix.

90 Jacob Biba and Lyle C. May, "The Geriatric Ward: North Carolina's Aging Death Row Population Faces Looming Health Care Crisis," *The Intercept* (November 20, 2021), https://theintercept.com.

91 Biba and May, "The Geriatric Ward."
92 "ACLU: Condemned Inmates Denied Care," *Seattle PI* (October 15, 2008), www.seattlepi.com.
93 "Bureau of Justice Statistics Reports Number on Death Row Down, Average Time on Death Row Approaches 19 Years," *Death Penalty Information Center* (June 25, 2021), https://deathpenaltyinfo.org.
94 "Number on Death Row Down," DPIC.
95 See, e.g., Jensen v. Shinn, 609 F. Supp. 3d 789, 890 (D. Ariz. 2022).
96 Chris Parker, "Schuylkill Inmates Sue Over Food," *Times News Online* (July 1, 2014), www.tnonline.com. Tennessee inmate Fred Williams lost 78 pounds in less than one year at the Schuylkill County Jail because he could not afford to supplement the jail's diet with commissary food.
97 Steve Visser, "Gordon County Inmates Underfed, Human Rights Group Alleges," *The Atlanta Journal-Constitution* (October 28, 2014), www.ajc.com.
98 Paul Nelson, "Lawsuit Says Jail Skimps on Food," *Times Union* (July 30, 2014), www.timesunion.com.
99 Nelson, "Jail Skimps on Food."
100 Nelson, "Jail Skimps on Food."
101 Parker, "Schuylkill Inmates."
102 Jensen v. Shinn, 609 F. Supp. 3d 789, 890 (D. Ariz. 2022).
103 Stop the Musick Coalition, "Cold, Rotting and Moldy Meals: Food Oppression in the Orange County Jails" (December 15, 2021): 3, www.stopthemusick.net.
104 Stop the Musick Coalition, "Cold, Rotting and Moldy Meals," 7.
105 Eric Lach, "Joe Arpaio Brags About Serving Inmates 56 Cent Thanksgiving Dinner," *TPM* (November 29, 2013), https://talkingpointsmemo.com. The dinner consisted of five ounces of turkey soy casserole, one cup each of mashed potatoes and glazed carrots, half a cup of fruit, a brownie (donated), a dinner roll, and margarine.
106 Ashley Broughton, "Sheriff Jailed for Pocketing Money Meant for Inmate Meals," *CNN*, last accessed September 13, 2023, www.cnn.com.
107 See, e.g., Complaint, United States v. Makos, Mag. No. 21–13331 (D.N.J. Sept. 29, 2021), www.justice.gov/usao-nj/press-release/file/1438041/download (complaint alleging torture by guards in a New Jersey prison, including punching and kicking inmates, handcuffing inmates to a fence while punching them, and forcing inmates to eat hot peppers); Affidavit of Sergeant Dale Hunt, Tennessee v. Taylor, www.aclu.org (corrections officer admitting that guards on Tennessee's death row singled out and tortured a particular death row inmate, including denying him food, hitting him with billy clubs, shutting off his water, ripping up his clothes, refusing to let him leave his cell, and threatening to hang him); Second Amended Complaint, Jones v. St. Louis, No. 4:21-cv-600 (E.D. Mo. Mar. 15, 2022), www.documentcloud.org (class action alleging abuse by officers in at St. Louis jail, including macing inmates unnecessarily and leaving them naked and without water in cells filled with mace).

108 See generally Andrea Jacobs, "Prison Power Corrupts Absolutely: Exploring the Phenomenon of Prison Guard Brutality and the Need to Develop a System of Accountability," *California Western Law Review* 41, no. 1 (2004), https://scholarlycommons.law.cwsl.edu.
109 See, e.g., Affidavit of Sergeant Dale Hunt in *Tennessee v. Taylor* (corrections officer explaining that he and fellow guards tortured a severely mentally ill death row inmate because "we wanted to make it horrible for him there" and because "I wanted him to suffer as much as he could").
110 Porter v. Nussle, 534 U.S. 516, 532 (2002).
111 See, e.g., Abney v. County of Nassau, 237 F. Supp. 2d 278 (E.D.N.Y. 2002) (an inmate requested an internal grievance form after an alleged assault by prison guards, but one was never provided to him).
112 Jacobs, "Prison Power," 295–96.
113 Jacobs, "Prison Power," 296. For example, a New York inmate who was beaten by corrections officers wrote a handwritten letter to the facility's Grievance Coordinator describing the incident and asking for a grievance form, but the form was never provided. See Abney v. County of Nassau, 237 F. Supp. 2d 278, 279 (E.D.N.Y. 2002).
114 See, e.g., Mendoza v. Goord, No. 00 Civ. 0146(GEL), 2002 WL 31654855 (S.D.N.Y. Nov. 21, 2002). Mendoza filed an excessive force grievance and followed up with another grievance when he never received a ruling. After the second grievance, the prison informed him that it had dismissed the first grievance without notifying Mendoza. The court dismissed his action on the grounds that he had failed to exhaust all administrative remedies. Another New York inmate filed an excessive force grievance, was never notified of its status, and repeatedly attempted to follow up the filing with guards. Eventually, he was informed that no record existed of the initial grievance and that he could not refile the complaint because of the amount of time that had passed. The court nonetheless denied his claim on the grounds that the inmate failed to appeal the grievance. Taylor v. Bermudez, No. 03 Civ. 0087(NRB), 2003 WL 21664673 (S.D.N.Y. 2003).
115 Robert Johnson, *A Study of the Modern Execution Process* (Belmont, CA: Wadsworth, 1998).
116 Michel Foucault, *Discipline and Punish*, trans. Alan Sheridan (New York: Vintage Books, 1975).
117 Press Release, Tex. Office of the Att'y Gen., David Martin Long Scheduled to Be Executed (December 7, 1999), available at www.texasattorneygeneral.gov.
118 Michael Graczyk, "Killer Executed 2 Days After Suicide Try," *Fort Worth Star-Telegram* (December 9, 1999), www.newspapers.com.
119 Jim Yardley, "Texan Who Took Overdose Is Executed," *New York Times* (December 9, 1999), http://www.nytimes.com.
120 Yardley, "Texan Who Took Overdose Is Executed."
121 Yardley, "Texan Who Took Overdose Is Executed."
122 Michael Graczyk, "Killer Executed Two Days After Suicide Try," *Fort Worth Star-Telegram* (December 9, 1999), www.newspapers.com. Texas literally spent

hundreds of thousands of dollars to preserve Long for execution, but at his trial, despite his obvious mental illness, he was denied funding for necessary mental health experts.

123 Howard Schneider, "A Common Thread Links 14 Deaths—Pee Wee Gaskins," *The State* (March 25, 1983), www.newspapers.com.

124 Art Harris, "The Seeds of Vengeance," *Washington Post* (June 24, 1983), www.washingtonpost.com.

125 Ivy Moore, "Former Sheriff Examines Gaskins' Claims," *The Item* (Nov. 14, 2010), www.newspapers.com.

126 Margaret N. O'Shea, "State Executes Gaskins," *The State* (September 6, 1991), www.newspapers.com.

127 O'Shea, "Gaskins."

128 O'Shea, "Gaskins."

129 O'Shea, "Gaskins." The use of valuable donated blood to resuscitate a person whom the state intends to kill the next day is worth noting.

130 O'Shea, "Gaskins."

131 O'Shea, "Gaskins." In the interests of full disclosure, one of the authors of this article represented both Long and Gaskins.

132 Ford v. Wainwright, 477 U.S. 399 (1986).

133 Ford v. Wainwright, 477 U.S. 399, 417 (1986). Due to the previously discussed deficits in medical care on death row and in prisons generally, it is difficult to know with certainty the number of death row inmates who suffer from mental illness. However, research indicates that 50 percent or more of death row inmates exhibit symptoms of severe mental illness. See "Report: 75% of 2015 Executions Raised Serious Concerns About Mental Health or Innocence," *Death Penalty Information Center*, archived at https://perma.cc/QQJ8-DDQD (finding that of the 28 people executed in 2015, seven suffered from serious mental illness, and another seven suffered from serious intellectual impairment or brain injury); Robert J. Smith, Sophie Cull, and Zoe Robinson, "The Failure of Mitigation?," *Hastings Law Journal* 65 (2014): 1245 ("Over half (fifty-four) of the last one hundred executed offenders had been diagnosed with or displayed symptoms of a severe mental illness."); Brandi Grissom, "Trouble in Mind," *Texas Monthly* (March 2013), archived at https://perma.cc/JZ7K-ZFU6 ("On Texas's death row, more than 20 percent of the 290 inmates are considered mentally ill").

134 Ford v. Wainwright, 477 U.S. 399, 409 (1986).

135 David M. Adams, "Belief and Death: Capital Punishment and the Competence-for-Execution Requirement," *Criminal Law and Philosophy* 10 (2016): 23. Adams notes that, to be executed, a person's understanding of his impending punishment must comport with the community's understanding of why that punishment is warranted—he must "endorse the reasons the state has for so punishing [him]."

136 Ford v. Wainwright, 477 U.S. 399, 422 (1986) (Powell, J., concurring).

137 Ford v. Wainwright, 477 U.S. 399, 425 n.5 (1986) (Powell, J., concurring).

138 Panetti v. Quarterman, 551 U.S. 930, 960 (2007).

139 ABA, "Severe Mental Illness and the Death Penalty," 2.
140 State v. Perry, 610 So. 2d 746 (La. 1992).
141 Singleton v. State, 437 S.E.2d 53 (S.C. 1993).
142 Singleton v. Norris, 319 F.3d 1018, 1021 (8th Cir. 2003). This section is based on Alan A. Stone, "Condemned Prisoner Treated and Executed," *Death Penalty Information Center* (March 2004), https://deathpenaltyinfo.org.
143 Singleton v. Norris, 319 F.3d 1018, 1030 (8th Cir. 2003).
144 Singleton v. Norris, 319 F.3d 1018, 1030–31 (8th Cir. 2003).
145 Singleton v. Norris, 319 F.3d 1018, 1031 (8th Cir. 2003).
146 Singleton v. Norris, 319 F.3d 1018, 1031–33 (8th Cir. 2003).
147 Singleton v. Norris, 319 F.3d 1018, 1031 (8th Cir. 2003).
148 Singleton v. Norris, 319 F.3d 1018, 1031 (8th Cir. 2003).
149 Singleton v. Norris, 319 F.3d 1018, 1025 n.3 (8th Cir. 2003).
150 Singleton v. Norris, 319 F.3d 1018, 1021 (8th Cir. 2003).
151 Washington v. Harper, 494 U.S. 210 (1990).
152 Singleton v. Endell, 870 S.W.2d 742 (Ark. 1994).
153 Singleton v. Norris, 319 F.3d 1018 (8th Cir. 2003).
154 Singleton v. Norris, 319 F.3d 1018 (8th Cir. 2003).
155 Singleton v. Norris, 319 F.3d 1018, 1026 (8th Cir. 2003).
156 Singleton v. Norris, 124 S. Ct. 74 (2003) (*cert. denied*); Scott Gottlieb, "Murderer Can Be Forced to Take Medication to Become Sane Enough to Be Executed," *BMJ* (October 18, 2003), www.ncbi.nlm.nih.gov/pmc/articles/PMC218842.
157 Gottlieb, "Murderer Can Be Forced to Take Medication."
158 "Singleton Dies; 2nd Execution Stopped," *Russellville Courier* (January 7, 2004).
159 State v. Perry, 610 So. 2d 746, 747 (La. 1992).
160 State v. Perry, 610 So. 2d 746, 754 (La. 1992).
161 Singleton v. State, 437 S.E.2d 53, 61 (1993).
162 Singleton v. State, 437 S.E.2d 53, 61 (1993).
163 Singleton v. State, 437 S.E.2d 53, 62 (1993).
164 Singleton v. State, 437 S.E.2d 53, 59 (1993).
165 Again, in the interest of disclosure, one of the authors of this article represented and currently represents Wilson.
166 John H. Blume and Sheri Lynn Johnson, "Killing the Non-Willing: Atkins, the Volitionally Incapacitated, and the Death Penalty," *South Carolina Law Review* 55, no. 93 (2003): 96–97, https://scholarship.law.cornell.edu.
167 Blume and Johnson, "Killing the Non-Willing," 98.
168 Blume and Johnson, "Killing the Non-Willing," 99.
169 "18 Years on Death Row: The Shootings," *WIS 10 News* (November 13, 2006), www.wistv.com.
170 Blume and Johnson, "Killing the Non-Willing," 94–95.
171 Blume and Johnson, "Killing the Non-Willing," 103.
172 Jeffrey Collins, "School Shooter Gets Temporary Reprieve," *Go Upstate* (July 10, 2004), www.goupstate.com.

173 See, e.g., Keri Blakinger and Maurice Chammah, "From Last Meals to Last Words, What Can Death Row Prisoners Request Before They Die?," *The Marshall Project*, September 7, 2021, www.themarshallproject.org.
174 Oklahoma Department of Corrections, "Execution of Inmates Sentenced to Death,"https://oklahoma.gov, last accessed January 26, 2024.
175 Florida Department of Corrections, "Death Row," last accessed January 26, 2024, https://fdc.myflorida.com.
176 Keri Blakinger and Maurice Chammah, "From Last Meals to Last Words, What Can Death Row Prisoners Request Before They Die?," *The Marshall Project*, September 7, 2021, www.themarshallproject.org.
177 Brian Price, "The Last Supper," *Legal Affairs* (2004): 31.
178 See John H. Blume, "On 'Death Houses' and 'Kill Boxes:' The Death Penalty and Animal Slaughter," *Cornell Law Review* 109 (2024).
179 Twenty-nine jurisdictions (27 states, the federal government, and the military) retain the death penalty. "State by State," *Death Penalty Information Center* (2023), https://deathpenaltyinfo.org/state-and-federal-info/state-by-state. Of those jurisdictions, eight offer the inmate a choice of execution methods, 20 offer no choice, and one (Missouri) is unclear. "State-by-State Execution Protocols," *Death Penalty Information Center* (2023), https://deathpenaltyinfo.org.
180 Baze v. Rees, 553 U. S. 35, 52 (2008).
181 Bucklew v. Precythe, 139 S. Ct. 1112, 1124 (2019).
182 Bucklew v. Precythe, 139 S. Ct. 1112, 1120 (2019).
183 "Missouri Executes Russell Bucklew Despite Concerns over Rare Medical Condition," *CBS News* (October 1, 2019), www.cbsnews.com.
184 Bucklew v. Precythe, 139 S. Ct. 1112, 1121 (2019).
185 Bucklew v. Precythe, 139 S. Ct. 1112, 1129 (2019).
186 Bucklew v. Precythe, 139 S. Ct. 1112, 1143 (2019) (Breyer, J., dissenting).
187 AMA Code of Medical Ethics, Opinion 9.7.3, "Capital Punishment," https://code-medical-ethics.ama-assn.org.
188 Leonidas Koniaris et al., "Inadequate Anaesthesia in Lethal Injection for Execution," *The Lancet* 365 (April 2005): 1412; Stephanie Mencimer, "State Executioners: Untrained, Incompetent, and 'Complete Idiots,'" *Mother Jones* (May 7, 2014), www.motherjones.com.
189 Elizabeth Weil, "The Needle and the Damage Done," *New York Times* (February 11, 2007), www.nytimes.com.
190 Jimmy Jenkins, "Republic Reporter: Witnessing a Man Put to Death 'Changed Me,'" *Arizona Republic* (June 9, 2022). Atwood had originally selected to be executed by nitrogen hypoxia, but because Arizona only provided for execution by lethal injection or cyanide poisoning, the state rejected his selection and imposed its default method of lethal injection.
191 Jenkins, "Witnessing a Man Put to Death."
192 Jenkins, "Witnessing a Man Put to Death."
193 Jenkins, "Witnessing a Man Put to Death."

194 "Private Autopsy Documents 'Carnage' Experienced by Alabama Death-Row Prisoner Joe Nathan James During Longest Botched Lethal-Injection Execution in History," *Death Penalty Information Center* (August 16, 2022), https://deathpenaltyinfo.org.
195 "Alabama Governor Halts Executions After Latest in Series of Execution Failures," *Death Penalty Information Center* (November 23, 2022), https://deathpenaltyinfo.org.
196 Rule 8(d)(1), Ala. R. App. P.
197 Order, Alabama Supreme Court (January 12, 2023), https://judicial.alabama.gov/docs/rules/Rule_8(d)(1),Ala.R.App.P.Order.pdf.
198 "Methods of Execution," *Death Penalty Information Center* (2023), https://deathpenaltyinfo.org/executions/methods-of-execution.
199 See, e.g., Joel B. Zivot et al., "Execution by Lethal Injection: Autopsy Findings of Pulmonary Edema" (preprint 2022), www.medrxiv.org/content/10.1101/2022.08.24.22279183v1.full.pdf (finding that inmates executed by lethal injection suffered from pulmonary edema before death); Koniaris et al., "Inadequate Anaesthesia," 1412 (concluding that individuals executed by lethal injection have continued to breathe after the injection of thiopental, and their hearts have continued to beat following injection of potassium, which means that the inmate likely experienced asphyxiation while conscious and paralyzed, and intense burning pain throughout the body from injection of potassium).
200 S.C. Code § 24-3-530; "South Carolina Completes Preparations for Firing-Squad Executions," *Death Penalty Information Center* (March 21, 2022), https://deathpenaltyinfo.org.
201 S.C. Code § 24-3-530; Order Granting Declaratory and Injunctive Relief, Owens v. Stirling, No. 2021-CP-4002306 (Sept. 6, 2022).
202 Order Granting Declaratory and Injunctive Relief, Owens v. Stirling, No. 2021-CP-4002306 (Sept. 6, 2022).
203 S.C. Code Ann. § 24-3-580 (2023).
204 "South Carolina Ready to Resume Executions by Lethal Injection After Acquiring Drugs," *Death Penalty Information Center* (September 23, 2023), https://deathpenaltyinfo.org.
205 Owens v. Stirling, 904 S.E.2d (S.C. 2024).
206 Owens v. Stirling, 904 S.E.2d 580, 608 (S.C. 2024).
207 "Idaho Governor Signs Firing Squad Execution Bill into Law," *Associated Press* (March 25, 2023), https://apnews.com.
208 "Idaho Bill Would Bring Back Execution by Firing Squad," *KUOW* (February 23, 2023), www.kuow.org.
209 "Execution Costs in Idaho Take Center Stage with New Firing Squad Law," *Death Penalty Information Center* (July 6, 2023), https://deathpenaltyinfo.org.
210 "Overview of Lethal Injection Protocols," *Death Penalty Information Center*, https://deathpenaltyinfo.org.
211 E.g., Michael J. Zoosman, "The Unconscionable Nazi Legacies of Executions by Gas and Lethal Injection," *JURIST* (February 7, 2024), www.jurist.org/commen-

tary/2024/02/the-unconscionable-nazi-legacies-of-executions-by-gas-and-lethal-injection.

212 Lauren Gill, "'Agony' and 'Suffering' as Alabama Experiments with Nitrogen Executions," *Bolts* (October 8, 2024), https://boltsmag.org/alabama-nitrogen-executions; Kim Chandler, "What Happened at the Nation's First Nitrogen Gas Execution: An AP Eyewitness Account," *Associated Press* (January 27, 2024), https://apnews.com/article/death-penalty-nitrogen-gas-alabama-kenneth-smith-54848cb06ce32d4b462a77b1bb25e656.

ABOUT THE CONTRIBUTORS

JOHN H. BLUME is the Samuel F. Leibowitz Professor of Trial Techniques and the Director of the Cornell Death Penalty Project. His writings include articles on federal habeas corpus law and practice, racial discrimination in the criminal law and capital cases in particular, and capital punishment and intellectual disability.

CLAUDIA CENTER is the Legal Director for the Disability Rights and Education Fund. She was previously a Senior Staff Attorney in the Disability Rights Program of the national ACLU Foundation and Director of the Disability Rights Program at Legal Aid At Work. In 2009, she received the Paul G. Hearne Award for Disability Rights from the ABA Commission on Disability Rights.

DORON DORFMAN is Professor of Law at Seton Hall Law School. His research and teaching focus on disability law, health law, torts, employment law, law and psychology, and family law.

ALLISON FRANZ is Staff Attorney at Justice 360 in Columbia, South Carolina, and Adjunct Professor of Law at Cornell Law School, supervising the Capital Punishment Clinic and Juvenile Justice Clinic.

SUSANNA LEE is Professor of French and Francophone Studies and Comparative Literature at Georgetown University. She is widely published in the areas of literature and moral authority, intellectual history, law and humanities, detective fiction, popular culture, and literary theory.

KIMBERLY MUTCHERSON is Co-Dean and Professor of Law at Rutgers Law School in Camden. Dean Mutcherson is a reproductive justice scholar whose work sits at the intersection of bioethics, health law, and family. She has a particular focus on assisted reproduction, abortion, disability, and medical decision-making for children and pregnant women.

WENDY E. PARMET is Matthews Distinguished University Professor of Law at Northeastern University School of Law. A leading expert on health, disability, and public health law, she directs the law school's Center for Health Policy and Law.

VICTORIA RODRÍGUEZ-ROLDÁN is Senior Policy Manager for AIDS United. Particular areas of expertise and focus are the issues affecting people living at the intersections of transgender identity, disability, and mental illness from a social justice lens. Before joining AIDS United, she was Senior Policy Counsel at the National LGBTQ Task Force, where she led the Trans/GNC Justice Project and the Disability Justice Project.

AUSTIN SARAT is William Nelson Cromwell Professor of Jurisprudence and Political Science at Amherst College in Amherst, Massachusetts. He has written, cowritten, or edited more than one hundred books in the fields of law and political science; his primary research interest is the death penalty,

ALLISON M. WHELAN is Assistant Professor of Law at Georgia State University College of Law. Her research and teaching encompass a broad set of medical, science, and social policy issues at the intersection of administrative law, health and FDA law, constitutional law, bioethics, and reproductive justice.

INDEX

AAPD. *See* American Association of People with Disabilities
ableism, 105, 166–68, 178–79
abortions, 3–4, 9–11, 17–18, 19n9, 29, 38, 114; access to, 8, 12, 30, 127, 129, 133–40, 152; bans on, 5, 8, 15–16, 31, 125–53, 154n3, 160n108, 165n203; illegal, 129, 135; legalization of, 138; medically necessary, 131–32; medications for, 129–30, 150; minors seeking, 82; out-of-state, 129, 156n27; physicians and, 135–36, 138–39, 151, 158n76; rights to, 2, 16, 82, 125, 132, 135, 139–41, 145, 147, 184. *See also specific court cases*
access, accessibility and, 13, 70–71, 131; to abortions, 8, 12, 30, 127, 129, 133–40, 152; to gender-affirming care, 17, 63–64, 83, 166–70, 174–76; to medical services for death row inmates, 193, 196–98, 201–2, 218n75, 222n133; to natural light, 18, 187, 193
accidental incest, 44
ADA. *See* Americans with Disabilities Act
Adams, David M., 222n135
Adams, Eric, 108
ADHD. *See* Attention-Deficit/Hyperactivity Disorder
adolescents, 67, 82; transgender, 4, 166, 174
adoptions, 40, 46–47, 52, 59nn68–69
adult-onset diseases, 14, 68–69, 90
Adverse Events (Fisher), 7
Affordable Care Act, U.S., 74, 167–68, 172, 179–80
Afghanistan, 110

age, 5, 23, 67; consent and, 14; of death row inmates, 198; gender-affirming care and, 1, 172–73
AI. *See* artificial insemination
Alabama, 178, 195, 199–200, 210–12, 217n59, 218n63
Alexander, Michelle, 8
Alito, Samuel, 9–11, 142–43, 145
Alliance for Hippocratic Medicine v. Food & Drug Administration, 150
ALS. *See* amyotrophic lateral sclerosis
American Association of People with Disabilities (AAPD), 112
American College of Pediatricians, 175, 184n37
American Contagions (Witt), 7
American Law Institute, 138–39
American Medical Association, 135, 139, 210
American Psychiatric Association, 168, 190
American Public Health Association, 139
American Society for Reproductive Medicine (ASRM), 24–26, 29–30, 33–35, 52, 55n14, 58n51
Americans with Disabilities Act (ADA), U.S., 102, 109, 112–13, 123n101, 167–68, 172, 179–80, 181n8, 186n64
amyotrophic lateral sclerosis (Lou Gehrig's disease, ALS), 14, 61
Anderson, Nancy, 20n28
anonymity, sale of gametes and, 13, 22, 30, 45–49
antiabortion movement, 3–4, 8–10, 89, 135

229

anti-maskers, anti-mask sentiment and, 4, 102
antipsychotic medications, 190, 204–7
anti-trans rhetoric, laws and, 16, 166–70, 172, 174–80
antitrust laws, 33–34
antivaccine (vaccine freedom) movements, 16, 137, 149–50, 159n96
Arizona, 199, 210, 224n190
Arkansas, 174–75, 204
Arpaio, Joe, 199
arrests, 5, 8
Arsenault, Trent, 43
artificial insemination (AI), 21, 27, 33, 37–38, 56n22
Asian people, 105, 113
ASRM. *See* American Society for Reproductive Medicine
assisted reproduction, 24, 37–40, 45–46, 49–50, 53
Attention-Deficit/Hyperactivity Disorder (ADHD), 166–68, 170–72, 176–77, 180
Atwood, Frank, 210, 224n190
authority, medical, 126, 139–40, 149, 150–51, 164n197, 182n15
authority, parental, 66, 78, 81, 87
autism, 110, 137, 166–68, 171–72, 174–77, 286n66
Autistic Self Advocacy Network, 171
Autistic Women and Nonbinary Network, 171
autonomy, bodily, 2–6, 9–12, 18, 87, 145, 163n168; of children, 14–15, 72–73, 75–76; of death row inmates, 187–91, 196, 200–201, 208–10, 212–13; individual, 16, 126–28, 134, 139, 144
avian influenza pandemic, 137

Bader Ginsburg, Ruth, 3, 142
Bailey, Michael, 174
Banking on the Body (Swanson), 33
banks, gamete-selling, 21–22, 26–27, 30, 32–42, 45, 57n46

bans, abortion, 5, 8, 15–16, 31, 125–53, 154n3, 160n108, 165n203
Barber, James, 211
Barr, William, 142
Barrett, Amy Coney, 142, 145, 150–51
Being and Owning (Wall), 7
Bellotti v. Baird, 82
Bennett, Barbara, 79
Bernstein, Anita, 7
biases, 10–11, 17, 117n5, 167, 172–73, 178–79
Biden, Joseph, 102, 141, 144
Bill of Rights, U.S., 85
biocertification, 111
biological parents, 46–52
biological weapon, 137
birth control, 138
birth defects, 5
Black Lives Matter movement, 107–8
Blackmun, Harry, 4, 139
Blackness, 39, 108
Black people, 17, 37, 192; police violence and, 107–8; slavery impacting, 2–3
The Black Reproductive (Clarke), 7
Blakeney-Williams, Nikita, 108
Blanchard, Raymond, 174
blood plasma, 29, 34
Blume, John H., 17–18
Bodies of Law (Hyde), 6
body, regulation of the. *See specific topics*
bombings, prison, 202
Borderline Personality Disorder (BPD), 177, 184n46
Boston, Massachusetts, 133
bounty hunters, 114
Bowers v. Hardwick, 3
BPD. *See* Borderline Personality Disorder
breach of warranty, sperm banks and, 37
breast reductions, 1
Brewer, David J., 135–36
Brewer, Henry, 207–8
Breyer, Stephen, 209–10
Bucklew, Russell, 209–10
Buck v. Bell, 136, 138

Buddhism, 195
Bush, George W., 137
Byrn, Robert, 9–10

California, 9, 34, 137, 139, 142–43, 199, 214n11, 218n75; genetic testing and, 74–75; independent living movement and, 109
Calvary Chapel Dayton Valley v. Sisolak, 142
Calvert, James, 191–92
cancer, 68, 70–71, 198
Cantor, James, 177–78
capital punishment, 187–90, 205, 213, 224n179. *See also* death row inmates
carcerality, 6, 8
Catholicism, 9
cavernous hemangioma, 209
CDC. *See* Centers for Disease Control and Prevention
censorship, 6, 188, 207
Census Bureau, U.S., 170
Center, Claudia, 16–17
Center for American Progress, 113
Centers for Disease Control and Prevention (CDC), U.S., 15, 23, 100–101, 104, 110, 112, 130
Centers for Medicare and Medicaid Services, 144
cerebral palsy, 110
cesarean section (C-sections), 149
Chapman, Jay, 210
chemotherapy, 66
Chen, Mel, 101
Chicago, Illinois, 110
childbirth, 131, 149
children: bodily autonomy of, 14–15, 72–73, 75–76; consent and, 75–77, 85–86, 90; decision-making and, 72–73, 76–77, 81; gender-affirming care for, 6, 63–64, 83; genetic information of, 12, 14–15, 73–76, 80, 85–86, 88–91; health care decisions and, 64–83; PPGT on, 14, 61–64, 67–77, 80, 82–91; privacy and, 61, 75–76, 83–88; rights of, 64–65, 73, 75–76, 79–81, 89, 92n12; socioemotional wellbeing of, 70–72; vaccine laws and, 127–28, 131, 133–138, 143. *See also* transgender children
Christianity, 146, 151
cisgender people, 168, 170
Citron, Danielle, 75, 86
civil death, 187, 213n1
Civil War, U.S., 133
class, 12
class-action suits, 199
Clayton, Ellen Wright, 76
cloning, 42
coital reproduction, 43–44, 49, 53
Colb, Sherry F., 148–49
Colgrove, James, 136
Collins, Francis, 117n7
colonoscopies, 107
Colorado, 110
commissary items, 198–99, 220n96
common-law, 11, 64, 84, 135
The Common Law Inside the Female Body (Bernstein), 7
communicable diseases, 26
comorbidities, 100, 105; mental health and, 174–77, 185n50
compensation, for the sale of gametes, 21–22, 32–35
competency, 172, 214n17; execution contingent on, 202–7, 222n135; forcible, 189–90, 201, 204–5
conception, 48–50, 53, 61
conjugal visitation, for death row inmates, 196
consent, 14, 64–66, 136; children and, 75–77, 85–86, 90; informed, 32, 56n28, 67, 137, 175, 177, 207; parental, 67–68, 82, 87–88, 90; trans disabled individuals and, 17, 172, 177
conservators, state-appointed, 17, 172–73

232 | INDEX

Consortium for Constituents with Disabilities, 168
Constitution, U.S., 8, 12, 19n8, 83, 160n113; rights, 1–2, 14, 16, 20n26, 53, 53n2, 61, 64–65, 82, 86, 126, 132, 135–40, 145. *See also specific Amendments*
contact visitation, for death row inmates, 194
conversion therapy, 173
corporate law, 104
corrections officers, guards and, 193–94, 200, 207–8, 210–13, 214n11, 214n14, 220n107, 221n109, 221n111, 221nn113–14
cost-benefit analysis, 197, 199, 207–8, 219n87
counsel, right to, 190
COVID-19 pandemic, 1–2, 5, 16, 121, 125, 132, 141; death row inmates and, 198–99; people with disabilities and, 100; preventative measures against, 101–3; social distancing for, 107–8, 111, 142; vaccinations, 2, 4, 106, 126–27, 130, 134, 142–45, 148, 152. *See also* mask mandates, COVID-19
Cox, Kate, 5
Cramblett, Jennifer, 37–41
criminalization: of abortion, 5; of care, 17, 169–70; of homosexual sex, 3; of sex work, 29
Crisp, Bryan, 110–11
critical race theory, 114
cruel and unusual punishments, 197, 210
C-sections. *See* cesarean section
CT scans, 70
Cumings, Susan, 105
custody, child, 58
cyanide poisoning, execution by, 224n190

daycare, 127
deaf people, 173
DeAngelo, Joseph James, 74–75
death row inmates, 1, 12, 17, 222n129; access to medical services for, 193, 196–98, 201–2, 218n75, 222n133; bodily autonomy of, 187–91, 196, 200–201, 208–10, 212–13; corrections officers and, 193–94, 200, 207–8, 210–13, 214n11, 214n14, 220n107, 221n109, 221n111, 221nn113–14; dehumanization of, 187–88, 192–93, 200–201, 213, 214n11, 217n51; deprived of sexual stimulation, 193, 196; execution competence and, 202–7, 222n135; executions of, 187–88, 194–95, 200–213, 222n135, 224n179; exposed to violence of, 187–88, 193, 200, 210–13, 220n107, 221n109, 221nn113–14; exposure to violence of, 187–88, 193, 200; forced medication of, 18, 187, 189–90, 201, 203–5; forcible competence and, 189–90, 201, 204–5; free will and, 188–89; grievance processes, for, 200, 221n111, 221n114; illusory choices of, 187–88, 190, 197–98, 200–201, 208–10, 212–13, 224n179; last words of, 188, 201, 205, 207–8; mental illnesses of, 202–7, 218n75, 221n109, 221n112, 222n133; as nonhuman entities, 187, 200; nutrition and, 193, 198–200, 220n96, 220n105; rehumanization of, 188–89, 200–208; rights of, 187, 190, 194–96, 199, 202–3, 205, 219n75, 219n88; "serious medical needs" of, 197, 219nn84–87; shackling of, 189, 191–92, 215n29, 215n32, 216n33; solitary confinement of, 192–96, 200, 214n11, 216n46, 217n47, 217n49, 217n51; spiritual advisers for, 187, 195–96, 217n59, 218n63; torture of, 188, 208, 217n51, 220n107, 221n109
deaths, 5, 18, 158, 198, 202, 204; civil, 187, 213n1; COVID-19, 121
death sentences, 18, 187–89, 192, 206, 223n179
decision-making, 14, 17, 61, 63, 65, 153, 173, 205–7; children and, 72–73, 76–77, 81; medical, 67, 69, 81, 82, 89–90, 130, 139

Deck v. Missouri, 191, 215n32
dehumanization, 187–88, 192–93, 200–201, 213, 214n11, 217n51
Dellapenna, Joseph, 10
Del Toro, Israel, 110
Democrats, 127, 141, 148
Demons (Dostoevsky), 11, 20n28
dental health, 198
Department of Health and Human Services, U.S., 146–47
DeSantis, Ron, 106
deservingness, 109–10, 115, 121n74
Destro, Robert, 9
deterrent goals, 103, 213
Diagnostic and Statistical Manual (DSM-5-TR), American Psychiatric Association, 168–69, 171, 179–80, 186n64
diphtheria–pertussis–tetanus vaccine, 136
direct-to-consumer (DTC) genetic tests, 62, 74
disability law, 114–15
disabled people, disabilities and, 7, 15, 24, 117n3; discrimination against, 172–73, 178–80, 181n5; immunocompromised, 100, 105, 112–13; masking and, 100–103, 109–14; parking permits for, 114–15; rights and, 100, 109–10, 112, 168, 171–72, 178–80; transgender, 16–17, 166–80, 180n2
discrimination, 16, 53, 63, 72, 165n205; disability, 172–73, 178–80, 181n5; gender, 3, 7; genetic, 73–75; sex, 6, 19n9; against transgender people, 166–67, 170–73, 180
Disneyland, 137
Dispelling the Myths of Abortion History (Dellapenna), 10
District of Columbia, 23, 127, 136, 173
Dobbs v. Jackson Women's Health Organization, 29, 86–87, 145–46, 165n203
Dobbs v. Whole Women's Health Center, 4–5, 8–11, 16, 125, 127, 132
domestic violence, 105

donor-conceived people, 13, 47–49, 51, 53n1
Dorf, Michael C., 148–49
Dorfman, Doron, 15, 125
Dostoevsky, Fyodor, 11, 20n28
Douglas, William O., 138–40
drag performers, 1, 6
DSM-5-TR. *See* Diagnostic and Statistical Manual
DTC genetic tests. *See* direct-to-consumer
Due Process Clause, Fourteenth Amendment, 81, 86–87, 133, 139, 158n76
dysphoria, gender, 168–70, 174–80, 181n8, 182n15, 186n63

education, 17, 63, 87–88, 167, 169–70; masking and, 106; parental rights and, 67; public school, 78, 133; vaccine mandates and, 127–28, 133, 136
Eighth Amendment, U.S. Constitution, 197, 202–3, 209
electrocution, execution by, 202, 211–12
Ellis, Katie, 105
Ely, John Hart, 3, 19n8
embryos, 27–28, 36, 49–50, 132
employment, 17, 167, 170; genetic discrimination and, 73–74; vaccine mandates and, 127–28, 144–45, 148
Employment Division v. Smith, 137
endocrinology, reproductive, 13, 22
Estelle v. Gamble, 219n76
ethics, medical, 7, 68–70, 72–73, 90, 137, 150, 205, 210
eugenics, eugenicists and, 53, 135–36
exclusivity, 35
executions, death row inmates and, 187–88, 194–95, 200–213, 222n135, 224n179
expertise, scientific, 140, 149–51
ex post facto laws, 136
extralegal abortions, 129, 135

Facebook, 33
Fallopian tubes, 136

false positives, testing and, 72
"family planning," 138
FDA. *See* Food and Drug Administration
Feinberg, Joel, 73
felony prosecution, 5, 135
feminism, 6, 150
fertility fraud, 13
fertility industry, 13, 25–27, 56n24. *See also* gamete industry
fetal personhood laws, 89
fetuses, fetal tissue and, 5, 49, 62, 89, 129, 131–32, 152, 161n149
Fifth Amendment, U.S. Constitution, 85
Fineman, Martha, 127
firing squad, execution by, 211–12
First Amendment, U.S. Constitution, 1, 128, 134, 137, 142–43, 146–47, 195–96
First Things (journal), 10
Fisher, Jill, 7
Fleming, Cheri, 110
Florida, 15, 58n50, 104–6, 178, 207
Food and Drug Administration (FDA), U.S., 26, 36, 43, 129–30, 150
forced parenthood, 51
Ford v. Wainwright, 202–4
foster care system, 46
Foucault, Michel, 7
Fourteenth Amendment, U.S. Constitution, 78, 85, 134, 145; Due Process Clause, 81, 86–87, 133, 139, 158n76
Fourth Amendment, U.S. Constitution, 85
Franz, Allison, 17–18
fraud, fertility, 13, 22
freedom, personal, 1, 102
Free Exercise Clause, First Amendment, 134, 137, 142–43, 146–47
free-speech, 6
free will, 188–89, 207
From the War on Poverty to the War on Crime (Hinton), 8
Fugitive Slave Acts, U.S., 114
Fulton v. City of Philadelphia, 143

future disease, predispositions for, 14, 62, 76
future privacy, right to, 61, 73–74, 76, 79–80, 83–89, 91

gamete industry, gametes sales and, 12–14, 132; anonymity in, 13, 22, 30, 45–49; compensation in, 21–22, 32–35; infertility and, 23–25; regulation of, 25–53; role of gamete banks in, 21–22, 26–27, 30, 32–42, 45, 57n46. *See also* ova, sale of; sperm, sperm donors and
Gaskins, Donald Henry "Pee Wee," 202
GEDmatch, 74–75
gender, 2–5, 12, 19n9, 100, 126, 214n14; compensation for gamete sales and, 21–22, 32–35; discrimination, 3, 7; dysphoria, 168–70, 174–80, 181n8, 182n15, 186n63; identity, 168–71, 175, 177–80, 186nn63–64; natal, 168–69; roles, 135, 151–53; stereotypes, 107, 152–53
gender-affirming care, 1–2, 185n54; access to, 17, 63–64, 83, 166–70, 174–76; ADA and, 179–80; for children, 6, 63–64, 83; discrimination and, 172–73; hormone therapy in, 169, 178, 181n14, 182n15, 185n49
gender identity disorder, 186nn63–64
gender theory, 6
general population, 7, 170–71, 183n26
genetic counseling, 71–72
genetic information and: of children, 12, 14–15, 73–76, 80, 85–86, 88–91; sale of gametes and, 13, 26
Genetic Information Nondiscrimination Act (GINA), U.S., 73
genetic parents, 46–52
genetic predispositions, 71, 73
genetic testing, 50, 61–62, 82–83, 131; on gametes, 26–27. *See also* pediatric predisposition genetic testing
genital surgeries, 169
Georgia, 81, 174, 178, 192, 199

gestational surrogates, 25, 45, 56n22
GINA. *See* Genetic Information Nondiscrimination Act
Glover, Enoch, 108
Goggin, Gerard, 105
Gonzales v. Carhart, 31, 141
Goodwin, Michele, 7
Gorsuch, Neil, 143, 162n160
Graves, Anthony, 194
grievance processes, for death row inmates, 200, 221n111, 221n114
Griswold v. Connecticut, 85, 138–40
guardians, legal, 63, 172–73, 207
Guillain-Barré syndrome, 130
Gutierrez, Ruben, 195

hanging, execution by, 212
harassment: masking and, 15; of trans people, 170–71
Harlan, Marshall, 134, 136
Hauser, Daniel, 66
Hawker v. People of New York, 135
headaches, 5
Health Freedom Defense Fund, Inc. v. Biden, 15, 104
health insurance, 23, 70–74
Health Insurance Portability and Accountability Act (HIPAA), U.S., 74, 76, 102
hearing impairments, 113
Heller, Beth, 105
helmets laws, motorcycle, 1–2
Helms, Jesse, 179, 181n8
hepatitis C, 198
herd immunity, 131
hierarchies, 39–40, 110
Hinton, Elizabeth, 8
HIPAA. *See* Health Insurance Portability and Accountability Act
Hippocratic oath, 205
HIV/AIDS activism, 149
Ho, James, 150
Hodgkin's lymphoma, 66

Holmes, James, 191, 215n29
Holmes, Oliver Wendell, 136
Holquist, Michael, 11
homosexuality, 2–3, 6, 37–39, 45–46, 50, 107, 185n60
hormone therapy, gender-affirming, 169, 178, 181n14, 182n15, 185n49
hospitals, 5, 15, 72, 81, 201, 206
HPV vaccine, 159n96
Hruz, Paul W., 177–78
Hughes, Herman, 198
The Human Body and the Law (Meyer), 6
Human Genome Project, 62
Human Life Review (journal), 9
human rights, 21, 53n2, 216n46
Huntington's disease, 14, 61, 68
Hyde, Alan, 6–7

Idaho, 212
I/DD. *See* intellectual/developmental disability
identity, 15, 48, 80, 111, 135; gender, 168–71, 175, 177–80, 186nn63–64; racial, 39–40
identity politics, 7
illegal abortions, 129, 135
Illinois, 174
immunization, vaccines and, 128
immunocompromised people, 15, 100, 105–9, 112–13
incest, 44, 129, 138
inclusion, 15, 24
independent living movement, 109
individual autonomy, 16, 126–28, 134, 139, 144
individual liberties, 1, 80, 140
individuals, individualization and, 11–12
inequalities, bodily regulation, 2–3, 7, 11–18
infertility, 5, 23–25, 30–32, 34, 36, 54n9, 55n14, 152
influenza, 117n8, 127, 131
informed consent, 32, 56n28, 67, 137, 175, 177, 207

innocence, presumption of, 191
intellectual/developmental disability (I/DD), 168, 171–73, 175, 183n27, 186n66
intellectual property, 104
intersectionality, 7, 115
invasive procedures, 70
in vitro fertilization (IVF), 21, 28, 54n7, 62
involuntary medication, 18, 187, 189–90, 201, 203–5
involuntary sterilization, 136, 138
Ives-Rublee, Mia, 113
Ivey, Kay, 211
IVF. *See* in vitro fertilization

Jacobson, Henning, 134
Jacobson v. Massachusetts, 128, 134–35, 137–40, 142–43, 145–46
James, Joe Nathan, Jr., 211
juries, trial, 190–92, 215n31

Kahan, Dan, 103–4
Kamakahi, Lindsay, 33–34
Kaplan, Sara Clarke, 7
Kennedy, Anthony, 31
Kennedy, Robert, Jr., 146–47
Klonick, Kate, 104

Ladau, Emily, 113–14
Lancaster University, 111
The Lancet (journal), 137
last meal, of death row inmates, 188, 201, 207–8
last words, of death row inmates, 188, 201, 205, 207–8
laws regulating the body. *See specific topics*
legal capacity, 166, 176–77
lesbians, 37–39
Lessig, Lawrence, 107
lethal injection, execution by, 202, 208–12, 224n190, 225n199
libertarianism, 154
liberty, individual, 1, 80, 140
life in prison, sentencing, 202, 204

lived experiences, 4, 13, 105, 115, 167
Long, David, 201–2, 221n112
Lou Gehrig's disease (amyotrophic lateral sclerosis), 14, 68
Louisiana, 203, 205–7
lupus, 105

MacKinnon, Catharine, 19n9
malnourishment, 199, 220n96
marginalized groups, marginalization and, 17–18, 25, 53, 72, 167
marijuana, 1
marriage, 9, 23, 90, 135, 138
masculinity, 107
masking, COVID-19: disabled people and, 100–103, 109–14; as a preventive measure, 15, 101–3; race and, 100, 107–8; stigmatization and, 15, 100, 103–7; as a voluntary practice, 15, 104–5
mask mandates, COVID-19, 2, 4, 12, 104, 144; enforcement of, 15, 100, 103, 114–16; executive orders for, 102–3; politicization of, 100, 102, 109, 116, 118n16
Massachusetts, 82
Massaro, Toni M., 103
mastectomies, 71, 169
masturbation, 27, 196
McGee, Ryan, 106
McReynolds, James Clark, 78
Means, Cyril, 9
measles, 136–37
measles–mumps–rubella vaccine, 137
Medicaid, 23, 54n9, 109, 167
medical authority, 126, 139–40, 149–51, 164n197, 182n15
medical contraindications, 128, 131
medical decision-making, 67, 69, 81, 82, 89–90, 130, 139
medical ethics, 7, 21, 68–70, 72–73, 90, 137, 150, 205, 210
medical freedom, health freedom and, 16, 125–28, 132, 134, 141, 143–44, 146–54, 154nn1–2

medical infertility, 23–25
medication, forced, 18, 187, 189–90, 201, 203–4
Meijer, Jonathan Jacob, 42
menstrual cycles, 27
mental capacity, 166, 176–77
mental hospitals, 81
mental illness, mental health and, 30, 130, 173, 183n26, 185n60; of death row inmates, 202–7, 218n75, 221n109, 221n112, 222n133; trans people and, 168, 170–72, 174–77, 180n2, 185n50
Meyer, David, 6
Meyer v. Nebraska, 78–79
midwives, 135
mifepristone ("abortion pills"), 129, 150
military, U.S., 74, 137
Miller, Alan, 211
Mingus, Mia, 112
Minnesota, 66
miscarriages, 5, 8
misinformation, 101–2, 117n7
Mississippi, 143, 155n21
Missouri, 175, 209
Mor, Sagit, 110, 122n83
mRNA COVID-19 vaccines, 130
Mullen, Arthur F., 78
murder, 202, 204
Murphy, Patrick Henry, 195
mutations, genetic, 14
Mutcherson, Kimberly, 13–14, 132
mutilation, bodily, 188, 208, 211
mutual social responsibility, 105
"My body, my choice" (slogan), 4, 16, 125
myocarditis, 130

Nagel, Ari, 43
Nario-Redmond, Michelle, 117n5
natal gender, 168–69
National Center for Transgender Equality, 168, 170
National School Climate Survey, GLSEN, 170

National Vaccine Information Center, 136–37
natural light, access to, 18, 187, 193
Nazi Germany, 148, 212
Netherlands, 42–43
neuroleptic medications, 190
New Hampshire, 212
New Jersey, 220n107
The New Jim Crow (Alexander), 8
New York, 3, 5, 9–10, 90, 105–6, 135, 199, 221n113; masking and, 108–9; sperm donors in, 43
New Zealand, 111–12
Ninth Amendment, U.S. Constitution, 85
nitrogen hypoxia, execution by, 208, 212, 224n190
nonbinary people, 171
nongenetic risks of disease, 72
nonhuman entities, death row inmates as, 187, 200
nonviable fetuses, 5
Norman Bloodsaw v. Lawrence Berkeley Laboratory, 85–86
North Carolina, 108, 178, 198
Nossiff, Rosemary, 138
nuclear families, 50
Nussbaum, Martha, 103
nutrition, for death row inmates, 193, 198–200, 220n96, 220n105

obesity, 104
obstetricians, 149
Occupational Safety and Health Administration (OSHA), 16, 144–45
O'Connor, Sandra Day, 77
Ohio, 5, 8, 174, 176
Oklahoma, 138, 207
Olmstead v. L.C. ex rel. Zimrin, 109
one-way masking, 102
online shaming, 104
oophorectomy, 71
Oregon, 78
organs, selling of, 29

OSHA. *See* Occupational Safety and Health Administration
out-of-state abortions, 129, 156n27
ova, sale of, 13, 21–22, 27–30, 32–36, 45, 47, 58n56
ovarian hyperstimulation syndrome, 28

pain, 188, 197–98, 208–9, 211–13, 218n75, 225n199
Palmore v. Sidoti, 58n50
Panetti v. Quarterman, 203
parents, 17, 104; authority of, 66, 78, 81, 87; biological, 46–52; consent of, 67–68, 82, 87–88, 90; gamete sellers *vs.*, 32, 45–47; PPGT and, 14, 61–64, 67–77; rights of, 12, 14, 46–47, 61, 63–67, 77–80, 82–83, 91, 92n12, 92n15, 96n63, 136–37, 143–44; of trans children, 6, 63–64, 172–73; vaccine laws and, 128, 134–37, 143–44
parent–state–child triad, 82–83, 92n12
Parham v. J.R., 81–82
parking permits, disabled, 114–15
Parmet, Wendy E., 15
partisanship, 125–26, 140–41, 148, 153–54
patriarchy, 7, 80, 135
pediatric predisposition genetic testing (PPGT), 14, 61–64, 67–77, 80, 82–91
Pennsylvania, 199
People v. Belous, 139
pericarditis, 130
Perry, Rick, 201–2
personal liberties, 79, 85, 101–2, 140
personhood, fetal, 89
PGD. *See* preimplantation genetic diagnosis
PGT. *See* preimplantation genetic testing
physical effects of long-term solitary confinement, 193–94
physician-assisted suicide, 17
physicians, abortions and, 135–36, 138–39, 151, 158n76
Pierce v. Society of Sisters, 78–79

Planned Parenthood of Minnesota v. Rounds, 141
Planned Parenthood of Southeastern Pennsylvania v. Casey, 140
poisoning, 135
police, police officers and, 5, 16–17, 110–11, 134–35, 149; violence, 107–8
Policing the Womb (Goodwin), 7
polio, 65–66, 131, 136
polycystic ovary syndrome, 23, 36
populism, 150–51, 164n199
Posner, Eric, 103
potential harm, 3, 5, 72
poverty, 17, 167
Powell, Lewis, 203
PPGT. *See* pediatric predisposition genetic testing
predispositions, genetic, 71, 73
pregnancies, 1–2, 36–37, 41, 89, 127–29; through AI, 27, 37–38, 56n22; complications during, 131–32, 138; infertility and, 23–25; IVF, 28; legal beginning of life, 135; miscarriages and, 5, 8; "natural order" of, 148; purchased gametes and, 21; termination of, 16, 38, 135, 139, 145. *See also* abortions
preimplantation genetic diagnosis (PGD), 62, 69–70, 89
preimplantation genetic testing (PGT), 62, 69–70, 89
prejudices, 107, 117n5, 190–92
preventive measures, care and, 70–72; masking as a, 15, 101–3
preventive medicine, 69, 107
Prince v. Massachusetts, 79
privacy, rights to, 3–4, 9–11, 14–15, 53, 111, 138–40, 205; children and, 61, 75–76, 83–88; DTC genetic testing and, 74–75; future privacy and, 61, 73–74, 76, 79–80, 83–89, 91
private schools, 78
"pro-choice" sentiment, 9
"pro-life" sentiment, 5, 9–10, 18, 20n26

Protestants, 135
psychiatric hospitals, 206
psychiatry, psychiatrists and, 175, 204, 207, 218n75
psychological effects of long-term solitary confinement, 193–94, 217n49, 219n51
psychosis, 204, 206
psychotropic medications, 190, 204
puberty blockers, 169, 185n49
public health, 4, 8, 15–16, 126, 130–31, 133, 149; authority of states and, 135–36, 142–45, 153–54; masking and, 100–102, 106, 115
public libraries, 6
public schools, 78, 133
public spaces, 15
Puerto Rico, 126
punitive regulations, 6–7, 166, 197
purity, vaccine, 133

quality of life, 167

race, 12, 37–41, 58; mask-wearing and, 100, 107–8
racial discrimination, 7
racial disparities, infertility and, 23–24, 58n51
racial homogeneity, 39–40
racial segregation, 39–40, 58n52
racial stereotypes, 192
racism, 72, 113
radiological imaging, 70
Ramirez, John, 195, 218n68
Ramirez v. Collier, 196
rape, 9–10, 129, 138, 196
Reagan, Ronald, 4
regret, gamete sellers and, 30–31
regulations, bodily. *See specific topics*
Rehabilitation Act, U.S., 179–80, 185m60
rehumanization, of death row inmates, 188–89, 200–208

religious freedoms, 67, 128, 195–96; vaccine mandates and, 130, 134, 136–38, 141–44, 147, 162n150
Religious Land Use and Institutionalized Persons Act (RLUIPA), U.S., 185–86, 218n68
reproduction, reproductive rights and, 4–7, 12, 53n2, 62, 136, 145, 148, 152, 154n3; assisted, 24, 37–40, 45–46, 49–50, 53; cloning and, 42; coital, 43–44, 49, 53; commodification of, 21–22, 46–47, 52; infertility and, 22–25. *See also* abortions
reproductive endocrinologists, 13
reproductive freedom, 6, 138, 153
Republicans, conservative states and, 63–64, 74, 127, 140–41, 146–48, 150–51, 159n96
resistance, vaccine, 136
retributive, regulations, 4, 188–89, 201–3 213
rights, 150, 199, 213n1; abortion, 2, 16, 82, 125, 132, 135, 139–41, 145, 147, 184; of children, 64–65, 73, 75–76, 79–81, 89, 92n12; constitutional, 1–2, 14, 16, 20n26, 53, 53n2, 61, 64–65, 82, 86, 126, 132, 135–40, 145; of death row inmates, 187, 190, 194–96, 199, 202–3, 205, 219n75, 219n88; disability, 100, 109–10, 112, 168, 171–72, 178–80; to future privacy, 61, 73–74, 76, 79–80, 83–89, 91; human, 21, 53n2, 216n46; parental, 12, 14, 46–47, 61, 63–67, 77–80, 82–83, 91, 92n12, 92n15, 96n63, 136–37, 143–44; to procreate, 48, 53n2; to right to represent oneself in court, 191–92; to sell gametes, 13, 22. *See also* privacy, rights to; reproduction, reproductive rights and
right-to-life, 9
risks, health, 30, 61, 65–77, 130, 133, 141
RLUIPA. *See* Religious Land Use and Institutionalized Persons Act

Roberts, John, 142
Rodriguez-Roldán, Victoria, 16–17
Roe v. Wade, 3–4, 8–11, 16, 19nn8–9, 29, 135, 139, 145–46, 149–50
Román, Sven, 177

safety of gametes, regulating the, 26–27
same-sex couples, 45–46, 50. *See also* homosexuality
Samuels, Ellen, 111
Sandel, Michael, 34
SART. *See* Society for Assisted Reproductive Technology
Scalia, Antonin, 137
scarcity, gamete industry and, 35
schizophrenia, 201–2, 204, 206–7
Schragger, Richard, 146
Schwartzman, Micah, 146
scientific expertise, 140, 149–51
screening procedures, gamete, 36–37, 41
seatbelt laws, 1, 3
secondary sex characteristics, 169, 181n13
secular liberties, 144
segregation, racial, 39–40, 58n52
self-harm, 88, 193–94
Sell v. United States, 189–90
separation of powers, 144, 162n160
serial sperm donors, 13, 22, 42–45, 58n56, 58n63
"serious medical need," death row inmates and, 197, 219nn84–87
sex discrimination, 6, 19n9
sexual deprivation, 193, 196
sexually transmitted infections, 26, 43, 90
sexual stimulation, restrictions on, 193, 196
sex work, 29
shackling, of death row inmates, 189, 191–92, 215n29, 215n32, 216n33
shaming, shame and, 71; masking and, 15, 100, 102–16
sign language, 167, 173, 184n31
Silverman, Ross, 104

Singleton, Charles, 204–6
Singleton v. State, 206
Skinner v. Oklahoma, 138
slavery, 2–3, 7, 114, 192
smallpox, 133, 137
Smith, Kenneth, 211
Smith, Willie, 195
social capital, 104
social distancing, COVID-related, 107–8, 111, 142
social infertility, 24–25
social media, 33, 104–5, 112–14
Social Security Administration, U.S., 170
Society for Assisted Reproductive Technology (SART), 25–26, 33
solitary confinement, of death row inmates, 192–96, 200, 214n11, 216n46, 217n47, 217n49, 217n51
South Bay United Pentecostal Church v. Newsom, 142
South Carolina, 197–98, 202–3, 205–7, 211–12
Southwest airlines, 110–11
sperm, sperm donors and, 21, 56nn23–24; sales, 26–27, 33–37, 45–47; serial sperm donors, 13, 22, 42–45
spiritual advisers, 187, 195–96, 217n59, 218n63
Spivack, Carla, 10
starvation, 198–99
state laws, U.S., 1–4, 11, 13, 15, 74, 90; on death row inmates, 18, 188–213, 224n179; gender-affirming care and, 83, 173–79; on medical contraindications, 128; private enforcement of, 114–15; on vaccine mandates, 16, 126–53. *See also specific laws; specific states*
State v. Oakley, 59n64
State v. Perry, 205
Steele, Claude, 108
stereotypes, 109, 176; gendered, 107, 152–53; racial, 192

sterilization, involuntary, 49, 53, 136, 138
stigmatization, 184n46; masking and, 15, 100, 103–7; of trans people, 171
Storer, Horatio, 135
strep throat, 65
stun belts, stun cuff and, 191–92, 215n32
suicides, suicide attempts and, 1, 17, 88, 193–94, 201–2, 218n75; trans people and, 171, 174, 177
supported decision-making, 173
Supreme Court, Alabama, 49–50, 211
Supreme Court, Arkansas, 204
Supreme Court, California, 139
Supreme Court, Louisiana, 205
Supreme Court, South Carolina, 205–6, 212
Supreme Court, Texas, 5, 129
Supreme Court, U.S., 2–4, 9–11, 16, 78, 129, 139–44, 176, 205; on death penalty, 195–96, 209; on the Eighth Amendment, 202–3; on forced medication, 189–90, 203–4; on the Fourteenth Amendment, 134; on involuntary sterilization, 136, 138; on parental rights, 14, 64, 67, 78–80, 92n15. *See also specific cases*
surgeries, gender-affirming, 169
surrogacy, gestational, 25, 45, 56n22
Swanson, Kara, 33
syphilis study, Tuskegee, 150
systemic: dehumanization, 187; inequality, 7

Tandon v. Newsom, 142–43
Target, 110–11
Targeted Restrictions on Abortion (TRAP) laws, 140–41
technologies, medical, 53, 62–63, 67, 77, 90–91
Tennessee, 176–78, 220n107
testify, rights to, 190
tetanus, 133

Texas, 55n13; abortion and, 5, 8, 151; death row, 194–96, 201–2, 207–8, 217n59, 221n112
therapeutic abortions, 135
Third Amendment, U.S. Constitution, 85
Thomas, Clarence, 86–87, 143, 157n45
tobacco industry, 150
torture, of death row inmates, 188, 208, 217n51, 220n107, 221n109
transgender adolescents, 4, 166, 174
transgender children, 168, 177–78; access to gender-affirming care for, 166–67, 169–70, 174–76; discrimination against, 166, 170, 172–73; parents of, 6, 63–64, 172–73
transgender people, 1, 154n2; disabled, 16–17, 166–79
transit mask order, Centers for Disease Control and Prevention, 15
transmissible diseases, 24
transvaginal ultrasound, 28
transvestitism, 185n60
TRAP laws. *See* Targeted Restrictions on Abortion laws
trauma, 17, 167, 173, 184n46, 217n49
trisomy 18 (genetic condition), 5, 129
Troxel v. Granville, 78
Trump, Donald, 9, 107, 118n16, 129–30, 146–47
Tsai, Robert L., 148
Tuskegee syphilis study, 150
23andMe, 45, 47, 62
Tyner, Rudolph, 202
Type One decisions, medical, 67, 69
Type Two decisions, medical, 67–79

Uhlmann, Michael, 20n26
"unborn human beings," 49–50, 132
United Kingdom, 111
unlicensed sperm donors, 43–44
unprotected sex, 23
U.S. Trans Survey, National Center for Transgender Equality, 170–71
Utah, 212

vaccinations, 12, 155n18; COVID-19, 2, 4, 106, 126–27, 130, 134, 142–45, 148, 152; polio, 65–66, 131, 136; smallpox, 133, 137
vaccine freedom (antivax) movements, 16, 137, 149–50, 159n96
vaccine-hesitancy, 104, 117n7
vaccine mandates, 2, 15–16, 125–29, 160n10, 161n130; religious freedoms and, 130, 134, 136–38, 141–44, 147, 162n150
ventilators, 201–2
veterans, 110
vigilantism, 114–15
violence, 100, 105, 191, 196, 199, 202; death row inmates exposed to, 187–88, 193, 200, 210–13, 220n107, 221n109, 221nn113–14; police, 107–8
voluntary practice, masking as a, 15, 104–5
vulnerability theory, 127–28

Wakefield, Andrew, 137
Walensky, Rochelle, 106
Wall, Jesse, 7
Wallach, Karen L., 133
war on drugs, 3
Washington, 78
Washington v. Harper, 204–5
Watson, Simon, 43
West Virginia v. Environmental Protection Agency, 162

Whatley, Frederick, 192
Whelan, Allison M., 14, 131
White, Byron, 139–40
whiteness, 40
white passing, 39, 41
white-supremacy, 7, 39–40
Whitman, James Q., 103
Whole Woman's Health v. Hellerstedt, 141
Wiley, Lindsey, 104
William and Mary Law Review (journal), 10
Williams, Fred, 220n96
Wilson, Jamie, 206–7
Wisconsin v. Yoder, 78
Witt, John Fabian, 7
Wollman, Roger, 204–5
women, 7, 11–12, 19n8, 104, 150; Black, 23–24; childbearing function of, 9, 135, 152–53; ova sold by, 13, 22–23; sale of ova by, 13, 21–22, 27–30, 32–36, 45, 47, 58n56
women's health movement, 149, 164n197
wrongful birth claims, sperm banks and, 37–39

X (formerly Twitter), 112–13
X-rays, 70

Zeigler, Mary, 148